D0378421

THE JOHN HARVARD LIBRARY

PURITANS

AMONG THE

INDIANS

Accounts of Captivity and Redemption

1676–1724

EDITED BY

Alden T. Vaughan & Edward W. Clark

THE BELKNAP PRESS
OF HARVARD UNIVERSITY PRESS
Cambridge, Massachusetts
and London, England

To Lynn Vaughan
and the memory of
Martha Clark Gibson

Copyright © 1981 by the President and Fellows of Harvard College
All rights reserved
Printed in the United States of America
10 9 8 7 6 5 4 3 2
Library of Congress Cataloging in Publication Data
Main entry under title:

Puritans among the Indians.

(John Harvard library)
Bibliography: p.
Includes index.
CONTENTS: Cups of common calamity: Puritan
captivity narratives as literature and history.—
Rowlandson, M. The sovereignty and goodness
of God.—[etc.]
1.   Indians of North America—New England—
Captivities.   2.   Puritans—Biography.   3.   New England—
History—Colonial period, ca. 1600–1775.   I.   Vaughan,
Alden T., 1929–   II.   Clark, Edward W., 1943–
III.   Series.
E85.P87   974'.02   80-26033
ISBN 0-674-73901-9
(cloth)
ISBN 0-674-73899-3
(paper)

CONTENTS

EDITORS' PREFACE

This anthology, drawn from the best New England accounts of Indian captivity, presents the captivity narrative at its peak as an American literary phenomenon and as an important expression of Puritan theological and social thought. The New England focus permits a coherent collection: the chronology is limited to half a century; the geography is confined to northern New England and adjacent Canada; and the captives can be roughly described as Puritan and their captors as Algonquian-Iroquoian or occasionally French Canadian.

The narratives are arranged in the chronological order of their authors' captivity, not publication dates, for two reasons. First, the dates of publication often lagged several years behind dates of authorship, which in turn were sometimes many years after the end of the captivities. If the narratives were read in order of publication, some events would seem anachronistic. Second, a sequence based on historical events allows the reader to understand the captives' experiences and observations in the order of their occurrence. In short, this anthology treats Puritan captivity narratives as histories of their times as well as an evolving literary form.

Our text for each narrative was the most authentic available. In most instances we chose the earliest surviving edition, which was also the last edition in which the author is believed to have participated. (Most captivity narratives had subsequent editions with substantial revisions by publishers or editors.) For the narratives reported secondhand by Cotton Mather, however, we used his last version, rather than any of his earlier accounts, on the assumption that the author's final revision reflected his best judgment.

To make these Puritan captivity narratives more accessible to modern readers, we have modified many of the original texts' outmoded forms. We have made capitalization, punctuation, abbreviations, and spelling (except for proper nouns) conform to modern practices. Because many personal and place names, especially Indian names, had no universally accepted form, and because the author's original spelling (usually phonetic) sometimes gives clues to obscure identifications, we have left proper nouns as the authors spelled them. Excessively long sentences and paragraphs have been divided where appropriate. But while imposing a uniform orthography and visual format, we have scrupulously respected each writer's vocabulary and syntax. The narratives in this volume contain every word, including archaic terms, of the original texts. For the reader's convenience, we have modernized obsolete verb forms if they involved only very slight changes in pronunciation; for example, "fetcht" becomes "fetched," "shew" becomes "show." The only additions are a few clarifying words enclosed in brackets. Thus the narratives are substantively the same as they appeared in the seventeenth and eighteenth centuries. To give a sense of the visual and orthographic character of the original texts, we have included unaltered quotations in our general introduction and headnotes. Small doses of colonial typography are, we believe, highly palatable, although a steady diet would be indigestible.

The footnotes in this volume are intended, first, to identify the people, places, and major events mentioned by the narrators; second, to lead interested readers to further works, either colonial sources or modern studies, that amplify the annotations we have provided; and third, to explain certain aspects of the narratives, such as Indian customs or obsolete terms, that readers might otherwise misunderstand.

Where not otherwise specifically identified, the notes in this volume are based primarily on the following works. BIOGRAPHICAL INFORMATION: James Savage, *A Genealogical Dictionary of the First Settlers of New England* . . . , 4 vols. (Boston, 1860–1862); Sybil Noyes, Charles Thornton Libby, and Walter Goodwin Davis, *Genealogical Dictionary of Maine and New Hampshire*, 5 vols. (Portland, Me., 1928–1939; repr. in 1 vol., Baltimore, 1972); *Dictionary of Canadian Biography,* ed. George W. Brown et al., I–III (Toronto, 1966–1974); Emma Lewis Coleman, *New England Captives Carried to Canada between 1677 and 1760 during the French and Indian Wars,* 2 vols. (Portland, Me., 1925); and Charles H. Lincoln, ed., *Narratives of the Indian Wars, 1675–1699* (New York, 1913; repr. 1952). PLACE NAMES: John C. Huden, *Indian Place Names in New England* (New York, 1962); R. A. Douglas-Lithgow, *The American Indian Place and Proper Names of New England* (Salem, Mass., 1908); Ava Harriet Chadbourne, *Maine Place Names, and the Peopling of Its Towns* (Portland, Me., 1955); and the appendix to Coleman, *New England Captives.* ETHNOLOGY: Most of the ethnographic information in the notes is drawn from seventeenth- and eighteenth-century sources; a few come from Frederick Webb Hodge, ed., *Handbook of American Indians North of Mexico*, 2 vols. (Washington, D.C., 1978); and *Handbook of North American Indians*, XV, *Northeast*, ed. Bruce G. Trigger (Washington, D.C., 1978). LEXICOGRAPHY: For definitions of a few obsolete words that are not found in most dictionaries, we have relied on the *Oxford English Dictionary*, 20 vols. (Oxford, Eng., 1888–1928). Translations of Indian words that were not made by the narrators are taken from seventeenth-century syllabaries by William Wood, Roger Williams, and others, or from James Hammond Trumbull, *Natick Dictionary* (Washington, D.C., 1903).

If the modernized and annotated texts in this volume achieve our aim of clear, unhindered presentation, modern readers will be spared the distractions of odd spelling, irregular punctuation, and convoluted structure that make seventeenth- and eighteenth-century editions so unwieldy. Our edition, we hope, will permit more enjoyable and insightful reading and encourage the wider audience and deeper appreciation that Mary Rowlandson, John Gyles, and the other narrators richly deserve. Readers who wish to explore further the Puritan world that produced those writings or to read more deeply in the literature of captivities should consult the extensive bibliography at the end of this book.

WE ARE GRATEFUL to several institutions and scholars who contributed time, talent, and resources. The book had its inception in the stimulating surroundings of the Charles Warren Center for Studies in American History at Harvard University, was nourished in the helpful libraries of Columbia University and Winthrop College, and came to fruition in two disparate but congenial environs—the American Antiquarian Society, where Alden Vaughan used the unparalleled collection of early Americana, and the University of Valencia, where Edward Clark held a Fulbright Junior Lectureship. We thank the staffs of these institutions for their assistance and generosity. Earlier, Clark's National Endowment for the Humanities Fellowship in College Residence at Columbia University provided the opportunity for us to discover our mutual interest in New England captivity narratives, which resulted in our collaboration on this volume. The William A. Dunning Fund of the Columbia University History Department helped to defray the cost of typing and photocopying.

Our introductory essay was improved by the perceptive critiques of Sacvan Bercovitch and an anonymous reader for the Harvard University Press. Daniel K. Richter, Michael J. Crisafulli, and Mary Elizabeth

EDITORS' PREFACE

Brown provided valuable assistance, and Cornelius J. Jaenen greatly improved the Canadian sections of the bibliography. Katarina Rice was an ideal editor. Our sincere thanks to all.

A.T.V.

E.W.C.

PURITANS AMONG THE INDIANS

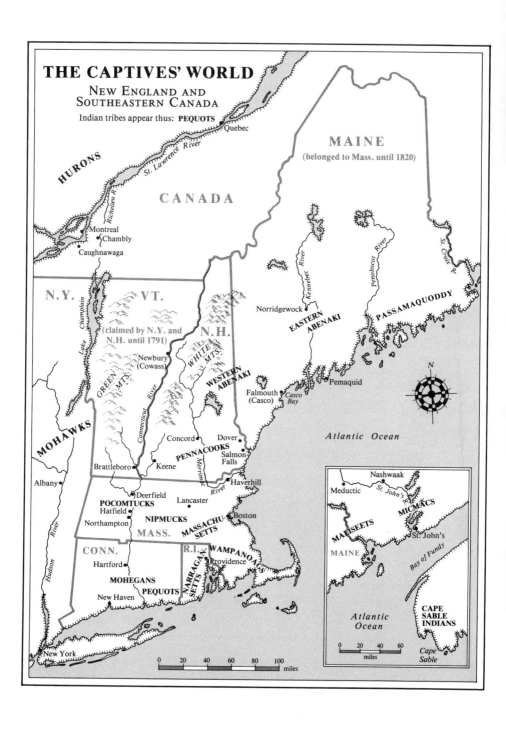

THE CAPTIVES' WORLD

NEW ENGLAND AND
SOUTHEASTERN CANADA

Indian tribes appear thus: **PEQUOTS**

HURONS

Quebec

MAINE
(belonged to Mass. until 1820)

St. Lawrence River

CANADA

Richelieu R.

Montreal
Chambly
Caughnawaga

N.Y.

VT.

(claimed by N.Y. and
N.H. until 1791)

Lake Champlain

GREEN MTS.

Newbury
(Cowass)

Connecticut River

WHITE MTS.

N.H.

Kennebec River

Penobscot River

St. Croix R.

Norridgewock

EASTERN ABENAKI

PASSAMAQUODDY

WESTERN ABENAKI

Pemaquid

MOHAWKS

Brattleboro

Albany

Concord
Keene

Merrimac River

Dover

PENNACOOKS

Salmon
Falls

Haverhill

Falmouth
(Casco)

Casco
Bay

Atlantic Ocean

N

Deerfield
POCOMTUCKS
Hatfield
Northampton

Lancaster

NIPMUCKS

MASS.

MASSACHU-
SETTS

Boston

Hudson River

CONN.

Hartford

MOHEGANS

New Haven

PEQUOTS

R.I.

NARRAGAN-
SETTS

WAMPANOAGS

Providence

New York

0   20   40   60   80   100
miles

Nashwaak

Meductic

St. John's River

MICMACS

MALISEETS

St. John's

MAINE

Bay of Fundy

Atlantic
Ocean

CAPE
SABLE
INDIANS

0   20   40   60
miles

Cape
Sable

·CUPS OF COMMON CALAMITY·
PURITAN CAPTIVITY NARRATIVES
AS LITERATURE AND HISTORY

"It is no new thing for Gods precious ones to drink as deep as others, of the Cup of common Calamity."
—PREFACE TO MARY ROWLANDSON,
The Soveraignty & Goodness of God, 1682

"Remarkable Mercies should be Faithfully Published, for the Praise of GOD the Giver."
—SERMON BY JOHN WILLIAMS, 1706

"It would be unaccountable stupidity in me," wrote a former captive of the Indians in 1707, "not to maintain the most Lively and Awful Sense of Divine Rebukes which the most Holy GOD has seen meet . . . to dispense to me, my Family and People in delivering us into the hands of those that Hated us, who Led us into a strange Land." But the redeemed captive, Reverend John Williams of Deerfield, Massachusetts, did not dwell on the Lord's rebukes. Like so many of his contemporaries in New England, Williams emphasized instead "The wonders of Divine Mercy, which we have seen in the Land of our Captivity, and Deliverance there-from [which] cannot be forgotten without incurring the guilt of the blackest Ingratitude."[1] A staunch Puritan, Williams believed—as earlier and later generations did not—that capture by the Indians was no military happenstance or secular accident. Captivity was God's punishment; redemption was His mercy; and New England must heed the lesson or suffer anew. Many survivors of the captivity ordeal proclaimed that message in stirring narratives which tell much about Puritan prisoners among the Indians and their French allies in the late seventeenth and early eighteenth centuries and reveal even more about the Puritan mind.

---

1. John Williams, *The Redeemed Captive Returning to Zion: A Faithful Narrative of Remarkable Occurrences in the Captivity and the Deliverance of Mr. John Williams* (Boston, 1707), A2v.

I

Puritans, of course, did not invent the captivity narrative. It is one of America's oldest literary genres and its most unique. Soon after Europe awakened to the existence of an inhabited western continent, stories of captivity by an alien culture began to excite the public imagination. Ironically, the earliest New World captivity tales must have been told by American natives: Spaniards, not Indians, first seized hapless victims to serve as guides, interpreters, hostages, or curiosities. But the Indians soon retaliated, and because Europeans long had a monopoly on the written word, most printed accounts related capture by Indians. Hence "captivity narrative" came to mean an account, usually autobiographical, of forced participation in Indian life. The literature of early American colonization is dotted with poignant and often gruesome tales of seizure, torture or adoption (sometimes both), and eventual escape or release. Such stories found a ready audience on both sides of the Atlantic, where they flourished, in one form or another, for three centuries.

Not until the late seventeenth century did captivity narratives emerge as a separate and distinct literary genre. Before then most captivity tales appeared as dramatic episodes in works of larger scope. That was true not only in Latin American literature—the accounts of Cabeza de Vaca and Juan Ortiz, for example—but also of North American settlement.[2] Captain John Smith's various versions of his capture by Powhatan Indians and his last-second rescue by Pocahontas is a case in point; they were embedded in Smith's chronicles of early Virginia.[3] Similarly, accounts of Father Isaac Jogues's incarceration, torture, release, recapture, and eventual death at the hands of the Iroquois were scattered through the annual Jesuit relations.[4] More than a century later, the earlier pattern of captivity narratives as a single stage in an unfolding adventure still survived: witness the stories of Daniel Boone's capture and adoption by the Shawnee.[5] But in the last quarter of the seventeenth century, writers in Puritan New En-

2. For bibliographic details see R. W. G. Vail, *The Voice of the Old Frontier* (Philadelphia, 1949), 90–91.

3. Edward Arber and A. G. Bradley, eds., *Travels and Works of Captain John Smith . . . 1580–1631*, 2 vols. (Edinburgh, 1910), I, 14–22; II, 395–401, 911–912.

4. Reuben Gold Thwaites, ed., *The Jesuit Relations and Allied Documents*, 73 vols. (Cleveland, 1896–1961), XXXI, 17–137. This version is in Fr. Jerome Lalemont's "Relation of 1647" and includes Jogues's death. Father Jogues also wrote an account of his first captivity (1642) in a letter of 1643 to Father Jean Filleau, which has been reprinted several times. In 1646 Jogues was recaptured by the Iroquois and killed.

5. Boone was a captive for seven days in 1769 and for several months in 1778. See John Filson, *The Discovery, Settlement and Present State of Kentucke* (Wilmington, Del., 1784; facs. repr. Ann Arbor, Mich., 1966), 51–53, 63–66.

gland began to issue narratives of Indian captivity in separate book-length works, though usually brief and sometimes bound with other items.

The Puritans approached the new genre cautiously at first—their initial narrative appeared more than five years after the event and was privately printed. When that volume achieved instant popularity, similar works soon followed. Thereafter captivity narratives, usually as separate works, enjoyed nearly two centuries of commercial success in colonial America and the United States, although not without important changes. From unpolished but intense religious statements in the Puritan period, captivity narratives had evolved by the late eighteenth century into ornate and often fictionalized accounts that catered to more secular and less serious tastes. By the late nineteenth century the genre had lost most of its historical and autobiographical integrity. It ultimately blended with the "penny-dreadfuls" of America's Victorian-age fiction.

PURITAN CAPTIVITY NARRATIVES began in 1682 with Mary Rowlandson's story of capture during the later stages of King Philip's War. Her brisk *Soveraignty & Goodness of God . . . Being a Narrative of the Captivity and Restauration of Mrs. Mary Rowlandson* sold quickly; three more issues appeared within the first year, and others followed periodically throughout the Puritan era.[6] Many subsequent New England narratives had almost as impressive literary careers and were the best-sellers of their day, and they remain among the most insightful clues to the tensions and expectations of Puritan society.

These stories were immensely popular because—like any successful literature—they served readers a hearty fare of literary and psychological satisfaction, peculiar to their time and place. In a society without fiction and plays, and almost barren of poetry, real-life dramas filled a crucial cultural void. Histories and accounts of warfare only partly met the need for dramatic literature. After 1676 tales of Indian captivity offered a more personal story: they told of raids and forced marches, of the wilderness and its native inhabitants, of the chilling efforts of Indians and Frenchmen to assimilate their captives into an alien culture. But the heart of the New

6. For bibliographic details see Vail, *Voice of the Old Frontier,* 167–169. A case could be made for John Underhill as the author of the first Puritan captivity narrative. Though not autobiographical, his account of the captivity and release of two girls from Wethersfield, Connecticut, in 1637 has many of the characteristics that later appear in Cotton Mather's secondhand accounts: drama, moral lessons, and pious rhetoric. See Underhill, *Newes from America . . .* (London, 1638; repr. in *Massachusetts Historical Society Collections,* 3rd ser., 6[1837]), 12–13, 17–23.

3

England narrative—the theme that made it truly Puritan and infused it with unusual dramatic force—was its introspective concentration on God's role in the life of the individual and the collective community. As Rowlandson's title proclaimed, she wrote only incidentally about deliverance from misery and potential death. More important, she portrayed "The Soveraignty & Goodness of GOD, Together with the Faithfulness of His Promises," while an appended posthumous sermon by her husband raised "the possibility of God's forsaking a people, that have been visibly near & dear to him." In sum, the Rowlandsons' publisher promised an intensely personal account of God's testing and eventual salvation of a tormented soul, and a broad hint that her experience might foretell in microcosm the fate of all Puritans. Those were compelling attractions to the deeply pietistic people of seventeenth-century New England, who sought desperately to comprehend their preordained roles in God's awesome universe.

Puritan authors wove the captivity narrative from several existing literary strands. One strand was spiritual autobiography; numerous seventeenth and early eighteenth-century New Englanders described their search for salvation to edify their children and other kin and occasionally to inspire the community at large. John Winthrop's "Christian Experience," Thomas Shepard's "My Birth & Life," Anne Bradstreet's "To My Dear Children," and Edward Taylor's "Spiritual Relation" are notable examples of an abundant theo-literary form.[7] The literary use of a representative life reaches much further back, to be sure, at least to the Reformation when Martin Luther developed the *exemplum fidei*, which stressed the spirit of Christ's life rather than his deeds.[8] That notion found congenial soil in Tudor-Stuart England, where the Puritans gave it added prominence and eventually carried it to their American Zion. The New England

---

7. Some Puritan autobiographies were published; most remained in manuscript. For discussions of the genre see Daniel Shea, *Spiritual Autobiography in Early America* (Princeton, N.J., 1968), and Owen C. Watkins, *The Puritan Experience: Studies in Spiritual Autobiography* (New York, 1972). Winthrop's account is in Massachusetts Historical Society, *Winthrop Papers*, 5 vols. (Boston, 1929–1947), I, 154–161; Shepard's is best consulted in Michael McGiffert, ed., *God's Plot: The Paradoxes of Puritan Piety, Being the Autobiography and Journal of Thomas Shepard* (Amherst, Mass., 1972), 33–77; Bradstreet's is in *The Works of Anne Bradstreet in Prose and Verse*, ed. John Harvard Ellis (Charlestown, Mass., 1867; repr. Gloucester, Mass., 1962), 3–10; and Taylor's is reprinted in Donald Stanford, ed., "Edward Taylor's 'Spiritual Relation,'" *American Literature*, 35 (1963–1964), 467–475.

8. Sacvan Bercovitch, *The Puritan Origins of the American Self* (New Haven, 1976), 9–10.

4

branch of the Puritan movement, and still later the Quakers in Pennsylvania, encouraged spiritual autobiography as a vital expression of the search for personal salvation. The principal authority on this early American literary form observes that "the spiritual autobiographer is primarily concerned with the question of grace: whether or not the individual has been accepted into divine life, an acceptance signified by psychological and moral changes which the autobiographer comes to discern in his past experience."[9] But the search for salvation was fraught with torments, doubts, and relapses, in almost perfect parallel to the experiences reported in the captivity narratives. In spiritual autobiographies, God and Satan wrestled for the sinner's soul; in captivity autobiographies, the captive, with God's help, battled Satan's agents. In both cases, of course, God eventually prevailed: the weary pilgrim survived the ordeal because his faith wavered but did not break, and because God's mercy was stronger than His wrath.

During and after his captivity by Indians, the victim pondered how his own experience coincided with God's plan. A redeemed captive usually saw his ordeal, and even the ordeal of his loved ones, as punishment for his past sins or present impiety. The survivor often concluded that he had gained measurably from the chastisement, and he almost invariably offered his experience as a lesson to neighbors of the ephemeral security of this world and the awesomeness of God's sovereignty. Mary Rowlandson, for one, came to appreciate God's omnipotence: "I then remembered how careless I had been of Gods holy time: how many Sabbaths I had lost and mispent, and how evily I had walked in Gods sight; which lay so close unto my spirit, that it was easie for me to see how righteous it was with God to cut off the threed of my life, and cast me out of his presence forever. Yet the Lord still showed mercy to me, and upheld me; and as he wounded me with one hand, so he healed me with the other."[10] "Redemption," a frequent term in captivity titles and texts, thus had a double meaning—spiritual as well as physical. Similarly, captivity stories combined individual catharsis and public admonition. Implicitly, at least, they exhorted the reader to find his or her own spiritual redemption. Rowlandson's title page explains that her story is directed "Especially to her dear Children and Relations." God would not have subjected her to such an ordeal had He

9. Shea, *Spiritual Autobiography*, xi.

10. Mary Rowlandson, *The Soveraignty & Goodness of God*, 2nd ed. (Cambridge, Mass., 1682), 9.

not intended her spiritual pilgrimage to enlighten her family and neighbors. Everything had a purpose. As Reverend John Williams insisted after his own harrowing ordeal, the Lord "has enjoyned us, to shew forth His praises in rehearsing to others the Salvations, and Favours we have been the Subjects of."[11]

Astute ministers such as Cotton Mather made sure the lesson was not missed. Serving as Hannah Swarton's amanuensis, Mather wrote an epitome of the abasement-salvation theme which offered hope and courage to those in doubt of their own fate. Swarton laments, "I was neither fit to live nor fit to die; and brought once to the very Pit of Despair about what would become of my Soul." But she found in her Bible the account of Jonah's troubles and resolved to pray as her biblical prototype had: "In the Meditation upon this Scripture the Lord was pleased by his Spirit to come into my Soul, and so fill me with ravishing Comfort, that I cannot express it."[12] And in *Humiliations Followed With Deliverances* Mather related the now-legendary story of Hannah Dustan's escape from the Indians after tomahawking her sleeping captors. In his initial recitation of the episode, Mather addressed a congregation in which she sat; he observed that "there happens to be at this very Time, in this Assembly, an *Example*, full of Encouragement unto these *humiliations,* which have been thus called for."[13] Presumably Hannah Dustan served many New Englanders as a living example of Christian piety and courage. In the same vein, Reverend John Williams wrote an extensive account of his own captivity and redemption; it went through several editions and ranks as one of the most forceful Puritan statements.[14]

A second source of inspiration for early New England captivity narratives was the sermon, that quintessential Puritan expression to which several generations of congregational preachers and settlers were addicted. In addition to the usual two Sunday sermons, there were Lecture Day sermons (usually on Thursday evening), election day sermons, fast and humiliation sermons, thanksgiving sermons, artillery company sermons, funeral sermons, even execution sermons. Most were delivered by cler-

11. Williams, "Reports of Divine Kindness," appended to *Redeemed Captive,* 97.

12. Cotton Mather, *Magnalia Christi Americana: or the Ecclesiastical History of New-England, from . . . 1620 unto . . . 1698* (London, 1702), Bk. VI, 13.

13. *Humiliations,* 40.

14. Williams, *Redeemed Captive.* The best modern version is edited by Edward W. Clark (Amherst, Mass., 1976). For bibliographic details on the early editions see Vail, *Voice of the Old Frontier,* 201–202, 209, 265, 296, 300, 304, 387, 407–410.

gymen, but occasionally laymen indulged as well.[15] John Winthrop's ship-board "Model of Christian Charity" is the most famous lay sermon, but there were many others, and they formed an important, if smaller, part of the same rhetorical type. And while most sermons—lay or clerical—were never published, an impressive number were put into print and widely read. Moreover, many parishioners took notes on sermons for later meditation, and schoolchildren were required to discuss Sunday's sermon in Monday morning's class. Not surprisingly, Puritan captivity narratives borrowed liberally from sermon themes and language. Especially evident are their emphasis on moral lessons and their extensive use of biblical citations to bolster almost every argument. At root, captivity narratives were lay sermons (or, when recited secondhand by an Increase or Cotton Mather, clerical sermons) in the guise of adventure stories.

Third, and perhaps most significant, the Puritan captivity narrative owed much of its tone and content to "jeremiads"—those peculiar laments by Puritan clergymen (and, again, sometimes by laymen) that accused New England of backsliding from the high ideals and noble achievements of the founders, of God's evident or impending wrath, and of the need for immediate and thorough reformation.[16] That theme emerged as early as the 1650s, sometimes in the pronouncements of the founding generation itself, but not until the 1660s and 1670s did the jeremiad become a literary cliché. Usually it appeared in sermons, but it also took other forms, such as Michael Wigglesworth's poetic *God's Controversy with New England* and the report of the Reforming Synod of 1679, which epitomized

15. Puritan sermons have been studied from diverse perspectives. Suggestive if not always convincing analyses include John Brown, *Puritan Preaching in England* (New York, 1900); Babette M. Levy, *Preaching in the First Half Century of New England History* (Hartford, Conn., 1945); Bruce A. Rosenberg, *The Art of the American Folk Preacher* (New York, 1970); Horton Davies, *Worship and Theology in England*, vols. I–II (Princeton, N.J., 1970–1975); and Emory Elliott, *Power and the Pulpit in Puritan New England* (Princeton, N.J., 1975). Convenient anthologies of Puritan sermons include Phyllis M. Jones and Nicholas R. Jones, eds., *Salvation in New England: Selections from the Sermons of the First Preachers* (Austin, Tex., 1977); and A. W. Plumstead, ed., *The Wall and The Garden: Selected Massachusetts Election Sermons, 1670–1775* (Minneapolis, 1968). Many sermons are reprinted in the Arno Press, "Library of American Puritan Writings: The Seventeenth Century," selected by Sacvan Bercovitch (New York, 1979).

16. The best discussion of the jeremiad is Sacvan Bercovitch, *The American Jeremiad* (Madison, Wis., 1978), chaps. 1–2. Important earlier analyses include Perry Miller, *The New England Mind: From Colony to Province* (Cambridge, Mass., 1953; repr. Boston, 1968), *passim;* and Bercovitch, "Horologicals to Chronometricals: The Rhetoric of the Jeremiad," *Literary Monographs*, III (Madison, Wis., 1970).

the jeremiad genre. (Even Cotton Mather's *Magnalia Christi Americana*, a massive ecclesiastical history of New England, is part jeremiad.) In 1662, Wigglesworth, the lugubrious Massachusetts minister-poet, interpreted a prolonged drought as a clear sign of God's growing wrath:

> For thinke not, O Backsliders, in your heart,
>   That I shall still your evill manners beare:
> Your sinns me press as sheaves do load a cart,
>   And therefore I will plague you for this geare
> Except you seriously, and soon, repent,
> Ile not delay your pain and heavy punishment.[17]

The impetus for such harangues came partly from an exaggerated sense of New England's "Golden Age" and chiefly from the Puritans' extreme biblicism. From close scrutiny of the Bible, Puritan divines drew parallels or types between the Old and New Testaments on which they based much of their religious and social doctrine. They used this typological system, for example, to justify their rejecting the corruptions of Old England for the wilderness of New England, thus reenacting the Israelites' flight from Egypt to the milk-and-honey land of Canaan. The ramifications of Puritan typology are too complex for adequate discussion here, but among them was the belief that God, in return for the colonists' suffering in the wilderness and establishing a new Zion, would protect and prosper His newly chosen people—*if* they remained true to His laws and steadfast in their faith.[18] Puritan enthusiasts such as Increase and Cotton Mather searched relentlessly for evidence of God's favor to New Englanders, which they duly published under titles such as *Illustrious Providences, Wonderful Works of God,* and *Remarkable Judgements of God.*[19] Predictably, the Mathers and their fellow seventeenth-century colonists found what they were looking for: miraculous deliverances from danger for the godly, divine retribution for the godless.

17. Wigglesworth, "God's Controversy with New England," *Massachusetts Historical Society Proceedings,* 12 (1871–1873), 89.
18. Among several modern studies of Puritan typology, see especially Sacvan Bercovitch, ed., *Typology and Early American Literature* (Amherst, Mass., 1972).
19. Increase Mather, *An Essay for the Recording of Illustrious Providences... Especially in New England* (Boston, 1684); Cotton Mather, *The Wonderful Works of God Commemorated...* (Boston, 1690); Cotton Mather, *Terribilia Dei: Remarkable Judgements of God, on Several Sorts of Offenders... among the People of New England...* (Boston, 1697). For additional works by the Mathers on the same subject see Thomas J. Holmes, *Increase Mather, A Bibliography of His Works,* 2 vols. (Cleveland, 1931); and Holmes, *Cotton Mather, A Bibliography of His Works,* 3 vols. (Cambridge, Mass., 1940).

8

This search for the Lord's guiding hand had implications far beyond individual rewards and punishments. Sins—especially a persistent flouting of the true faith—brought punishment to the entire community because of the Puritans' compact with the Lord; as John Williams explained, "the great God . . . hath taken us into *Covenant Relation* to Himself."[20] Accordingly, the righteous must suffer along with transgressors when He punished His flock for its accumulated wrongs. Mary Rowlandson was only the first of the Puritan captivity narrators to identify Indian depredations with God's retribution against the entire community: "It is said, *Psal.* 81. 13. 14. *Oh that my People had hearkned to me and* Israel *had walked in my ways, I should soon have subdued their Enemies, and turned my hand against their Adversaries.* But now our perverse and evil carriages in the sight of the Lord, have so offended him, that instead of turning his hand against them, the Lord feeds and nourishes them up to be a scourge to the whole Land."[21] Two decades later, John Williams opened his narrative with essentially the same message: "The History I am going to Write, proves, That Days of *Fasting* & *Prayer,* without REFORMATION, will not avail, to Turn away the Anger of God from a Professing People."[22]

Williams's contemporaries had frequently witnessed God's anger at incomplete reformation. In the 1670s and after, New England suffered a frightful series of major and minor calamities. The worst came in 1675–1676 when the region's most devastating Indian war claimed the lives of nearly a tenth of its adult colonial males—the highest mortality rate in American military history, before or since—and took a correspondingly heavy toll in property: twelve thousand homes burned, eight thousand head of cattle destroyed, innumerable farmlands laid waste. And the destruction did not end in 1676 with the death of Metacomet (King Philip); rather, it shifted to the relatively vulnerable northern frontier in Maine, New Hampshire, and western Massachusetts where Indians, often accompanied by their French allies, continued to raid isolated farms and villages. No wonder the Reforming Synod of Puritan ministers and lawyers concluded in 1679 that "God hath a Controversy with his New-England People"; the Indians, they believed, were His principal rod of chastisement.[23] No wonder too that Puritan captives looked inward for

20. Williams, "Reports of Divine Kindness," 97.
21. Rowlandson, *Soveraignty & Goodness of God,* 62.
22. Williams, *Redeemed Captive,* 1.
23. On King Philip's War see Douglas Edward Leach, *Flintlock and Tomahawk: New England in King Philip's War* (New York, 1958). The quote from the Reforming Synod is in [Increase Mather], *The Necessity of Reformation* . . . (Boston, 1679), 1.

9

signs of their own shortcomings. Most captives found convincing evidence; others acknowledged their failings but also recognized that even the innocent and the saintly must suffer when God punished an errant flock. "It is no new thing," wrote the anonymous author of the preface to Mary Rowlandson's narrative, "for Gods precious ones to drink as deep as others, of the Cup of common Calamity."[24]

Puritan readers responded enthusiastically to the captivity genre not only because it fused the prominent features of spiritual autobiography, lay sermon, and jeremiad with those of the secular adventure story. In its descriptions of the forced rending of Puritan families, the narratives unintentionally added an element of pathos that appealed profoundly to a society which placed unusual emphasis on family ties and responsibilities. This fundamental social unit was often revered in Puritan tracts and sermons and was frequently the subject of governmental legislation and proclamations. The importance Puritans gave to the family undoubtedly touched a universal chord among readers of the narratives and made more poignant their grief over the death of loved ones that so often accompanied captivities. Accounts of the murder of a husband, wife, or child are numerous, and the understated descriptions of their deaths helped the narrators weave their fascinating and sometimes horrifying tapestry of despair and salvation. A modern reader—like readers in the seventeenth and eighteenth centuries—cannot resist deep sympathy for Mary Rowlandson when her six-year-old daughter dies in her arms or for John Williams when he learns of his wife's death by an Indian tomahawk after she fell through a frozen river.

Despite the importance a Puritan attached to family love and security, he knew that these affections were ultimately temporal and must not supersede the love of God. Had not Jesus said that a true Christian should follow Him (Luke 14:26) and if necessary forsake his family? And Puritans were familiar with the lesson of Bunyan's *Pilgrim's Progress:* every Christian must turn his back on spouse and family, shoulder his burden of sins, and start out for the Celestial City. This ultimate reliance on the self and its relation to God often conflicted with the family communal bond. A Puritan whose family had been dispersed after capture suffered an enormous sense of loss and guilt, tempered only slightly by the dictates of religion. The narratives of Mary Rowlandson, John Williams, and Elizabeth Hanson bear witness to the depth of such heart-wrenching experiences.

24. Rowlandson, *Soveraignty & Goodness of God,* A2v.

PURITAN CAPTIVITY NARRATIVES have interest for modern readers beyond their poignant expression of religious fervor and individual anguish. As anthropological records they recount unique individual and group experiences; as observations of native tribes, many of which no longer exist, they provide rare descriptions of northeastern Indian life; and as ethnological histories they shed light on conflicts between disparate cultures—New England's against Algonquian-Iroquoian and, in some cases, New England's against French Canadian.

Modern readers of an Indian captivity narrative are likely to see what anthropologists term a rite of passage, or, more specifically, an initiation process by which a person moves from one set of perceptions to another. Several scholars have isolated the initiation process as a vital element in the captivity experience.[25] There is, however, a danger in focusing too intently on the initiation ordeal and overlooking the significance of the much longer and equally profound captivity experience itself. The day-to-day struggle with an alien culture is the mainspring of the experience and the driving force of the captive's attempt to understand the change he has undergone.

Anthropologist Victor Turner provides an explanation of the initiation process that permits a broader focus on the three stages of *rites de passage,* or transitions from one social position to another—separation, margin, and reaggregation.[26] Turner's analysis can be applied to captivity narratives. First, captives began to gain new knowledge about their own culture and American Indian culture when they were separated from their natal environment—in Puritan narratives, a New England town or frontier settlement. They then entered a "margin" (or "liminal") phase where they lost the security they had enjoyed as English subjects and usually suffered servitude in a culture they considered grossly inferior to their own. With their world in psychological as well as physical disarray, the captives initially saw

25. See, for example, Richard Slotkin, *Regeneration through Violence: The Mythology of the American Frontier, 1600–1860* (Middletown, Conn., 1973), 103–104. Because this work relies so heavily on Joseph Campbell's monomyth theory (*Hero with a Thousand Faces* [New York, 1949]), it should be used with discretion; it does, however, contain provocative ideas and a valuable bibliography. See also James Axtell, "The White Indians of Colonial America," *William and Mary Quarterly,* 3rd ser., 32 (1975), 55–88; and Richard VanDerBeets, "The Indian Captivity Narrative as Ritual," *American Literature,* 43 (1971–1972), 562.

26. Turner, *Dramas, Fields, and Metaphors: Symbolic Action in Human Society* (Ithaca, N.Y., 1974), 231–232. Turner expands and modifies Arnold Van Gennep's terms of separation, margin, and reaggregation.

their new social relationships and consequent obligations as punishment and humiliation; unfamiliarity with Indian language kept them from understanding even nonthreatening remarks. Later they became more flexible and began to comprehend, perhaps even to appreciate, their captors' beliefs and manner of living.[27] Finally, in the third stage, they were redeemed and reintegrated ("reaggregated") into their own culture.

During the liminal phase the captive witnessed the bulk of what he recorded in his narrative, for in that stage—the actual captivity—he was relatively free from the social strictures and cultural values of his previous life. His natal culture's values were called into question; he must adapt to foreign ways or starve or be killed. Cut loose from his normal guideposts of language and social relationships, he entertained ideas and values that colonial New England did not allow. Old patterns were abandoned and new ones acquired. Just to keep alive, for example, all captives had to eat food they previously considered inedible. Mary Rowlandson drank broth boiled from a horse's leg and ate bark from trees, and found them palatable; Hannah Swarton ate *"Groundnuts, Acorns, Purslain, Hogweed, Weeds, Roots,* and sometimes *Dogs Flesh";* Elizabeth Hanson scavenged "Guts and Garbage" of the beavers her masters had eaten.[28] And virtually every captive, even in time of war, eventually admired the Indians' ability to accommodate harsh conditions. A captive's admiration usually extended only to Indian clothing and housing or to personal stamina and ingenuity; he rarely appreciated the complexities of Algonquian spiritual life or the Indians' approach to social and political organization. But at least the captives' earlier prejudices lost some of their rigidity when confronted by the realities of Indian life.

27. Psychologists and other students of human behavior have long recognized the tendency of captives—whether they are taken by kidnappers, terrorists, or military forces—to develop sympathy for their captors. In some instances, the sympathy reflects a new awareness of the captors' viewpoint or culture—a true learning experience. But in other instances, captives admire, even emulate, captors who abuse and threaten them. The essential mechanism in this ostensibly illogical identification with the enemy is the captive's utter dependence on the captor for every necessity, even for life itself. For some widely diverse but highly suggestive writings on this matter, see Bruno Bettelheim, "Individual and Mass Behavior in Extreme Situations," *Journal of Abnormal and Social Psychology,* 38 (1943), 417–452; William Sargant, *Battle for the Mind: A Physiology of Conversion and Brainwashing* (New York, 1957); Dorothy Rabinowitz, "The Hostage Mentality," *Commentary,* 63 (June 1977), 70–72; and Walter Reich, "Hostages and the [Stockholm] Syndrome," *New York Times,* Jan. 15, 1980.

28. Rowlandson, *Soveraignty & Goodness of God,* 18–19, 21–22, 33; Swarton in Cotton Mather, *Magnalia Christi Americana,* Bk. VI, 10; Hanson, *God's Mercy Surmounting Man's Cruelty* (Philadelphia, 1728), 13.

Rarely was a captive taken singly. Usually he was part of a group, often survivors of the same attack. Seeing the death of a parent or sibling sometimes left him in a psychological trauma, too shocked to rebel. When captives shared such a crisis, a small community of sufferers emerged. Turner calls the resulting *esprit de corps* "communitas"— the group identity created by those in the same liminal experience.[29] Communitas can be seen in the New England narratives when captives gathered for group prayer. By praying together, Puritan hostages gained comfort from familiar religious rites and values while simultaneously restating their cultural separateness from their Indian or French captors. Both Indians and Frenchmen recognized the cohesive strength of group prayer and its detriment to acculturation, and both usually proscribed it.

Although collective activities strengthened common identity, Indian retribution against all captives when one of them escaped probably did more to cement communal bonds. When an English prisoner ran away, the captors usually threatened to kill one or more of those remaining. Few captives risked the responsibility, and the ensuing guilt, for such retaliation against their compatriots. John Williams reported one situation: "In the Night an *English* Man made his escape: in the Morning I was call'd for, and ordered by the General to tell the English, That if any more made their escape, they would burn the rest of the Prisoners."[30] Sometimes the Indians vented their wrath on those who escaped and were recaptured. John Gyles described his brother's fate: "My unfortunate Brother who was taken with me, after about three Years Captivity, deserted with an Englishman who was taken from *Casco-Bay,* and was retaken by the Indians at *New-Harbour* and carried back to *Penobscot Fort,* where they were both tortured at a Stake by Fire for some time; then their Noses and Ears were cut off, and they made to eat them; after which they were burned to Death at the Stake."[31] Such intimidating events worked paradoxically on a surviving captive: on one hand they forced him to endure, even to cooperate with his captors; on the other hand they heightened his resentment of the captors' culture and raised psychological barriers to acculturation.

Each captivity narrative was written during the postliminal period, usually soon after redemption, and reflects the profound impact of the li-

29. Turner, *Dramas, Fields, and Metaphors,* 231–232.

30. Williams, *Redeemed Captive,* 7. For a similar threat see "Quentin Stockwell's Relation" in Increase Mather, *An Essay for the Recording of Illustrious Providences* (Boston, 1684), 45–46.

31. John Gyles, *Memoirs of Odd Adventures, Strange Deliverances, etc., in the Captivity of John Gyles, Esq. . . .* (Boston, 1736), 11–12.

minal experience on the writer. And whatever the depth and variety of the impact, redeemed captives seemed compelled, like Coleridge's ancient mariner, to recite their tales. Among the scores of narratives that spanned the centuries and the continent, several distinct categories emerge.

First, some writers give the impression that they had not substantially changed, although former captives were obviously not quite the same psychologically as they had been before their ordeals. After redemption, once again in familiar surroundings, captives still vividly remembered their months in the wilderness. Mary Rowlandson, for one, could not forget: *"I can remember the time, when I used to sleep quietly without workings in my thoughts, whole nights together, but now it is other wayes with me.* When all are fast about me, and no eye open, but his who ever waketh, my thoughts are upon things past."[32]

For women especially, the return to New England society posed problems of readjustment and reacceptance. Although no ethnological evidence indicates that northeastern Indians ever raped women prisoners, as Plains Indians sometimes did, female captives sometimes felt a need to defend their sexual conduct. Rowlandson, for example, assured her readers that *"not one of them ever offered me the least abuse of unchastity to me, in word or action.* Though some are ready to say I speak it for my own credit, *But I speak it in the presence of God, and to his Glory."*[33] Similarly, Elizabeth Hanson insisted that the Indians were "very civil toward their captive Women, not offering any Incivility by any indecent Carriage (unless they be much overgone in Liquor[)]," and implied that no intoxicated Indians had molested her.[34]

Under captivity, when many undreamed-of things could occur, both fear and its opposite—temptation—were omnipresent. There was always the suspicion that redeemed captives had, consciously or unconsciously, found Indian ways irresistible, and that they had to some degree "gone savage." Such suspicions came easily in a culture that interpreted the form of God's displeasure as a reflection of its cause. "Christians in this Land, have become too like unto the Indians," the Reforming Synod declared, "and then we need not wonder if the Lord hath afflicted us by them."[35] Thus community group pressure urged captives to reaffirm their natal culture's values more fervently than ever and to deny the attractions of "savage" life. On the other hand, it was acceptable to admit, as Hannah

32. Rowlandson, *Soveraignty & Goodness of God,* 71.
33. Rowlandson, *Soveraignty & Goodness of God,* 64.
34. Hanson, *God's Mercy,* 35–36.
35. Increase Mather, *Necessity of Reformation,* 5.

Swarton repeatedly does, that she strayed from God's path so long as it was a torment of the soul, not the passions. Mather, Swarton's mouthpiece, defends her honor while steadily guiding her toward conversion.[36] Most New England narrators did not need such help. John Williams's *Redeemed Captive* and Mary Rowlandson's *Soveraignty & Goodness of God* emphatically reaffirm the Puritans' errand into the wilderness. It may not be coincidental that Williams was a clergyman and Rowlandson a clergyman's wife. The clerical class had the deepest commitment to Puritan values.

Narrators who gained empathetic insight into Indian culture constitute a second group. Although they reaffirm their natal ways, they acknowledge some Indian virtues. John Gyles is a good example. He admired the Indians' skill in hunting moose as well as the powwow's ability to forecast the hunt's success through dream visions; yet he considered Indian myths of no more value than fairy tales. Similarly, Gyles praised the Indians' adaptation to their environment but believed them too influenced by the unpredictable elements of nature and too addicted to feasting to plan for future needs. On the whole, adult Puritan captives successfully resisted efforts at assimilation by the French and Indians. Puritan indoctrination had been thorough, and a pervasive sense that an omniscient God kept close eye on His chosen flock was real enough to shield most adult New Englanders from cultural innovation.[37]

A third group of narratives was written by those who had difficulty adjusting to their natal culture after long exposure to Indian life. The number of such accounts is small and includes none of the New England captivities. However, as a matter of illustration, James Smith's *Account of the Remarkable Occurences in the Life and Travels of Col. James Smith* reflects a substantial assimilation of Indian habits.[38] Captured in 1755 on the Pennsylvania frontier by a Caughnawaga and two Delawares, Smith lived for four years with Indians in the Ohio territory. He did not publish his narrative until 1799 because he felt that "at that time [1760] the Americans were so little acquainted with Indian affairs, I apprehended a great

---

36. Cotton Mather, *Magnalia Christi Americana*, Bk. VI, 10–14 *passim*.

37. For a discussion of Puritan captives' attraction to Indian life and the reasons why most resisted it, see Alden T. Vaughan and Daniel K. Richter, "Crossing the Cultural Divide: Indians and New Englanders, 1605–1763," *American Antiquarian Society Proceedings*, 90 (1980), 23–99, especially 81–83. At most, about twelve percent of the captives who spent the last part of their captivities with the Indians, rather than with the French, remained permanently among them.

38. For bibliographic details see Vail, *Voice of the Old Frontier*, 447.

part of it would be viewed as fable and romance." Although Smith returned to white America, he sympathetically described his life among the Indians and so thoroughly absorbed their military tactics that he taught them to settlers on the Ohio frontier.[39] A more difficult adjustment is illustrated in John Tanner's narrative, published in 1830. Tanner spent over thirty years among the Ojibway tribe and, not surprisingly, his account offers a more accurate picture of Indian life than narratives by those who lived only briefly with their captors. When Tanner attempted to return to "civilized" society, he was rejected, and he probably rejoined the culture he had so thoroughly absorbed.[40]

Another category of narratives, this one hypothetical, could have been written by those who never returned to their natal culture. If captives who entirely forsook their original environment—who completely transculturated—had written of their experiences, we would have a still more sympathetic and knowledgeable portrayal of Indian life. This category would be filled mainly by those who had been captured as children; in most cases they forgot their mother tongue and hence could not easily have written their narratives. The Indians and the French were well aware, of course, that children did not have the physical or psychic strength to resist acculturation and had not yet acquired the political and cultural loyalties of adulthood. Although a captive child was not exactly a Lockean *tabula rasa* for his Indian captors, he readily learned a new language and new values. (By the same token, English missionaries made special efforts to indoctrinate Indian children into Christianity and European customs.) The most famous example of an unredeemed Puritan youngster's assimilation into Indian and French ways was Eunice Williams, daughter of John Williams. Aged seven when captured, Eunice remained in custody long after the rest of her family returned to New England, and she eventually succumbed to the alien culture. She was converted to Catholicism by Canadian nuns, married an Indian, and refused all subsequent efforts to reunite her with her Puritan family.[41] The fact that many children captives chose not to

39. James Smith, *Scoouwa: James Smith's Indian Captivity Narrative*, ed. John J. Barsotti (Columbus, Ohio, 1978), 16.

40. Tanner, *A Narrative of the Captivity of John Tanner* (New York, 1830).

41. For a discussion of captives from all parts of British America who were assimilated by Indians, see Axtell, "White Indians of Colonial America." The demographic aspects of Puritan captives—numbers, age, sex, and length of captivity—are analyzed in Vaughan and Richter, "Crossing the Cultural Divide." Eunice Williams's story is best followed in John Williams's narrative and Alexander Medlicott, Jr., "Return to the Land of Light: A Plea to an Unredeemed Captive," *New England Quarterly*, 38 (1965), 202–216. A valuable exam-

return to their families must have shaken New England's confidence. Perhaps these youthful expatriots are a bittersweet symbol of the failure of the concept of "progress," a notion to which the Puritans firmly subscribed and which became almost universal among nineteenth-century Americans.

DESPITE THE RELATIVE BREVITY of the captivity period for most captives (usually a few months to a few years), the narratives collectively provide a fascinating glimpse of Indian culture. It is only a glimpse; Puritan society had abundant legal and social strictures against imitating or admiring the Indians' "prophane course of life."[42] Indian ways were to be shunned, not emulated; "savagery" was feared and despised, not appreciated or respected. Hence captives had little incentive, save their own curiosity or a desire for dramatic detail, to describe native customs, and the few exceptions are marred by pervasive ethnocentricity.

Even if the captives had been willing and unbiased, the task of description would have been formidable. Most raiding parties probably had warriors from several tribes, each with a slightly—sometimes markedly—different cultural heritage; the same was often true of the villages to which the captives were taken. And although most Indian captors were from the northeastern Algonquian linguistic group, a significant minority were from the linguistically and culturally distant Iroquois Confederacy. Especially important among the latter were Mohawks who had converted to Roman Catholicism, nominally at least, and had moved to the Caughnawaga missionary settlement near Montreal. (Many Puritan captives, including Eunice Williams, were thus simultaneously confronted by Indian and French cultural pressures.) Most New England prisoners were taken to southeastern Canada, where French, Algonquian, and Iroquoian cultural influences were gradually but unevenly blending. Bewildered captives could scarcely have comprehended the complex and ever-changing Franco-Indian world of the late seventeenth and early eighteenth

---

ination of the legends that accumulate around famous unredeemed captives, especially Eunice Williams, is Dawn Lander Gherman, "From Parlour to Teepee: The White Squaw on the American Frontier" (Ph.D. diss., University of Massachusetts, 1975), 70–91. The most famous narrative of a captive who remained with her captors is the semi-autobiographical account by Mary Jemison of Pennsylvania. In 1755, at age twelve, she was taken by the Seneca, with whom she lived until her death in 1833. Her career was described by James Everett Seaver, who interviewed her in 1823, in *A Narrative of the Life of Mrs. Mary Jemison* (Canandaigua, N.Y., 1824). Many subsequent editions have been issued, some of them entitled *Deh-he-wa-mis . . . the White Woman of the Genessee*.

42. For example, J. Hammond Trumbull, ed., *The Public Records of the Colony of Connecticut . . .* , 15 vols. (Hartford, 1850–1890), I, 78.

centuries, but we can wish they had tried harder to describe, even if they could not understand or appreciate, their new surroundings.

When ethnographic material does appear in the captivity narratives, it is valuable and fascinating. Mary Rowlandson, for example, included a lively if not entirely sympathetic description of the ceremonial preparations for an attack on Sudbury, Massachusetts.[43] Elizabeth Hanson explained (unsympathetically) Indian eating customs.[44] John Gyles told much about Indian hunting and farming practices, methods of preserving food, and burial and marriage rites. Gyles, in fact, came closest of the Puritan narrators to providing comprehensive ethnographic information. Although he appears to have been a member in good standing of the Puritan community, his account is conspicuously less pietistic than the others; his relatively secular turn of mind allowed him to describe Indian and French customs more fully and even to devote several pages to the curious habits of the beaver.[45]

Several Puritan narrators dwelled on Indian maltreatment of captives—especially Quentin Stockwell and John Gyles, who were apparently handled more harshly than most New England captives. Gyles twice was saved from torture ceremonies, once by his master and once by a squaw and an Indian girl. In each instance, Gyles's savior pledged a gift to the tribe to reprieve him. Gyles later explained that "A Captive among the Indians is exposed to all manner of Abuse, and to the utmost Tortures, unless his Master, or some of his Master's Relations, lay down a Ransom, such as a Bag of Corn, or a Blanket, or such like: by which they may redeem them from their Cruelties." When Gyles's kindly master later traveled to Canada and left him with less friendly guardians, Gyles fell into the hands of Cape Sable Indians who inflicted the torture that he had earlier avoided.[46]

43. Rowlandson, *Soveraignty & Goodness of God*, 50–52.

44. Hanson, *God's Mercy*, 12–13, 15–17, 22, 24.

45. Gyles, *Memoirs of Odd Adventures, passim*, especially 24–27. Gyles was a captive from 1689 to 1695, but his narrative did not appear until 1736. By the later date the old Puritan enthusiasm had severely waned, and the new enthusiasm of the Great Awakening had yet to make its full impact. That may account for Gyles's secular tone; it may also reflect an editor's influence. For a summary of the ethnographic information to be found in captivity narratives throughout North America and over the span of three centuries, see Marius Barbeau, "Indian Captivities," *American Philosophical Society Proceedings*, 94 (1950), 522–548, especially 531–543.

46. Gyles, *Memoirs of Odd Adventures*, 5. For a comprehensive but somewhat muddled analysis of cruelty to captives, see Nathaniel Knowles, "The Torture of Captives by the Indians of Eastern North America," *American Philosophical Society Proceedings*, 82 (1940), 151–225.

Perhaps because he wrote his narrative long after the era of intense Puritan piety, Gyles attributed Indian compassion or cruelty to human inclination. Earlier captives saw the Indians as God's pawns, at least when it came to kindness. John Williams epitomized this aspect of the Puritan perspective: among "Passages of Divine Providence," he reported that "God hath made such . . . characters . . . as delighted in cruelty, to pity and compassionate such who were led into captivity by them. Made them bear on their Arms, and carry on their Shoulders our *Little Ones,* unable to Travel, Feed the Prisoners with the best of their Provisions: Yea, sometimes pinch themselves, as to their daily food, rather than their Captives."[47] Similarly, Cotton Mather attributed the Indian men's reluctance to molest female captives to "a wonderful Restraint from God upon the Bruitish Salvages."[48] But whether God or man got the credit, New England narratives clearly reveal that some Indians were kind, some were cruel, and that generally the treatment of women and children was as humane as wartime conditions allowed.

Puritan perceptions of how Indians treated captives may be partly explained by the narrators' norms for family structure and its responsibilities. The New England family centered on the conjugal relationship of husband, wife, and children. Servants who resided under the roof of a Puritan home were treated almost as family members. They called the patriarchal head of the family "master" and owed him loyal and industrious service. Masters, in turn, were obliged by law and custom to treat their servants humanely and to provide them with adequate food, shelter, clothing, education, and religious training. Master and servant, in short, had almost the same relationship as father and child.[49] (A sharp increase in African and Indian slaves in the eighteenth century helped to undermine the earlier master-servant relationship.) A Puritan captive of the Indians usually referred to his principal captor as master, which not only implied the captive's inferior status but also suggested that, in the captive's eyes, each had reciprocal obligations. In many of the Puritan narratives, captives—unconsciously thinking in terms of their culture alone—complain bitterly

47. Williams, *Redeemed Captive,* 98.
48. Cotton Mather, *Good Fetch'd Out of Evil* (Boston, 1706), 33–34.
49. For a valuable general account of the Puritan family, see Edmund S. Morgan, *The Puritan Family: Religion and Domestic Relations in Seventeenth Century New England,* rev. ed. (New York, 1966). Of special relevance is the final chapter on Puritan tribalism. Among the most extensive Puritan statements are Cotton Mather, *A Family Well-Ordered* . . . (Boston, 1699), and Benjamin Wadsworth, *The Well-Ordered Family* . . . (Boston, 1712).

of the failure of Indian masters to provide them with enough food or comfort. Yet a captive often realized, as he grew more accustomed to Indian ways, that he usually ate as well or as poorly as his captors; the ill treatment of Elizabeth Hanson and her children in the 1720s was an exception, not the rule.

The Puritan family centered primarily on the relationship of husband, wife, and children in what anthropologists call a cognatic descent group: all descendants, both male and female, are emphasized equally. Northeastern Indians, on the contrary, employed a complex mixture of unilineal descent groups, both matrilineal and patrilineal. The lineage groups of a particular clan of a tribe could be traced through either husband or wife. Thus, an Indian child could inherit a distinct group of rights and responsibilities from his mother and quite a different set from his father.[50] Moreover, in many tribes a man might have two or three wives, which not only offended the English captive but added to his bewilderment over the intricate matrix of Indian social bonds. In Elizabeth Hanson's narrative, for example, when her master ordered his son to beat her child, "the Indian boy's [maternal] grandmother, would not suffer him to do it." Hanson's protectoress later became so upset with her son-in-law's behavior that she moved out of his wigwam.[51]

Because all captives were prisoners of war, some animosity toward Indians or French captors was inevitable, whatever the treatment accorded the prisoners and whatever the reasons for it. Perhaps inevitable too was the combination of war-bred enmity with latent contempt for Indians that gradually shifted the New England captivity narrative from an essentially religious tract, with occasional insights into Indian culture, to what Roy Harvey Pearce has aptly called a "vehicle of Indian-hatred."[52] That motif had first appeared in the preface to Rowlandson's narrative—though significantly not in the narrative itself—in an assertion that "none can imagine what it is to be captivated, and enslaved to such atheisticall proud, wild, cruel, barbarous, bruitish (in one word) diabolicall creatures as these, the worst of the heathen."[53] But not until Cotton Mather's accounts, espe-

---

50. For a general introduction to the complexities of kinship, see two chapters in Robin Fox, *Encounter with Anthropology* (New York, 1968), "Comparative Family Patterns" (85–94) and "Kinship and Alliance" (95–112). Useful also for its information on tribes in northern New England and southern Canada is *Handbook of North American Indians*, XV, *Northeast*, ed. Bruce G. Trigger (Washington, D.C., 1978).

51. Hanson, *God's Mercy*, 26–28.

52. "The Significances of the Captivity Narrative," *American Literature*, 19 (1947), 5.

53. Rowlandson, *Soveraignty & Goodness of God*, A3v.

cially those published in *Decennium Luctuosum* (1699) and repeated in *Magnalia Christi Americana* (1702), did the anti-Indian and anti-French themes become blatant. Late in the seventeenth century Mather lashed out at "those Ravenous howling *Wolves*," and "these cursed Blood-Hounds"; by the turn of the century, Mather was ranting about "those *Dragons of the Wilderness*," and "the *Dark places* of *New-England*, where the *Indians* had their Unapproachable *Kennels* . . . *of Cruelty*."[54] That atrocities took place is undeniable; the point to be made here is that Mather began the transformation of captivity narratives into a new sub-genre. By 1740, as Pearce notes, "religious concerns came to be incidental at most; the intent of the typical writer of the narrative was to register as much hatred of the French and Indians as possible . . . The captivity narrative had become the American equivalent of the Grub Street criminal biography."[55] By then it had also ceased to be Puritan.

Most New England narratives before mid-eighteenth century praised the French for tempering the Indians' cruelty, providing material comfort, and arranging prisoner exchanges. That did not prevent Puritan writers from venting their contempt for the "Popish" or "Romish" religion, as can best be seen in the narratives by Williams and Swarton. Both accounts record extensive debates between the authors and their Catholic hosts, which forcefully illustrate how the Puritan mind continued to battle what it considered the regressive doctrines of Roman Catholicism. The Puritans' antagonists were seldom the Canadian laity, whom the narrators often thanked explicitly and abundantly, but rather the Jesuits and other clerics who assumed a God-directed edict to convert English captives— just as the Puritans assumed the opposite. Puritan captivity narratives thus suggest a cultural hostility between Canada and New England that in some ways paralleled the cultural chasm between English and Indians.

IN STYLE AS WELL AS SUBSTANCE, Puritan captivity narratives reflect the dominant characteristics of early New England. The narratives are distinguished not only by their religious fervor but (not surprisingly) by the clergy's close involvement in their composition, which gives them a distinct tone. Of the best New England narratives before 1750, only a few can be considered purely lay products. Several were written by clerics or their immediate kin; others were transcribed and embellished by cler-

---

54. Cotton Mather, *Souldiers Counselled and Comforted* (Boston, 1689), 28; *Fair Weather. Or, Considerations to Dispel the Clouds . . . of Discontent . . .* (Boston, 1691), 90; *Good Fetch'd Out of Evil* (Boston, 1706), 4; *Magnalia Christi Americana*, Bk. VII, 69.

55. Pearce, "Significances of the Captivity Narrative," 6–7.

gymen, especially Cotton Mather. Even John Gyles, the most secular of the Puritan narrators, may have leaned heavily on a local chaplain for stylistic guidance.

Authors with clerical affiliation or assistance were not reluctant to arouse the reader's emotions, though they were less inclined to sensationalism than were later writers. Cotton Mather especially employed attention-grabbing devices usually suited for oral delivery, such as alliteration, exaggerated emphasis, and exclamations. And because of his concern with communal rather than individual experience, Mather often resorted to generalized diction. This tendency is evident in his attempts to deal with the physical landscape. When Mather writes of Mary Plaisted's journey into captivity, his description is not tactile but mental, filtered through a mind more concerned with spiritual than with physical reality. "But she must now Travel many Days," he wrote, "thro' Woods, and Swamps, and Rocks, and over Mountains, and Frost and Snow, until she could stir no farther."[56] By contrast, John Williams had experienced captivity firsthand. Although his diction too is often general, he can recall physical details precisely; he writes, for instance, "Each night I wrung blood out of my stockings," and "My shins also were very sore, being cut with crusty snow."[57]

Although Mary Rowlandson cited biblical sources more than Williams did, she balanced spiritual generalities with precise observations. For example, in her chilling description of the attack on Lancaster, she and other victims were "standing amazed, with the blood running down to our heels."[58] Williams was more concerned with the Canadian Jesuits' attempts to convert his flock to Roman Catholicism than with an accurate rendering of the physical details of his wilderness experience. His narrative, in fact, is more precise in its Canadian than its New England portions. Rowlandson, on the other hand, displayed an acute understanding of the psychology of her Indian captors. She described with keen insight the second wife of her Indian master. Weetamoo, she tells us, was "a severe and proud Dame . . . bestowing every day in dressing her self neat as much time as any of the Gentry of the land: powdering her hair, and painting her face, going with neck-laces, with Jewels in her ears, and Bracelets upon her hands: When she had dressed her self, her work was to make Girdles of *Wampum* and *Beads.*" Rowlandson thus reveals her mis-

56. Cotton Mather, *Magnalia Christi Americana*, Bk. VII, 71.
57. Williams, *Redeemed Captive*, 16.
58. Rowlandson, *Soveraignty & Goodness of God*, 4.

tress's preoccupation with cosmetic baubles; Weetamoo's vanity becomes obvious.[59]

Gyles, too, presents his observations more carefully than his clerical counterparts. He can be meticulous in his description, even excruciating in detail. For example, Gyles contracted a severe case of frostbite, and wrote: "Soon after the Skin came off my Feet from my Ankles whole like a Shoe, and left my Toes naked without a Nail, and the ends of my great Toe-Bones bare, which in a little time turn'd black, so that I was obliged to cut the first Joint off with my Knife."[60] Later writers of captivity narratives would strive for such sensational effects, but Gyles does not indulge in gory detail for its own sake. His narrative unfolds with honesty and simplicity—no pious ejaculations nor infants with bashed-in skulls. He does not see his Indian companions through Rousseau-colored glasses; rather he identifies with them, often using "we" and "our" when referring to his captors.

Gyles's structural form also sets his narrative apart from earlier New England captivity accounts. Although it follows the usual chronological sequence, some of its chapters interrupt the narrative flow. Chapter VI, for example, presents a "description of several creatures commonly taken by the Indians on St. John's River." That Gyles would pause in his story to include such an account suggests a subtle shift in author-audience relations. It is difficult to imagine Mather, Williams, or Rowlandson succumbing to such a natural history urge. Thus, by the time Gyles published his story, captivity narratives were in the process of becoming a sub*literary* genre; its audience expected not only a truthful tale but information about Indians, the landscape, and animals of which most townsfolk had no first-hand knowledge. Perhaps such pressure encouraged editors to "improve" the narratives for better reception.

Although Elizabeth Hanson was Quaker, her story belongs within the New England captivity narrative framework. The writer of the three-paragraph preface to her narrative of *God's Mercy Surmounting Man's Cruelty* alludes to biblical themes as well as contemporary historians, including, apparently, Cotton Mather. Hanson was captured in Maine and she, like other New Englanders, was bought from her captors by the Canadian French.[61] When compared to another famous Quaker captivity

59. Rowlandson, *Soveraignty & Goodness of God*, 47–48.
60. *Memoirs of Odd Adventures*, 16–17.
61. For full bibliographic information see Vail, *Voice of the Old Frontier*, 216–218, 248, 272, 274, 309, 313, 336, 362–363.

narrative, Jonathan Dickinson's *God Protecting Providence*, Hanson's account—with its focus on New England terrain, on family trials, and on the moral lesson of the "kindness and goodness of God"—is clearly within the New England mold. Dickinson's narrative, published in 1699, is set in East Florida and Carolina. Moreover, Dickinson is more properly considered an Englishman than an American, and he does not conclude his narrative in the usual New England manner by asking the reader to see in the captive experience evidence of God's over-arching plan. Dickinson merely hopes "that I with all those of us that have been spared hitherto, shall never be forgetful nor unmindful of the low estate we were brought into."[62]

Hanson's work, however, stands at the end of the New England school and at the beginning of a more personal and secular response to Indian captivity. Her narrative illustrates an increasingly conscious literary attempt to arouse the reader's sentiments. The drama of her family's ordeal and her husband's death while trying to redeem one of their children proved too tempting for later editors, who liberally embellished her story.[63]

As the narratives progress chronologically over the years, biblical quotations—another evidence of Puritan piety and clerical influence—decrease. John Gyles's book (1736) has few. Instead Gyles quotes *The Odyssey*, Dryden's *Virgil*, and even Mather's *Magnalia Christi Americana*. Elizabeth Hanson's narrative (1724) contains no biblical citations. Although religious tracts and sermons remained popular literary forms well into the eighteenth century, the focus of New England captivity narratives shifted from communal to personal, from religious to secular. Later, in narratives published during the Revolution and the early national period, the emphasis shifted again to a combination of personal experiences and national spirit. Puritan narratives, like Puritanism itself, had given way to new modes of expression.

62. For full bibliographic information on Dickinson's narrative, see ibid., 191–194, 207–208, 223, 225–226, 244, 267, 292, 335, 350, 360, 370–372. The quote is from Jonathan Dickinson, *Journal; or, God's Protecting Providence, Being the Narrative of a Journey from Port Royal in Jamaica to Philadelphia between August 23, 1696 and April 1, 1697,* ed. Evangeline Walker Andrews and Charles McLean Andrews (New Haven, Conn., 1961), 78.

63. Compare, for example, the early American and English editions. The latter is conveniently reprinted, with frequent comparative passages from the 1754 American edition, in Richard VanDerBeets, *Held Captive by Indians: Selected Narratives, 1642–1836* (Knoxville, Tenn., 1973), chap. 4.

EMBELLISHMENT AND DIFFUSION marked the narratives' subsequent career. Beginning in the latter half of the eighteenth century, publishers of captivity narratives increasingly exercised a heavy editorial hand. Often they sought to imitate the sentimental fiction in vogue in England; sometimes they merely heightened the drama and polished the prose. The earlier narratives, especially those in Puritan New England, had exhibited a simple, unadorned style. Authors were not overly concerned with careful sentence patterns or orchestration of tone. Most narrators told their stories in chronological order and in a sparse, vital style that effectively conveyed the immediacy of the author's life-and-death struggle. Even when an editor's ghostly hand seemed to hover over the narrative, its emphasis remained substantive rather than rhetorical.

In the second half of the eighteenth century, the literary image of women captives also underwent significant alteration. Mary Rowlandson, Hannah Swarton, and Elizabeth Hanson achieved fame during their lifetimes as resilient and resourceful women. The gothic vogue of the late eighteenth and early nineteenth centuries stereotyped female captives: the woman became a passive mother who witnessed the murder of her baby and the abduction of her older children by a cruel man-monster. Although the actual experience of captive women often justified a more assertive image, the usual picture in the public mind was of a frail woman submissively kneeling before her Indian captor, waiting for a death stroke from a raised tomahawk. Various components of this icon may be found in the woodcut depictions of later narratives and ultimately in Horatio Greenough's massive sculpture, "The Rescue Group."[64]

In the early nineteenth century, captivity narratives presented fewer unadorned firsthand experiences and more rhetorical flourishes, often verging on fantasy. Even then, however, some of the captivity accounts contained important ethnographic detail, as in the narrative of John Tanner (1830) on which Longfellow drew extensively for his epic poem *Hiawatha*. But Tanner was exceptional. More representative of the later genre were dime novels such as *Nathan Todd; or The Fate of the Sioux' Captive* (1860), which catered to an audience more interested in sensa-

---

64. Slotkin, *Regeneration through Violence*, 94. See also Gherman, "From Parlour to Teepee," which successfully counters the prevailing image of the American white woman on the frontier as a genteel carrier of Western culture. For a vivid example of the nineteenth century's image of the woman captive as submissive mother, see John Mix Stanley's oil painting, "Osage Scalp Dance" (1845), reproduced in *Smithsonian*, 9, no. 4 (July 1978), 52–53.

tion than verisimilitude.[65] Even though authentic narratives about life among the western Plains Indians appeared as late as 1871, when Fanny Kelly's *My Captivity among the Sioux Indians* was published, popular fiction had largely absorbed the genre years before.[66]

In the 1830s Andrew Jackson's removal policy transplanted most eastern Indians permanently beyond the Mississippi River. As aggressive white farmers and land speculators moved onto confiscated Indian lands, the Indian, no longer viewed as a serious threat by easterners, became the sympathetic subject of popular dramas and novels. In 1829, King Philip, having lain silent for a century and a half, was resurrected by John Augustus Stone in *Metamora, or the Last of the Wampanoags*. The lead role secured Edwin Forrest an enduring fame and a small fortune as well; he played the part for forty years. In 1855 the stage Indian was so noble and so ethereal that John Brougham aimed a satiric arrow at pompous portrayals of Indians by actors such as Forrest; his burlesque *Po-ca-hon-tas* also made fun of James Nelson Barker's early drama *The Indian Princess* (1808) and George Washington Custis's *Pocahontas* (1830).[67]

The themes, imagery, and language of the captivity narrative occurred frequently in the more serious realms of American literature. As Richard Slotkin has pointed out, eighteenth-century works such as Jonathan Edwards's evangelical sermon, "Sinners in the Hands of an Angry God," employed the captivity rhetoric.[68] In the early nineteenth century, when writers in the young republic increasingly turned their attention to American topics, the captivity genre helped to create a new national mythology. Here was the stuff of New World experience, something that contemporary Europe could not offer. Charles Brockden Brown's novel *Edgar Huntly* (1799) employed the capture-escape-flight theme so congenial to an audience familiar with captivity narratives. Brown's application of the wilderness landscape to reflect the tangled battle between reason and emotion in his hero's psyche parallels the Puritan's use of the wilderness to symbolize the struggle between the spiritual and physical worlds.

65. Henry Nash Smith, *Virgin Land: The American West as Symbol and Myth* (New York, 1950), 99–135.

66. It is indicative of the "degenerate" state of the captivity narrative that Fanny Kelly's publishers felt compelled to verify her experience by appending several affidavits from United States military officers who rescued Mrs. Kelly. See Fanny Kelly, *My Captivity among the Sioux Indians* (Hartford, Conn., 1871; repr. Secaucus, N.J., 1962).

67. *Metamora* and *Po-ca-hon-tas* are included in Richard Moody, ed., *Dramas from the American Theatre, 1762–1909* (Boston, 1966), 199–228, 397–422.

68. Slotkin, *Regeneration through Violence*, 103–106.

Other early American novelists used the captivity theme more explicitly: by 1823 at least fifteen American novels included a captivity episode.[69]

Poets as well as prose writers responded to the quickening pace of American interest in Indian material in the early decades of the nineteenth century. The extremely popular *Yamoyden, a Tale of the Wars of King Philip* (1820), a long narrative poem written by James W. Eastburn and Robert C. Sands, focused on the plight of a fictional Nipnet chieftain and his white wife, Nora. With its shopworn imagery, sentimental description, and well-established romantic conventions, the poem nevertheless illustrates the sympathy which writers of imaginative literature then extended toward the Indian. The captivity theme and its underlying drama of the clash between Indian and European cultures reached its zenith, however, in the writer who first systematically exploited the myth of the American frontier, James Fenimore Cooper. The five volumes of the Leatherstocking tales delighted the American public: the initial novel of the series, *The Pioneers* (1823), sold 3,500 copies in its first day of publication.[70] Although Cooper killed off his hero, Natty Bumppo, in *The Prairie* (1827), the wilderness theme was so effective that he resurrected the hunter and wrote three more novels about Bumppo's youth. Cooper's portrayal of the inevitable demise of his Noble Savage, Chingachgook, was more than lively reading; it was grist for the mills of those who cried Manifest Destiny in the 1830s and after, and thus encouraged American expansion as well as American literary themes. Cooper was not the only prominent writer of the early nineteenth century whose work reflected America's perception of the taming of the wilderness. Southern novelists such as William Gilmore Simms, most notably in *The Yemasee* (1835), echoed Cooper's message.

Later writers also exploited the metaphors of the hunter and the hunted that were central to captivity narratives. Nathaniel Hawthorne reconstructed the famous Hannah Dustan story, making the husband the hero. Mather's account of the tomahawk-wielding frontierswoman also in-

69. Dorothy Forbis Behan, "The Captivity Story in American Literature, 1577–1826" (Ph.D. diss., University of Chicago, 1952), *passim.*

70. For the popular reception of the Leatherstocking Tales see James D. Hart, *The Popular Book: A History of America's Literary Taste* (New York, 1950), 80. One of Cooper's lesser known novels (*The Wept of Wish-Ton-Wish: A Tale*, 2 vols. [New York, 1829]) focused directly on Puritan New England and the dilemmas of captivity and assimilation, and one of his better known (*The Last of the Mohicans*) was strongly influenced by the captivity theme.

trigued Henry David Thoreau. In *A Week on the Concord and Merrimack Rivers* (1849), Thoreau underscores the ambiguities of Indian-European relations; the climactic moment of the "Thursday" section of the book retells the Dustan story differently: "The family of Hannah Dustin all assembled alive once more except the infant whose brains were dashed out against the apple tree, and there have been many who in later times have lived to say that they have eaten of the fruit of that apple tree."[71] Thoreau's most famous work, *Walden* (1854), chronicles a mid-nineteenth-century American's attempt to confront nature on a level parallel to the Indians of earlier centuries. Herman Melville's first novel, *Typee* (1846), is based on the captivity-escape plot in which Toby, the main character, flees not from Indians but from South Sea islanders he suspects of cannibalism. Melville's awareness of the cruelties of both frontiersmen and Indians is found in its most mature form in *The Confidence-Man* (1857) in a perceptive chapter called "Metaphysics of Indian-Hating."[72]

By mid-nineteenth century the captivity narrative had become fully integrated into American literature. If it had largely lost its standing as a reliable and introspective autobiographical account, and had wholly lost its religious fervor, it had nonetheless assumed an important role in the minds of America's most prominent authors. Through the voluminous and popular works of Cooper, Melville, Simms, Thoreau, and many others, the setting if not always the plot and substance of wilderness captivities had entered the mainstream of American literature.

71. *A Week on the Concord and Merrimack Rivers* (Boston, 1896), 426–427. For an interesting and provocative analysis of the Hannah Dustan story and how it fits into the American literary canon, see Leslie A. Fiedler, *The Return of the Vanishing American* (New York, 1968), 98–108.

72. *The Confidence-Man: His Masquerade,* ed. Elizabeth S. Foster (New York, 1954), 163–171.

ONE

A

NARRATIVE

OF THE

CAPTIVITY, SUFFERINGS AND REMOVES

OF

Mrs. *Mary Rowlandson,*

Who was taken Prisoner by the INDIANS with several others,
and treated in the most barbarous and cruel Manner by those
vile Savages : With many other remarkable Events during her
Travels.

Written by her own Hand, for her private Use, and now made
public at the earnest Desire of some Friends, and for the Benefit of the afflicted.

BOSTON :

Printed and Sold at John Boyle's Printing-Office, next Door
to the *Three Doves* in Marlborough-Street. 1773.

Title page of the tenth edition (1773) of Mary Rowlandson's *Soveraignty &
Goodness of God,* with a more secular title, a more provocative subtitle, and a primitive woodcut. Courtesy of the American Antiquarian Society.

·MARY ROWLANDSON·
"THE SOVEREIGNTY
AND GOODNESS OF GOD"

In the spring of 1675, New England suffered its first prolonged clash with the Indians. King Philip's war brought to a sudden and violent end a half-century of generally cordial relations between the English settlers and the Algonquian tribes of southern New England. Partly because the native population had been sharply reduced by epidemics early in the century, and partly because both the Indians and the colonists made substantial efforts to avoid lethal confrontations, friction between them had been infrequent and brief. The only significant exception, the Pequot War of 1636–1637, pitted Connecticut and Massachusetts against the most powerful tribe in New England. The outcome, however, was gratifying to the English, for most of the other tribes remained neutral or aided the English. The subsequent destruction of the Pequots thoroughly satisfied the colonists and awed the Indians. As Cotton Mather later explained in his *Magnalia Christi Americana* (1702), "The marvellous Providence of God immediately extinguished that *war*, by prospering the *New-English* arms, unto the utter subduing of the Quarrelsome nation and affrightening of all the other natives."

They did not remain permanently "affrightened." By 1675 several tribes, especially the Wampanoag, had accumulated grievances they could no longer bear. The immediate causes of the war are unclear even from the hindsight of three centuries; it is certain, however, that the Wampanoag chief Metacomet—who had earlier been dubbed "Philip" by the English—harbored deep resentment toward Plymouth Colony for encroaching on his tribal lands, curtailing his authority, and treating him and his tribesmen with disdain. The Plymouth magistrates suspected Philip of scheming the colony's destruction and of causing the murder of a Christian Indian. More than once they preemptorily ordered Philip to Plymouth for explanations and confiscated his firearms. In June 1675 a Plymouth colonist shot an Indian at Swansea, a town close to Wampanoag territory. In retaliation, some of Philip's warriors attacked the settlement. The ensuing war soon embroiled all of the New England colonies and nearly all of the tribes; most of the Indians supported Philip's cause, although some, especially those who had converted to Christianity, aided the colonists. During more than a year of vicious fighting, colonial troops pursued elusive Indians through forest and swamp while Indian raiding parties assaulted dozens of English settlements. Both sides suffered heavy mortality and destruction.

In February 1676, a contingent of Narragansetts struck Lancaster, Massachusetts, a frontier community of perhaps fifty families. Among the captives was Mary White Rowlandson (c. 1635–c. 1678), daughter of one of the town's founders and wife of its clergyman. She was ransomed eleven weeks later, shortly before the war ended. The following year Mrs. Rowlandson and the surviving members of her family moved to Wethersfield, Connecticut, where her husband had accepted a new pastorate. Sometime in the next year or two Mary Rowlandson recorded her experiences, but they were not published until 1682. Nothing is known of her subsequent life. She may have died before 1682; if so, the anonymous preface—perhaps by Increase Mather—is strangely silent on her fate. But it is equally strange that no record survives of the death and burial of such a prominent author.

No complete copies survive of the first edition, which was issued in Boston and included her husband Joseph's last sermon (delivered in November 1678), plaintifully entitled "The possibility of God's forsaking a people, that have been visibly near and dear to him, together with the misery of a people thus forsaken." The following version of Mary Rowlandson's narrative is based on *The Soveraignty & Goodness of God, Together, with the Faithfulness of His Promises Displayed; Being a Narrative of the Captivity and Restauration of Mrs. Mary Rowlandson. Commended by her, to all that desires to know the Lords doings to, and dealings with Her . . . The Second Addition Corrected and amended.* This second "Addition" was issued in Cambridge later in 1682 by Samuel Green, Sr. The first London edition also appeared in 1682. The entire text is reprinted here except for the preface, which chastises the Indians and assures the reader that this "Narrative of the wonderfully awfull, wise, holy, powerfull, and gracious providence of God, towards that worthy and precious Gentlewoman" had indeed been written by Mrs. Rowlandson and had been made public for the edification of its readers and their countrymen. Since its first publication, this most famous of the New England narratives has appeared in scores of editions and anthologies.

On the tenth of February 1675 [1676]¹ came the Indians with great numbers upon Lancaster. Their first coming was about sunrising. Hearing the noise of some guns, we looked out; several houses were burning and the smoke ascending to heaven. There were five persons taken in one house; the father and the mother and a sucking child they knocked on the head; the other two they took and carried away alive. There were two others, who being out of their garrison upon some occasion were set upon; one was knocked on the head, the other escaped. Another there was who running along was shot and wounded and fell down; he begged of them his life, promising them money (as they told me), but they would not hearken to him but knocked him in [the] head, stripped him naked, and split open his bowels. Another, seeing many of the Indians about his barn, ventured and went out but was quickly shot down. There were three others belonging to the same garrison who were killed; the Indians, getting up upon the roof of the barn, had advantage to shoot down upon them over their fortification. Thus these murderous wretches went on, burning and destroying before them.

At length they came and beset our own house,² and quickly it was the dolefullest day that ever mine eyes saw. The house stood upon the edge of a hill. Some of the Indians got behind the hill, others into the barn, and others behind anything that could shelter them; from all which places they shot against the house so that the bullets seemed to fly like hail; and quickly they wounded one man among us, then another, and then a third.

1. Before 1752, the British empire adhered to the Julian calendar, which had been replaced in most other European nations in 1582 by the more accurate Gregorian calendar. The principal difference between the two calendars was the beginning date of the new year: March 25 in the Julian calendar and January 1 in the Gregorian. By the seventeenth century there was also a discrepancy of ten days between calendar dates; to transpose dates from Julian ("old style") to Gregorian ("new style"), ten days must be added to the former in the seventeenth-century, eleven in the eighteenth. Thus Mrs. Rowlandson was captured on February 20, 1676, according to modern reckoning. Dates in this volume have been left as originally written, but the new-style year has been added in brackets where appropriate.

2. The Rowlandson house contained thirty-seven persons, including Mrs. Rowlandson, her three children, her two sisters (Hannah White Divoll and Elizabeth White Kerley) with their families, and several neighboring families.

About two hours (according to my observation in that amazing time) they had been about the house before they prevailed to fire it (which they did with flax and hemp which they brought out of the barn, and there being no defense about the house, only two flankers at two opposite corners and one of them not finished). They fired it once, and one ventured out and quenched it, but they quickly fired it again and that took.

Now is that dreadful hour come that I have often heard of (in time of war as it was the case of others), but now mine eyes see it. Some in our house were fighting for their lives, others wallowing in their blood, the house on fire over our heads, and the bloody heathen ready to knock us on the head if we stirred out. Now might we hear mothers and children crying out for themselves and one another, "Lord, what shall we do?" Then I took my children (and one of my sisters, hers) to go forth and leave the house, but as soon as we came to the door and appeared, the Indians shot so thick that the bullets rattled against the house as if one had taken an handful of stones and threw them so that we were fain to give back. We had six stout dogs belonging to our garrison, but none of them would stir although another time, if any Indian had come to the door, they were ready to fly upon him and tear him down.[3] The Lord hereby would make us the more to acknowledge His hand and to see that our help is always in Him. But out we must go, the fire increasing and coming along behind us roaring, and the Indians gaping before us with their guns, spears, and hatchets to devour us. No sooner were we out of the house, but my brother-in-law [John Divoll] (being before wounded, in defending the house, in or near the throat) fell down dead; whereat the Indians scornfully shouted, hallooed, and were presently upon him, stripping off his clothes. The bullets flying thick, one went through my side, and the same (as would seem) through the bowels and hand of my dear child in my arms. One of my elder sister's children, named William [Kerley], had then his leg broken, which the Indians perceiving, they knocked him on the head. Thus were we butchered by those merciless heathen, standing amazed, with the blood running down to our heels.

My eldest sister [Elizabeth] being yet in the house and seeing those woeful sights, the infidels hailing mothers one way and children another and some wallowing in their blood, and her elder son telling her that her son William was dead and myself was wounded, she said, "And, Lord, let

3. Many English colonists kept large dogs, preferably mastiffs, as protective weapons. The Indians' dogs were relatively small and docile.

me die with them." Which was no sooner said, but she was struck with a bullet and fell down dead over the threshold. I hope she is reaping the fruit of her good labors, being faithful to the service of God in her place. In her younger years she lay under much trouble upon spiritual accounts till it pleased God to make that precious scripture take hold of her heart, 2 Cor. 12:9, "And he said unto me, my grace is sufficient for thee." More than twenty years after I have heard her tell how sweet and comfortable that place was to her. But to return: the Indians laid hold of us, pulling me one way and the children another, and said, "Come go along with us." I told them they would kill me. They answered, if I were willing to go along with them they would not hurt me.

Oh, the doleful sight that now was to behold at this house! "Come, behold the works of the Lord, what desolation He has made in the earth." Of thirty-seven persons who were in this one house none escaped either present death or a bitter captivity save only one, who might say as he, Job 1:15, "And I only am escaped alone to tell the news." There were twelve killed, some shot, some stabbed with their spears, some knocked down with their hatchets. When we are in prosperity, oh, the little that we think of such dreadful sights, and to see our dear friends and relations lie bleeding out their heart-blood upon the ground! There was one who was chopped into the head with a hatchet and stripped naked, and yet was crawling up and down. It is a solemn sight to see so many Christians lying in their blood, some here and some there, like a company of sheep torn by wolves, all of them stripped naked by a company of hell-hounds, roaring, singing, ranting and insulting, as if they would have torn our very hearts out. Yet the Lord by his almighty power preserved a number of us from death, for there were twenty-four of us taken alive and carried captive.

I had often before this said that if the Indians should come I should choose rather to be killed by them than taken alive, but when it came to the trial, my mind changed; their glittering weapons so daunted my spirit that I chose rather to go along with those (as I may say) ravenous beasts than that moment to end my days. And that I may the better declare what happened to me during that grievous captivity, I shall particularly speak of the several removes we had up and down the wilderness.

The First Remove

Now away we must go with those barbarous creatures with our bodies wounded and bleeding and our hearts no less than our bodies. About a

35

mile we went that night up upon a hill within sight of the town where they intended to lodge. There was hard by a vacant house (deserted by the English before for fear of the Indians). I asked them whether I might not lodge in the house that night, to which they answered, "What, will you love English men still?" This was the dolefullest night that ever my eyes saw. Oh, the roaring and singing and dancing and yelling of those black creatures in the night, which made the place a lively resemblance of hell. And as miserable was the waste that was there made of horses, cattle, sheep, swine, calves, lambs, roasting pigs, and fowl (which they had plundered in the town), some roasting, some lying and burning, and some boiling to feed our merciless enemies who were joyful enough though we were disconsolate. To add to the dolefulness of the former day and the dismalness of the present night, my thoughts ran upon my losses and sad bereaved condition. All was gone: my husband gone (at least separated from me, he being in the Bay,[4] and to add to my grief, the Indians told me they would kill him as he came homeward), my children gone, my relations and friends gone, our house and home and all our comforts within door and without, all was gone except my life, and I knew not but the next moment that might go too. There remained nothing to me but one poor wounded babe, and it seemed at present worse than death that it was in such a pitiful condition bespeaking compassion, and I had no refreshing for it nor suitable things to revive it. Little do many think what is the savageness and brutishness of this barbarous enemy, ay, even those that seem to profess more than others among them when the English have fallen into their hands.

Those seven that were killed at Lancaster the summer before upon a Sabbath day and the one that was afterward killed upon a week day were slain and mangled in a barbarous manner by one-eyed John and Marlborough's praying Indians[5] which Capt. Mosely[6] brought to Boston, as the Indians told me.

4. Rev. Joseph Rowlandson had gone to Boston, capital of the Massachusetts Bay Colony, to request aid in the defense of Lancaster. He returned soon after the attack to find his home in ashes and his family gone.

5. Marlborough's "praying Indians" were residents of one of the villages set up by missionary John Eliot for Indians who chose to exchange their religion and customs for Christianity and English ways. When war broke out, many of the praying Indians, especially at Marlborough, Massachusetts, joined Philip's side. One-eyed John was a Nipmuc sachem whose Indian names were Monoco and Apequinash.

6. Capt. Samuel Moseley of Boston was a principal leader of New England forces. He earned a controversial reputation—admired by most soldiers, distrusted by most missionaries—for his rough treatment of friendly Indians.

MARY ROWLANDSON

The Second Remove

But now, the next morning, I must turn my back upon the town and travel
with them into the vast and desolate wilderness, I knew not whither. It is
not my tongue or pen can express the sorrows of my heart and bitterness
of my spirit that I had at this departure, but God was with me in a wonderful manner, carrying me along and bearing up my spirit that it did not
quite fail. One of the Indians carried my poor wounded babe upon a horse;
it went moaning all along, "I shall die, I shall die." I went on foot after it
with sorrow that cannot be expressed. At length I took it off the horse and
carried it in my arms till my strength failed, and I fell down with it. Then
they set me upon a horse with my wounded child in my lap. And there
being no furniture [saddle] upon the horse['s] back, as we were going
down a steep hill, we both fell over the horse's head, at which they like
inhuman creatures laughed and rejoiced to see it, though I thought we
should there have ended our days, as overcome with so many difficulties.
But the Lord renewed my strength still and carried me along that I might
see more of His power; yea, so much that I could never have thought of
had I not experienced it.

After this it quickly began to snow, and when night came on, they
stopped.[7] And now down I must sit in the snow by a little fire and a few
boughs behind me, with my sick child in my lap and calling much for
water, being now (through the wound) fallen into a violent fever. My own
wound also [was] growing so stiff that I could scarce sit down or rise up;
yet so it must be that I must sit all this cold winter night upon the cold,
snowy ground with my sick child in my arms, looking that every hour
would be the last of its life, and having no Christian friend near me either
to comfort or help me. Oh, I may see the wonderful power of God that my
spirit did not utterly sink under my affliction! Still the Lord upheld me
with His gracious and merciful spirit, and we were both alive to see the
light of the next morning.

The Third Remove

The morning being come, they prepared to go on their way. One of the
Indians got up upon a horse, and they set me up behind him with my poor
sick babe in my lap. A very wearisome and tedious day I had of it what
with my own wound and my child's being so exceeding sick in a lamenta-
ble condition with her wound. It may be easily judged what a poor feeble

7. At Princeton, Massachusetts.

condition we were in, there being not the least crumb of refreshing that came within either of our mouths from Wednesday night to Saturday night except only a little cold water. This day in the afternoon about an hour by sun we came to the place where they intended, *viz.* an Indian town called Wenimesset,[8] nor[th]ward of Quabaug.[9] When we were come, oh, the number of pagans (now merciless enemies) that there came about me that I may say as David, Psal. 27:13, "I had fainted, unless I had believed," etc. The next day was the Sabbath. I then remembered how careless I had been of God's holy time, how many Sabbaths I had lost and misspent and how evilly I had walked in God's sight, which lay so close unto my spirit that it was easy for me to see how righteous it was with God to cut the thread of my life and cast me out of His presence forever. Yet the Lord still showed mercy to me and upheld me, and as He wounded me with one hand, so He healed me with the other.

This day there came to me one Robert Pepper (a man belonging to Roxbury) who was taken in Captain Beers his fight[10] and had been now a considerable time with the Indians and up with them almost as far as Albany to see King Philip, as he told me, and was now very lately come into these parts. Hearing, I say, that I was in this Indian town, he obtained leave to come and see me. He told me he himself was wounded in the leg at Captain Beers his fight and was not able some time to go, but, as they carried him, and as he took oaken leaves and laid to his wound, and through the blessing of God, he was able to travel again. Then I took oaken leaves and laid to my side, and, with the blessing of God, it cured me also. Yet before the cure was wrought, I may say, as it is in Psal. 38:5, 6, "My wounds stink and are corrupt, I am troubled, I am bowed down greatly, I go mourning all the day long." I sat much alone with a poor wounded child in my lap, which moaned night and day, having nothing to revive the body or cheer the spirits of her, but instead of that sometimes one Indian would come and tell me one hour that, "Your master will knock your child in the head." And then a second, and then a third, "Your master will quickly knock your child in the head."

This was the comfort I had from them. "Miserable comforters are ye all," as He said. Thus nine days I sat upon my knees with my babe in my

8. Now New Braintree, Massachusetts. Usually spelled Menameset.

9. Present-day Brookfield.

10. Capt. Richard Beers of Watertown, Massachusetts, and several of his men were killed in a skirmish with Connecticut River Indians near Northfield, Massachusetts, in late August 1675.

lap till my flesh was raw again; my child being even ready to depart this sorrowful world, they bade me carry it out to another wigwam[11] (I suppose because they would not be troubled with such spectacles), whither I went with a heavy heart, and down I sat with the picture of death in my lap. About two hours in the night my sweet babe like a lamb departed this life on Feb. 18, 1675 [1676], it being about six years and five months old. It was nine days from the first wounding in this miserable condition without any refreshing of one nature or other except a little cold water. I cannot but take notice how at another time I could not bear to be in the room where any dead person was, but now the case is changed; I must and could lie down by my dead babe side by side all the night after. I have thought since of the wonderful goodness of God to me in preserving me in the use of my reason and senses in that distressed time that I did not use wicked and violent means to end my own miserable life.

In the morning when they understood that my child was dead, they sent for me home to my master's wigwam. (By my master in this writing must be understood Quanopin who was a sagamore and married [to] King Philip's wife's sister, not that he first took me, but I was sold to him by another Narragansett Indian who took me when first I came out of the garrison.) I went to take up my dead child in my arms to carry it with me, but they bid me let it alone. There was no resisting, but go I must and leave it. When I had been at my master's wigwam, I took the first opportunity I could get to go look after my dead child. When I came, I asked them what they had done with it. Then they told me it was upon the hill. Then they went and showed me where it was, where I saw the ground was newly digged, and there they told me they had buried it. There I left that child in the wilderness and must commit it and myself also in this wilderness condition to Him who is above all.

God having taken away this dear child, I went to see my daughter Mary who was at this same Indian town at a wigwam not very far off, though we had little liberty or opportunity to see one another. She was about ten years old and taken from the door at first by a praying Indian and afterward sold for a gun. When I came in sight, she would fall a-weeping at which they were provoked and would not let me come near her but bade

11. For seventeenth-century descriptions of Algonquian wigwams see Thomas Morton, *New English Canaan* (London, 1637; repr. New York, 1972), 24–26; and Roger Williams, *A Key into the Language of America,* ed. John J. Teunissen and Evelyn J. Hinz (Detroit, 1973), 117–128. A modern discussion is Charles C. Willoughby, *Antiquities of the New England Indians* (Cambridge, Mass., 1935), 289–292.

me be gone, which was a heart-cutting word to me. I had one child dead, another in the wilderness I knew not where; the third they would not let me come near to. "Me," as he said, "have ye bereaved of my children, Joseph is not, and Simeon is not, and ye will take Benjamin also, all these things are against me" [Gen. 42:36]. I could not sit still in this condition but kept walking from one place to another. And as I was going along, my heart was even overwhelmed with the thoughts of my condition and that I should have children and a nation which I knew not ruled over them. Whereupon I earnestly entreated the Lord that He would consider my low estate and show me a token for good, and if it were His blessed will, some sign and hope of some relief.

And indeed quickly the Lord answered in some measure my poor prayers; for, as I was going up and down mourning and lamenting my condition, my son [Joseph] came to me and asked me how I did. I had not seen him before since the destruction of the town, and I knew not where he was till I was informed by himself that he was amongst a smaller parcel of Indians whose place was about six miles off. With tears in his eyes he asked me whether his sister Sarah was dead and told me he had seen his sister Mary and prayed me that I would not be troubled in reference to himself. The occasion of his coming to see me at this time was this. There was, as I said, about six miles from us a small plantation of Indians where it seems he had been during his captivity, and at this time there were some forces of the Indians gathered out of our company and some also from them (among whom was my son's master) to go to assault and burn Medfield.[12] In this time of the absence of his master his dame brought him to see me. I took this to be some gracious answer to my earnest and unfeigned desire.

The next day, viz. to this, the Indians returned from Medfield all the company, for those that belonged to the other small company came through the town that now we were at. But before they came to us, oh, the outrageous roaring and whooping that there was! They began their din about a mile before they came to us. By their noise and whooping they signified how many they had destroyed, which was at that time twenty-three. Those that were with us at home were gathered together as soon as they heard the whooping, and every time that the other went over their number, these at home gave [such] a shout that the very earth rung again. And thus they continued till those that had been upon the expedition were come up to the sagamore's wigwam. And then, oh, the hideous insulting

12. Medfield, Massachusetts, was burned on February 21, 1676.

and triumphing that there was over some Englishmen's scalps that they had taken (as their manner is) and brought with them![13]

I cannot but take notice of the wonderful mercy of God to me in those afflictions in sending me a Bible. One of the Indians that came from Medfield fight [who] had brought some plunder came to me and asked me if I would have a Bible; he had got one in his basket. I was glad of it and asked him whether he thought the Indians would let me read. He answered, "Yes." So I took the Bible, and in that melancholy time it came into my mind to read first the 28 chapter of Deut., which I did, and when I had read it, my dark heart wrought on this manner, that there was no mercy for me, that the blessings were gone and the curses come in their room, and that I had lost my opportunity. But the Lord helped me still to go on reading till I came to chapter 30, the seven first verses, where I found there was mercy promised again if we would return to him by repentance, and, though we were scattered from one end of the earth to the other, yet the Lord would gather us together and turn all those curses upon our enemies. I do not desire to live to forget this scripture and what comfort it was to me.

Now the Indians began to talk of removing from this place, some one way and some another. There were now besides myself nine English captives in this place, all of them children except one woman. I got an opportunity to go and take my leave of them, they being to go one way and I another; I asked them whether they were earnest with God for deliverance. They told me they did as they were able, and it was some comfort to me that the Lord stirred up children to look to Him. The woman, *viz.* Goodwife Joslin,[14] told me she should never see me again and that she could find in her heart to run away; I wished her not to run away by any means, for we were near thirty miles from any English town and she very big with child and had but one week to reckon and another child in her

13. The origin of scalping has been attributed by various writers to Europeans or Indians, often on the basis of assumption rather than research. The most authoritative discussion is James Axtell and William C. Sturtevant, "The Unkindest Cut, or, Who Invented Scalping," *William and Mary Quarterly*, 3rd ser., 37 (1980), 451–472. A briefer, undocumented statement is Axtell, "Who Invented Scalping?" *American Heritage*, 28, no. 3 (April 1977), 96–99. Both articles argue convincingly that Indians in several parts of North America practiced scalping before Europeans arrived in America and that it was a custom unknown to foreign observers. Of course Europeans had equally gruesome rituals, such as displaying a victim's head on a pole or gateway. American colonists expanded scalping among the Indians by offering bounties for enemy scalps.

14. Ann Joslin (or Josselyn), wife of Abraham Joslin of Lancaster. Part of her family was killed during the raid; her own fate is described in the next paragraph.

arms, two years old, and bad rivers there were to go over, and we were feeble with our poor and coarse entertainment. I had my Bible with me; I pulled it out and asked her whether she would read. We opened the Bible and lighted on Psalm 27, in which psalm we especially took notice of that *ver. ult.,* "Wait on the Lord, be of good courage, and He shall strengthen thine heart, wait I say on the Lord."

The Fourth Remove

And now I must part with that little company I had. Here I parted from my daughter Mary (whom I never saw again till I saw her in Dorchester, returned from captivity) and from four little cousins and neighbors, some of which I never saw afterward. The Lord only knows the end of them. Amongst them also was that poor woman before mentioned who came to a sad end, as some of the company told me in my travel. She, having much grief upon her spirit about her miserable condition, being so near her time, she would be often asking the Indians to let her go home; they, not being willing to that and yet vexed with her importunity, gathered a great company together about her and stripped her naked and set her in the midst of them. And when they had sung and danced about her (in their hellish manner) as long as they pleased, they knocked her on [the] head and the child in her arms with her. When they had done that, they made a fire and put them both into it and told the other children that were with them that if they attempted to go home they would serve them in like manner.[15] The children said she did not shed one tear but prayed all the while. But to return to my own journey, we traveled about half a day or [a] little more and came to a desolate place in the wilderness where there were no wigwams or inhabitants before;[16] we came about the middle of the afternoon to this place, cold and wet, and snowy, and hungry, and weary, and no refreshing for man but the cold ground to sit on and our poor Indian cheer.

Heartaching thoughts here I had about my poor children who were scattered up and down among the wild beasts of the forest. My head was light and dizzy (either through hunger or hard lodging or trouble or all together), my knees feeble, my body raw by sitting double night and day that I cannot express to man the affliction that lay upon my spirit, but the Lord helped me at that time to express it to Himself. I opened my Bible

15. For a scholarly discussion of Indian torture ceremonies see Nathaniel Knowles, "The Torture of Captives by the Indians of Eastern North America," *American Philosophical Society Proceedings,* 82 (1940), 151–225.

16. Near the Indian village of Nichewaug, in present-day Petersham.

to read, and the Lord brought that precious scripture to me, Jer. 31:16, "Thus saith the Lord, 'Refrain thy voice from weeping and thine eyes from tears, for thy work shall be rewarded, and they shall come again from the land of the enemy.' " This was a sweet cordial to me when I was ready to faint; many and many a time have I sat down and wept sweetly over this scripture. At this place we continued about four days.

The Fifth Remove

The occasion (as I thought) of their moving at this time was the English army,[17] it being near and following them. For they went as if they had gone for their lives for some considerable way, and then they made a stop and chose some of their stoutest men and sent them back to hold the English army in play whilst the rest escaped. And then, like Jehu, they marched on furiously with their old and with their young; some carried their old decrepit mothers; some carried one and some another. Four of them carried a great Indian upon a bier, but, going through a thick wood with him, they were hindered and could make no haste; whereupon they took him upon their backs and carried him, one at a time, till they came to Bacquaug River.[18] Upon a Friday a little after noon we came to this river. When all the company was come up and were gathered together, I thought to count the number of them, but they were so many and, being somewhat in motion, it was beyond my skill. In this travel because of my wound I was somewhat favored in my load; I carried only my knitting work and two quarts of parched meal.[19] Being very faint, I asked my mistress [Weetamoo] to give me one spoonful of the meal, but she would not give me a taste. They quickly fell to cutting dry trees to make rafts to carry them over the river, and soon my turn came to go over. By the advantage of some brush which they had laid upon the raft to sit upon, I did not wet my foot (which many of themselves at the other end were mid-leg deep) which cannot but be acknowledged as a favor of God to my weakened body, it being a very cold time. I was not before acquainted with such kind of doings or dangers. "When thou passeth through the waters I will be with thee, and through the rivers they shall not overflow thee," Isai. 43:2. A certain number of us got over the river that night, but it was the

17. A contingent of Massachusetts and Connecticut troops under Captain Thomas Savage.

18. Present-day Miller's River in Orange, Massachusetts.

19. For a contemporary description of the Indians' travel diet see William Wood, *New England's Prospect,* ed. Alden T. Vaughan (Amherst, Mass., 1977), 87.

night after the Sabbath before all the company was got over. On the Saturday they boiled an old horse's leg which they had got, and so we drank of the broth as soon as they thought it was ready, and when it was almost all gone, they filled it up again.

The first week of my being among them I hardly ate anything; the second week, I found my stomach grow very faint for want of something; and yet it was very hard to get down their filthy trash. But the third week, though I could think how formerly my stomach would turn against this or that and I could starve and die before I could eat such things, yet they were sweet and savory to my taste. I was at this time knitting a pair of white cotton stockings for my mistress and had not yet wrought upon a Sabbath day. When the Sabbath came, they bade me go to work; I told them it was the Sabbath day and desired them to let me rest and told them I would do as much more tomorrow, to which they answered me they would break my face. And here I cannot but take notice of the strange providence of God in preserving the heathen. They were many hundreds, old and young, some sick and some lame, many had papooses at their backs. The greatest number at this time with us were squaws, and they traveled with all they had, bag and baggage, and yet they got over this river aforesaid. And on Monday they set their wigwams on fire, and away they went. On that very day came the English army after them to this river and saw the smoke of their wigwams, and yet this river put a stop to them. God did not give them courage or activity to go over after us; we were not ready for so great a mercy as victory and deliverance. If we had been, God would have found out a way for the English to have passed this river, as well as for the Indians with their squaws and children and all their luggage. "Oh that my people had hearkened to me, and Israel had walked in my ways, I should soon have subdued their enemies and turned my hand against their adversaries," Psal. 81:13, 14.

The Sixth Remove

On Monday (as I said) they set their wigwams on fire and went away. It was a cold morning, and before us there was a great brook with ice on it; some waded through it up to the knees and higher, but others went till they came to a beaver dam, and I amongst them, where through the good providence of God I did not wet my foot. I went along that day mourning and lamenting, leaving farther my own country and traveling into the vast and howling wilderness, and I understood something of Lot's wife's temptation when she looked back. We came that day to a great swamp by the

44

side of which we took up our lodging that night.[20] When I came to the brow of the hill that looked toward the swamp, I thought we had been come to a great Indian town (though there were none but our own company). The Indians were as thick as the trees: it seemed as if there had been a thousand hatchets going at once. If one looked before one, there was nothing but Indians and behind one nothing but Indians, and so on either hand, I myself in the midst, and no Christian soul near me, and yet how hath the Lord preserved me in safety. Oh, the experience that I have had of the goodness of God to me and mine!

The Seventh Remove

After a restless and hungry night there we had a wearisome time of it the next day. The swamp by which we lay was, as it were, a deep dungeon and an exceeding high and steep hill before it. Before I got to the top of the hill, I thought my heart and legs and all would have broken and failed me. What through faintness and soreness of body it was a grievous day of travel to me. As we went along, I saw a place where English cattle had been. That was comfort to me, such as it was. Quickly after that we came to an English path which so took with me that I thought I could have freely laid down and died. That day, a little after noon, we came to Squakeag[21] where the Indians quickly spread themselves over the deserted English fields, gleaning what they could find; some picked up ears of wheat that were crickled [broken] down; some found ears of Indian corn; some found groundnuts, and others sheaves of wheat that were frozen together in the shock, and went to threshing of them out. Myself got two ears of Indian corn, and whilst I did but turn my back, one of them was stolen from me, which much troubled me. There came an Indian to them at that time with a basket of horse liver. I asked him to give me a piece. "What," says he, "can you eat horse liver?" I told him I would try if he would give a piece, which he did, and I laid it on the coals to roast, but before it was half ready they got half of it away from me so that I was fain to take the rest and eat it as it was with the blood about my mouth, and yet a savory bit it was to me: "For to the hungry soul every bitter thing is sweet." A solemn sight methought it was to see fields of wheat and Indian corn forsaken and spoiled and the remainders of them to be food for our merciless enemies. That night we had a mess of wheat for our supper.

20. In Northfield, Massachusetts.
21. Also in Northfield.

The Eighth Remove

On the morrow morning we must go over the river, i.e. Connecticot, to meet with King Philip. Two canoesful they had carried over; the next turn I myself was to go, but as my foot was upon the canoe to step in, there was a sudden outcry among them, and I must step back. And instead of going over the river, I must go four or five miles up the river farther northward. Some of the Indians ran one way and some another. The cause of this rout was, as I thought, their espying some English scouts who were thereabout. In this travel up the river about noon the company made a stop and sat down, some to eat and others to rest them. As I sat amongst them musing of things past, my son Joseph unexpectedly came to me. We asked of each other's welfare, bemoaning our doleful condition and the change that had come upon us. We had husbands and father, and children, and sisters, and friends, and relations, and house, and home, and many comforts of this life, but now we may say as Job, "Naked came I out of my mother's womb, and naked shall I return. The Lord gave, and the Lord hath taken away, blessed be the name of the Lord." I asked him whether he would read; he told me he earnestly desired it, [so] I gave him my Bible, and he lighted upon that comfortable scripture, Psal. 118:17, 18, "I shall not die but live and declare the works of the Lord: the Lord hath chastened me sore, yet he hath not given me over to death." "Look here, Mother," says he, "did you read this?" And here I may take occasion to mention one principal ground of my setting forth these lines, even as the psalmist says to declare the works of the Lord and His wonderful power in carrying us along, preserving us in the wilderness while under the enemy's hand and returning of us in safety again and His goodness in bringing to my hand so many comfortable and suitable scriptures in my distress.

But to return, we traveled on till night, and in the morning we must go over the river to Philip's crew. When I was in the canoe, I could not but be amazed at the numerous crew of pagans that were on the bank on the other side. When I came ashore, they gathered all about me, I sitting alone in the midst. I observed they asked one another questions and laughed and rejoiced over their gains and victories. Then my heart began to fail and I fell a-weeping, which was the first time to my remembrance that I wept before them. Although I had met with so much affliction and my heart was many times ready to break, yet could I not shed one tear in their sight but rather had been all this while in a maze and like one aston-ished. But now I may say as Psal. 137:1, "By the rivers of Babylon there

46

we sat down; yea, we wept when we remembered Zion." There one of them asked me why I wept; I could hardly tell what to say, yet I answered they would kill me. "No," said he, "none will hurt you." Then came one of them and gave me two spoonfuls of meal to comfort me, and another gave me half a pint of peas which was more worth than many bushels at another time. Then I went to see King Philip. He bade me come in and sit down and asked me whether I would smoke it (a usual compliment nowadays among saints and sinners), but this no way suited me. For though I had formerly used tobacco, yet I had left it ever since I was first taken. It seems to be a bait the devil lays to make men lose their precious time.[22] I remember with shame how formerly when I had taken two or three pipes I was presently ready for another, such a bewitching thing it is. But I thank God He has now given me power over it; surely there are many who may be better employed than to lie sucking a stinking tobacco pipe.

Now the Indians gather their forces to go against Northampton. Overnight one went about yelling and hooting to give notice of the design, whereupon they fell to boiling of groundnuts and parching of corn (as many as had it) for their provision, and in the morning away they went. During my abode in this place[23] Philip spoke to me to make a shirt for his boy, which I did, for which he gave me a shilling.[24] I offered the money to my master, but he bade me keep it, and with it I bought a piece of horseflesh. Afterwards he asked me to make a cap for his boy, for which he invited me to dinner. I went, and he gave me a pancake about as big as two fingers; it was made of parched wheat, beaten and fried in bear's grease, but I thought I never tasted pleasanter meat in my life. There was a squaw who spoke to me to make a shirt for her *sannup* [husband], for which she gave me a piece of bear. Another asked me to knit a pair of stockings, for which she gave me a quart of peas. I boiled my peas and bear together and

22. In the seventeenth century, as in the second half of the twentieth, the medical and moral reasons for smoking tobacco were hotly debated. Most Puritans frowned on the habit, partly because it wasted time, partly because it presented a serious fire hazard in an age of wooden buildings and thick forests.

23. In South Vernon, Vermont. Philip was en route from northern New York colony, where he had unsuccessfully sought aid from the powerful Mohawks, to southeastern New England.

24. The Indians had no woven cloth before the arrival of European traders and settlers, from whom they rapidly began to acquire it in considerable quantities. It took time, however, for the Indians to learn sewing skills, and they consequently took advantage of the talents of their captives. Cloth clothes supplemented, rather than replaced, the Indians' traditional animal-skin garments.

invited my master and mistress to dinner, but the proud gossip [i.e., companion], because I served them both in one dish, would eat nothing except one bit that he gave her upon the point of his knife.

Hearing that my son was come to this place, I went to see him and found him lying flat upon the ground. I asked him how he could sleep so. He answered me that he was not asleep but at prayer and lay so that they might not observe what he was doing. I pray God he may remember these things now he is returned in safety. At this place (the sun now getting higher) what with the beams and heat of the sun and the smoke of the wigwams, I thought I should have been blind. I could scarce discern one wigwam from another. There was here one Mary Thurston of Medfield who, seeing how it was with me, lent me a hat to wear, but as soon as I was gone, the squaw who owned that Mary Thurston came running after me and got it away again. Here was the squaw that gave one spoonful of meal. I put it in my pocket to keep it safe, yet notwithstanding somebody stole it but put five Indian corns in the room of it, which corns were the greatest provision I had in my travel for one day.

The Indians, returning from Northampton,[25] brought with them some horses, and sheep, and other things which they had taken. I desired them that they would carry me to Albany upon one of those horses and sell me for powder, for so they had sometimes discoursed. I was utterly hopeless of getting home on foot the way that I came. I could hardly bear to think of the many weary steps I had taken to come to this place.

The Ninth Remove

But instead of going either to Albany or homeward, we must go five miles up the river and then go over it. Here we abode awhile.[26] Here lived a sorry Indian who spoke to me to make him a shirt. When I had done it, he would pay me nothing. But he living by the riverside where I often went to fetch water, I would often be putting of him in mind and calling for my pay; at last he told me if I would make another shirt for a papoose not yet born, he would give me a knife, which he did when I had done it. I carried the knife in, and my master asked me to give it him, and I was not a little glad that I had anything that they would accept of and be pleased with. When we were at this place, my master's maid came home; she had been gone three weeks into the Narragansett country to fetch corn where they

25. Indians attacked Northampton, Massachusetts, on March 14, 1676, but were repulsed.

26. Somewhere in the Ashuelot Valley, New Hampshire, south of present-day Keene.

had stored up some in the ground. She brought home about a peck and [a] half of corn. This was about the time that their great captain, Naananto,[27] was killed in the Narragansett country. My son being now about a mile from me, I asked liberty to go and see him; they bade me go, and away I went. But quickly [I] lost myself, traveling over hills and through swamps, and could not find the way to him. And I cannot but admire at the wonderful power and goodness of God to me in that though I was gone from home and met with all sorts of Indians, and those I had no knowledge of, and there being no Christian soul near me, yet not one of them offered the least imaginable miscarriage to me.

I turned homeward again and met with my master; he showed me the way to my son. When I came to him, I found him not well, and withall he had a boil on his side which much troubled him. We bemoaned one another awhile, as the Lord helped us, and then I returned again. When I was returned, I found myself as unsatisfied as I was before. I went up and down mourning and lamenting, and my spirit was ready to sink with the thoughts of my poor children. My son was ill, and I could not but think of his mournful looks, and no Christian friend was near him to do any office of love for him either for soul or body. And my poor girl, I know not where she was nor whether she was sick or well, or alive or dead. I repaired under these thoughts to my Bible (my great comfort in that time) and that scripture came to my hand, "Cast thy burden upon the Lord, and He shall sustain thee," Psal. 55:22.

But I was fain to go and look after something to satisfy my hunger, and going among the wigwams I went into one and there found a squaw who showed herself very kind to me and gave me a piece of bear. I put it into my pocket and came home but could not find an opportunity to broil it for fear they would get it from me, and there it lay all that day and night in my stinking pocket. In the morning I went to the same squaw who had a kettle of groundnuts boiling; I asked her to let me boil my piece of bear in her kettle, which she did and gave me some groundnuts to eat with it, and I cannot but think how pleasant it was to me. I have sometime seen bear baked very handsomely among the English, and some like it, but the thoughts that it was bear made me tremble, but now that was savory to me that one would think was enough to turn the stomach of a brute creature.

One bitter cold day I could find no room to sit down before the fire. I went out and could not tell what to do, but I went into another wigwam where they were also sitting around the fire, but the squaw laid a skin for

27. Better known as Canonchet.

me, bid me sit down, gave me some groundnuts, bade me come again, and told me they would buy me if they were able, and yet these were strangers to me that I never saw before.

The Tenth Remove

That day a small part of the company removed about three-quarters of a mile, intending further the next day. When they came to the place where they intended to lodge and had pitched their wigwams, being hungry, I went again back to the place we were before at to get something to eat, being encouraged by the squaw's kindness who bade me come again when I was there. There came an Indian to look after me, who, when he had found me, kicked me all along. I went home and found venison roasting that night, but they would not give me one bit of it. Sometimes I met with favor and sometimes with nothing but frowns.

The Eleventh Remove

The next day in the morning they took their travel, intending a day's journey up the river.[28] I took my load at my back, and quickly we came to wade over the river and passed over tiresome and wearisome hills. One hill was so steep that I was fain to creep up upon my knees and to hold by the twigs and bushes to keep myself from falling backward. My head also was so light that I usually reeled as I went, but I hope all these wearisome steps that I have taken are but a forewarning of me to the heavenly rest. "I know, O Lord, that Thy judgments are right, and that Thou in faithfulness hast afflicted me," Psal. 119:71 [actually 75].

The Twelfth Remove

It was upon a Sabbath-day morning that they prepared for their travel. This morning I asked my master whether he would sell me to my husband; he answered me *nux* [yes], which did much rejoice my spirit. My mistress, before we went, was gone to the burial of a papoose, and, returning, she found me sitting and reading in my Bible. She snatched it hastily out of my hand and threw it out of doors; I ran out and catched it

28. The eleventh remove, in early April 1676, took Rowlandson to her northernmost location, in the vicinity of Chesterfield, New Hampshire. Thus she, unlike so many of the later captives, did not enter Canada.

up and put it into my pocket and never let her see it afterward. Then they packed up their things to be gone and gave me my load. I complained it was too heavy, whereupon she gave me a slap in the face and bade me go. I lifted up my heart to God, hoping the redemption was not far off, and the rather because their insolency grew worse and worse.

But the thoughts of my going homeward (for so we bent our course) much cheered my spirit and made my burden seem light and almost nothing at all. But (to my amazement and great perplexity) the scale was soon turned, for when we had gone a little way, on a sudden my mistress gives out. She would go no further but turn back again and said I must go back again with her. And she called her *sannup* and would have had him gone back also, but he would not but said he would go on and come to us again in three days. My spirit was upon this, I confess, very impatient and almost outrageous. I thought I could as well have died as went back; I cannot declare the trouble that I was in about it, but yet back again I must go. As soon as I had an opportunity, I took my Bible to read, and that quieting scripture came to my hand, Psal. 46:10, "Be still and know that I am God," which stilled my spirit for the present. But a sore time of trial, I concluded, I had to go through, my master being gone, who seemed to me the best friend that I had of an Indian both in cold and hunger, and quickly so it proved. Down I sat with my heart as full as it could hold, and yet so hungry that I could not sit neither. But, going out to see what I could find and walking among the trees, I found six acorns and two chestnuts which were some refreshment to me. Towards night I gathered me some sticks for my own comfort that I might not lie a-cold, but when we came to lie down they bade me go out and lie somewhere else, for they had company (they said) come in more than their own. I told them I could not tell where to go; they bade me go look. I told them if I went to another wigwam they would be angry and send me home again. Then one of the company drew his sword and told me he would run me through if I did not go presently. Then was I fain to stoop to this rude fellow and to go out in the night, I knew not whither. Mine eyes have seen that fellow afterwards, walking up and down Boston under the appearance of a friend-Indian and several others of the like cut.

I went to one wigwam, and they told me they had no room. Then I went to another, and they said the same; at last an old Indian bade me come to him, and his squaw gave me some groundnuts; she gave me also something to lay under my head, and a good fire we had. And through the good providence of God I had a comfortable lodging that night. In the morning another Indian bade me come at night, and he would give me six groundnuts, which I did. We were at this place and time about two miles from Connecticut River. We went in the morning to gather groundnuts to the river and went back again that night. I went with a good load at my back (for they, when they went though but a little way, would carry all their trumpery with them); I told them the skin was off my back, but I had no other comforting answer from them than this, that it would be no matter if my head were off too.

The Thirteenth Remove

Instead of going toward the Bay, which was that I desired, I must go with them five or six miles down the river into a mighty thicket of brush where we abode almost a fortnight.[29] Here one asked me to make a shirt for her papoose, for which she gave me a mess of broth which was thickened with meal made of the bark of a tree, and to make it the better she had put into it about a handful of peas and a few roasted groundnuts. I had not seen my son a pretty while, and here was an Indian of whom I made inquiry after him and asked him when he saw him. He answered me that such a time his master roasted him and that himself did eat a piece of him as big as his two fingers and that he was very good meat. But the Lord upheld my spirit under this discouragement, and I considered their horrible addictedness to lying and that there is not one of them that makes the least conscience of speaking of truth. In this place on a cold night as I lay by the fire, I removed a stick that kept the heat from me; a squaw moved it down again at which I looked up, and she threw a handful of ashes in mine eyes. I thought I should have been quite blinded and have never seen more, but lying down, the water run out of my eyes and carried the dirt with it that by the morning I recovered my sight again. Yet upon this and the like occasions I hope it is not too much to say with Job, "Have pity upon me, have pity upon me, oh, ye my friends, for the hand of the Lord has touched me."

And here I cannot but remember how many times sitting in their wigwams and musing on things past I should suddenly leap up and run out as if I had been at home, forgetting where I was and what my condition was. But when I was without and saw nothing but wilderness and woods and a company of barbarous heathens, my mind quickly returned to me, which made me think of that spoken concerning Sampson, who said, "I will go

29. Vicinity of present-day Hinsdale, New Hampshire.

out and shake myself as at other times, but he wished not that the Lord was departed from him."

About this time I began to think that all my hopes of restoration would come to nothing. I thought of the English army and hoped for their coming and being taken by them, but that failed. I hoped to be carried to Albany as the Indians had discoursed before, but that failed also. I thought of being sold to my husband, as my master spake, but instead of that my master himself was gone and I left behind so that my spirit was now quite ready to sink. I asked them to let me go out and pick up some sticks that I might get alone and pour out my heart unto the Lord. Then also I took my Bible to read, but I found no comfort here neither, which many times I was wont to find. So easy a thing it is with God to dry up the streams of scripture-comfort from us. Yet I can say that in all my sorrows and afflictions God did not leave me to have my impatience work towards Himself, as if His ways were unrighteous. But I knew that He laid upon me less than I deserved. Afterward, before this doleful time ended with me, I was turning the leaves of my Bible and the Lord brought to me some scriptures, which did a little revive me, as that Isai. 55:8, " 'For my thoughts are not your thoughts, neither are your ways my ways,' saith the Lord." And also that Psal. 37:5, "Commit thy way unto the Lord, trust also in Him, and He shall bring it to pass."

About this time they came yelping from Hadley where they had killed three Englishmen and brought one captive with them, viz. Thomas Read.[30] They all gathered about the poor man, asking him many questions. I desired also to go and see him, and when I came he was crying bitterly, supposing they would quickly kill him. Whereupon I asked one of them whether they intended to kill him; he answered me they would not. He being a little cheered with that, I asked him about the welfare of my husband; he told me he saw him such a time in the Bay, and he was well but very melancholy. By which I certainly understood (though I suspected it before) that whatsoever the Indians told me respecting him was vanity and lies. Some of them told me he was dead, and they had killed him. Some said he was married again, and that the governor wished him to marry and told him he should have his choice, and that all persuaded [him] I was dead. So like were these barbarous creatures to him who was a liar from the beginning.

As I was sitting once in the wigwam here, Philip's maid came in with

30. After his capture in an attack on Hadley, Massachusetts, he subsequently escaped.

the child in her arms and asked me to give her a piece of my apron to make a flap for it. I told her I would not. Then my mistress bade me give it, but still I said no. The maid told me if I would not give her a piece she would tear a piece off it. I told her I would tear her coat then; with that my mistress rises up and takes up a stick big enough to have killed me and struck at me with it, but I stepped out, and she struck the stick into the mat of the wigwam. But while she was pulling of it out, I ran to the maid and gave her all my apron, and so that storm went over.

Hearing that my son was come to this place, I went to see him and told him his father was well but very melancholy. He told me he was as much grieved for his father as for himself; I wondered at his speech, for I thought I had enough upon my spirit in reference to myself to make me mindless of my husband and everyone else, they being safe among their friends. He told me also that a while before his master, together with other Indians, were going to the French for powder,[31] but by the way the Mohawks met with them and killed four of their company which made the rest turn back again,[32] for which I desire that myself and he may bless the Lord. For it might have been worse with him had he been sold to the French than it proved to be in remaining with the Indians.

I went to see an English youth in this place, one John Gilberd of Springfield. I found him lying without doors upon the ground; I asked him how he did. He told me he was very sick of a flux with eating so much blood. They had turned him out of the wigwam and with him an Indian papoose almost dead (whose parents had been killed) in a bitter cold day without fire or clothes. The young man himself had nothing on but his shirt and waistcoat. This sight was enough to melt a heart of flint. There they lay quivering in the cold, the youth [curled] round like a dog, the papoose stretched out with his eyes, nose, and mouth full of dirt and yet alive and groaning. I advised John to go and get to some fire; he told me he could not stand, but I persuaded him still, lest he should lie there and die. And with much ado I got him to a fire and went myself home. As soon as I was got home, his master's daughter came after me to know what I had done with the Englishman; I told her I had got him to a fire in such a place. Now had I need to pray Paul's prayer, 2 Thess. 3:2, "That we may be delivered from unreasonable and wicked men." For her satisfaction I

31. By 1676 the Indians had acquired a considerable number of guns, despite periodic colonial laws forbidding the colonists from selling them to Indians. However, Indian gunmen persistently lacked powder and bullets.

32. This episode illustrates once again how the ancient hostility between the Mohawks and New England tribes seriously damaged King Philip's cause.

went along with her and brought her to him, but before I got home again, it was noised about that I was running away and getting the English youth along with me, that as soon as I came in they began to rant and domineer, asking me where I had been, and what I had been doing, and saying they would knock him on the head. I told them I had been seeing the English youth and that I would not run away. They told me I lied, and taking up a hatchet, they came to me and said they would knock me down if I stirred out again and so confined me to the wigwam. Now may I say with David, 2 Sam. 24:14, "I am in a great strait." If I keep in, I must die with hunger, and if I go out, I must be knocked in [the] head. This distressed condition held that day and half the next. And then the Lord remembered me, whose mercies are great.

Then came an Indian to me with a pair of stockings that were too big for him, and he would have me ravel them out and knit them fit for him. I showed myself willing and bid him ask my mistress if I might go along with him a little way; she said yes, I might, but I was not a little refreshed with that news that I had my liberty again. Then I went along with him, and he gave me some roasted groundnuts which did again revive my feeble stomach.

Being got out of her sight, I had time and liberty again to look into my Bible, which was my guide by day and my pillow by night. Now that comfortable scripture presented itself to me, Isa. 54:7, "For a small moment have I forsaken thee, but with great mercies will I gather thee." Thus the Lord carried me along from one time to another and made good to me this precious promise and many others. Then my son came to see me, and I asked his master to let him stay awhile with me that I might comb his head and look over him, for he was almost overcome with lice. He told me when I had done that he was very hungry, but I had nothing to relieve him but bid him go into the wigwams as he went along and see if he could get anything among them, which he did. And it seems [he] tarried a little too long, for his master was angry with him and beat him, and then sold him. Then he came running to tell me he had a new master, and that he had given him some groundnuts already. Then I went along with him to his new master who told me he loved him and he should not want. So his master carried him away, and I never saw him afterward till I saw him at Pascataqua in Portsmouth.

That night they bade me go out of the wigwam again. My mistress's papoose was sick, and it died that night, and there was one benefit in it that there was more room. I went to a wigwam and they bade me come in and gave me a skin to lie upon, and a mess of venison and groundnuts, which was a choice dish among them. On the morrow they buried the papoose and afterward, both morning and evening, there came a company to mourn and howl with her though I confess I could not much condole with them.[33] Many sorrowful days I had in this place, often getting alone "like a crane, or a swallow, so did I chatter; I did mourn as a dove, mine eyes fail with looking upward. Oh, Lord, I am oppressed; undertake for me," Isa. 38:14. I could tell the Lord as Hezekiah, ver. 3, "Remember now, O Lord, I beseech Thee, how I have walked before Thee in truth."

Now had I time to examine all my ways. My conscience did not accuse me of unrighteousness toward one or other, yet I saw how in my walk with God I had been a careless creature. As David said, "Against Thee, Thee only, have I sinned," and I might say with the poor publican, "God be merciful unto me a sinner." On the Sabbath days I could look upon the sun and think how people were going to the house of God to have their souls refreshed and then home and their bodies also, but I was destitute of both and might say as the poor prodigal, "He would fain have filled his belly with the husks that the swine did eat, and no man gave unto him," Luke 15:16. For I must say with him, "Father I have sinned against heaven and in thy sight," ver. 21. I remembered how on the night before and after the Sabbath when my family was about me and relations and neighbors with us, we could pray and sing, and then refresh our bodies with the good creatures of God, and then have a comfortable bed to lie down on. But instead of all this I had only a little swill for the body and then like a swine must lie down on the ground. I cannot express to man the sorrow that lay upon my spirit; the Lord knows it. Yet that comfortable scripture would often come to my mind, "For a small moment have I forsaken thee, but with great mercies will I gather thee."

The Fourteenth Remove

Now must we pack up and be gone from this thicket, bending our course toward the Bay towns, I having nothing to eat by the way this day but a few crumbs of cake that an Indian gave my girls the same day we were taken. She gave it me, and I put it in my pocket; there it lay till it was so moldy (for want of good baking) that one could not tell what it was made

33. For contemporary accounts of Algonquian mourning and burial customs, see Wood, *New England's Prospect*, 110–112; Morton, *New English Canaan*, 51–52; and Williams, *Key into the Lanugage*, 247–250.

of; it fell all to crumbs and grew so dry and hard that it was like little flints, and this refreshed me many times when I was ready to faint. It was in my thoughts when I put it into my mouth that if ever I returned I would tell the world what a blessing the Lord gave to such mean food. As we went along, they killed a deer with a young one in her; they gave me a piece of the fawn, and it was so young and tender that one might eat the bones as well as the flesh, and yet I thought it very good. When night came on we sat down. It rained, but they quickly got up a bark wigwam where I lay dry that night. I looked out in the morning, and many of them had laid in the rain all night [which] I saw by their reeking. Thus the Lord dealt mercifully with me many times, and I fared better than many of them. In the morning they took the blood of the deer and put it into the paunch and so boiled it; I could eat nothing of that, though they ate it sweetly. And yet they were so nice in other things that when I had fetched water and had put the dish I dipped the water with into the kettle of water which I brought, they would say they would knock me down for they said it was a sluttish trick.[34]

The Fifteenth Remove

We went on our travel. I having got one handful of groundnuts for my support that day, they gave me my load, and I went on cheerfully (with the thoughts of going homeward) having my burden more on my back than my spirit. We came to Baquaug River[35] again that day, near which we abode a few days. Sometimes one of them would give me a pipe, another a little tobacco, another a little salt which I would change for a little victuals. I cannot but think what a wolfish appetite persons have in a starving condition, for many times when they gave me that which was hot, I was so greedy that I should burn my mouth that it would trouble me hours after, and yet I should quickly do the same again. And after I was thoroughly hungry, I was never again satisfied. For though sometimes it fell out that I got enough and did eat till I could eat no more, yet I was as unsatisfied as I was when I began. And now could I see that scripture verified (there being many scriptures which we do not take notice of or understand till we are afflicted), Mic. 6:14, "Thou shalt eat and not be sat-

34. Rowlandson had apparently violated Indian custom by putting her dipper into the community kettle.
35. Miller's River in Orange, Massachusetts.

isfied." Now might I see more than ever before the miseries that sin hath brought upon us. Many times I should be ready to run out against the heathen, but the scripture would quiet me again, Amos 3:6, "Shall there be evil in the city, and the Lord hath not done it?" The Lord help me to make a right improvement of His word and that I might learn that great lesson, Mic. 6:8, 9, "He hath showed thee (Oh Man) what is good, and what doth the Lord require of thee, but to do justly and love mercy and walk humbly with thy God? Hear ye the rod and who hath appointed it."

The Sixteenth Remove

We began this remove with wading over Baquag River; the water was up to the knees and the stream very swift and so cold that I thought it would have cut me in sunder. I was so weak and feeble that I reeled as I went along and thought there I must end my days at last after my bearing and getting through so many difficulties. The Indians stood laughing to see me staggering along, but in my distress the Lord gave me experience of the truth and goodness of that promise, Isai. 43:2, "When thou passest through the waters, I will be with thee, and through the rivers, they shall not overflow thee." Then I sat down to put on my stockings and shoes with the tears running down mine eyes and many sorrowful thoughts in my heart, but I got up to go along with them. Quickly there came up to us an Indian who informed them that I must go to Wachuset to my master, for there was a letter come from the council to the sagamores about redeeming the captives and that there would be another in fourteen days and that I must be there ready. My heart was so heavy before that I could scarce speak or go in the path and yet now so light that I could run. My strength seemed to come again and recruit my feeble knees and aching heart, yet it pleased them to go but one mile that night, and there we stayed two days. In that time came a company of Indians to us, near thirty, all on horseback.[36] My heart skipped within me, thinking they had been Englishmen at the first sight of them, for they were dressed in English apparel, with hats, white neckcloths, and sashes about their waists, and ribbons upon their shoulders, but when they came near there was a vast

36. There were no horses in the Western Hemisphere when Europeans began colonization, although skeletal remains reveal that horses had been on the continent in prehistoric times. Most colonies passed strict laws against selling them to Indians, both because of the animals' importance to colonial agriculture and transportation and because of their potential threat in the hands of Indian enemies. The large number mentioned by Rowlandson had probably been taken in earlier raids on English settlements.

difference between the lovely faces of Christians and the foul looks of those heathens which much damped my spirit again.[37]

The Seventeenth Remove

A comfortable remove it was to me because of my hopes. They gave me a pack, and along we went cheerfully, but quickly my will proved more than my strength. Having little or no refreshing, my strength failed me, and my spirit were almost quite gone. Now may I say with David, Psal. 119:22, 23, 24, "I am poor and needy, and my heart is wounded within me. I am gone like the shadow when it declineth: I am tossed up and down like the locust; my knees are weak through fasting, and my flesh faileth of fatness."

At night we came to an Indian town,[38] and the Indians sat down by a wigwam discoursing, but I was almost spent and could scarce speak. I laid down my load and went into the wigwam, and there sat an Indian boiling of horses' feet (they being wont to eat the flesh first, and when the feet were old and dried and they had nothing else, they would cut off the feet and use them). I asked him to give me a little of his broth or water they were boiling in; he took a dish and gave me one spoonful of samp [corn mush] and bid me take as much of the broth as I would. Then I put some of the hot water to the samp and drank it up and my spirit came again. He gave me also a piece of the rough or ridding of the small guts, and I broiled it on the coals; and now may I say with Jonathan, "See, I pray you, how mine eyes have been enlightened because I tasted a little of this honey," 1 Sam. 14:29. Now is my spirit revived again, though means be never so inconsiderable; yet if the Lord bestow His blessing upon them, they shall refresh both soul and body.

The Eighteenth Remove

We took up our packs and along we went, but a wearisome day I had of it. As we went along I saw an Englishman stripped naked and lying dead upon the ground but knew not who it was. Then we came to another Indian town where we stayed all night.[39] In this town there were four En-

37. Most early descriptions of the Indians praise their appearance. Rowlandson's revulsion at "the foul looks of the heathens" undoubtedly reflects exaggerated wartime perceptions.

38. Probably Nichewaug in Petersham.

39. Probably Wanimesset in present-day New Braintree.

glish children, captives, and one of them my own sister's. I went to see how she did, and she was well, considering her captive condition. I would have tarried that night with her, but they that owned her would not suffer it. Then I went into another wigwam where they were boiling corn and beans, which was a lovely sight to see, but I could not get a taste thereof. Then I went to another wigwam where there were two of the English children. The squaw was boiling horses' feet; then she cut me off a little piece and gave one of the English children a piece also. Being very hungry, I had quickly eat up mine, but the child could not bite it, it was so touch and sinewy but lay sucking, gnawing, chewing, and slabbering of it in the mouth and hand. Then I took it of the child and ate it myself and savory it was to my taste. Then I may say [as] Job, chap. 6:7, "The things that my soul refused to touch are as my sorrowful meat." Thus the Lord made that pleasant refreshing which another time would have been an abomination. Then I went home to my mistress' wigwam, and they told me I disgraced my master with begging, and if I did so anymore they would knock me in [the] head. I told them they had as good knock me in [the] head as starve me to death.

The Nineteenth Remove

They said when we went out that we must travel to Wachuset[40] this day. But a bitter weary day I had of it, traveling now three days together without resting any day between. At last, after many weary steps, I saw Wachuset Hills but many miles off. Then we came to a great swamp through which we traveled up to the knees in mud and water, which was heavy going to one tired before. Being almost spent, I thought I should have sunk down at last and never got out, but I may say, as in Psal. 94:18, "When my foot slipped, Thy mercy, O Lord, held me up." Going along, having indeed my life but little spirit, Philip, who was in the company, came up and took me by the hand and said, "Two weeks more and you shall be mistress again." I asked him if he spake true. He answered, "Yes, and quickly you shall come to your master again who has been gone from us three weeks." After many weary steps we came to Wachuset where he was, and glad I was to see him. He asked me when I washed me. I told him not this month. Then he fetched me some water himself and bid me wash and gave me the glass to see how I looked and bid his squaw give me

40. In Princeton, Massachusetts. The Indians and their captives had virtually retraced their steps from Chesterfield, New Hampshire, to the site of the third remove.

something to eat. So she gave me a mess of beans and meat and a little groundnut cake. I was wonderfully revived with this favor showed me, Psal. 106:46, "He made them also to be pitied, of all those that carried them captives."

My master had three squaws, living sometimes with one and sometimes with another one.[41] This old squaw at whose wigwam [now] I was, my master had been [with] those three weeks. Another was Wettimore [Weetamoo], with whom I had lived and served all this while. A severe and proud dame she was, bestowing every day in dressing herself neat as much time as any of the gentry of the land, powdering her hair and painting her face, going with necklaces, with jewels in her ears, and bracelets upon her hands. When she had dressed herself, her work was to make girdles of wampum[42] and beads. The third squaw was a younger one by whom he had two papooses. By that time I was refreshed by the old squaw with whom my master was. Wettimore's maid came to call me home, at which I fell a-weeping. Then the old squaw told me, to encourage me, that if I wanted victuals I should come to her, and that I should lie there in her wigwam. Then I went with the maid and quickly came again and lodged there. The squaw laid a mat under me and a good rug over me; the first time I had any such kindness showed me. I understood that Wettimore thought that if she should let me go and serve with the old squaw, she would be in danger to lose not only my service but the redemption pay also. And I was not a little glad to hear this, being by it raised in my hopes that in God's due time there would be an end of this sorrowful hour. Then came an Indian and asked me to knit him three pair of stockings, for which I had a hat and a silk handkerchief. Then another asked me to make her a shift, for which she gave me an apron.

Then came Tom and Peter[43] with the second letter from the council about the captives. Though they were Indians, I got them by the hand and burst out into tears; my heart was so full that I could not speak to them, but recovering myself, I asked them how my husband did and all my friends and acquaintances. They said they [were] all very well but melan-

41. Some Indians, especially chiefs, had several wives. See, for example, Williams, *Key into the Language*, 205–209. On Weetamoo, a powerful sachem herself, see Samuel G. Drake, *The Aboriginal Races of North America*, 15th ed. (Philadelphia, 1859), 187–190; and Douglas Edward Leach, *Flintlock and Tomahawk: New England in King Philip's War* (New York, 1958), *passim*.

42. For a description of wampum, or wampompeage, used by the Indians as both currency and decoration, see Williams, *Key into the Language*, 210–220.

43. Christian Indians Tom Dublet (Nepanet) and Peter Conway (Tatatiquinea) from the praying town of Nashobah.

choly. They brought me two biscuits and a pound of tobacco. The tobacco I quickly gave away; when it was all gone, one asked me to give him a pipe of tobacco. I told him it was all gone. Then began he to rant and threaten. I told him when my husband came I would give some. "Hang [the] rogue," says he, "I will knock out his brains if he comes here." And then again in the same breath they would say that if there should come a hundred without guns they would do them no hurt, so unstable and like madmen they were, so that fearing the worst, I durst not send to my husband though there were some thoughts of his coming to redeem and fetch me, not knowing what might follow. For there was little more trust to them than to the master they served.

When the letter was come, the sagamores met to consult about the captives and called me to them to inquire how much my husband would give to redeem me. When I came, I sat down among them as I was wont to do as their manner is. Then they bade me stand up and said they were the General Court.[44] They bid me speak what I thought he would give. Now knowing that all we had was destroyed by the Indians, I was in a great strait. I thought if I should speak of but a little, it would be slighted and hinder the matter; if of a great sum, I knew not where it would be procured. Yet at a venture, I said twenty pounds yet desired them to take less, but they would not hear of that but sent that message to Boston that for twenty pounds I should be redeemed.[45] It was a praying Indian that wrote their letter for them. There was another praying Indian who told me that he had a brother that would not eat horse; his conscience was so tender and scrupulous (though as large as hell for the destruction of poor Christians). Then he said he read that scripture to him, 2 Kings, 6:25, "There was a famine in Samaria, and behold they besieged it, until an ass's head was sold for fourscore pieces of silver, and the fourth part of a kab of doves' dung for five pieces of silver." He expounded this place to his brother and showed him that it was lawful to eat that in a famine which is not at another time. And now, says he, he will eat horse with any Indian of them all.

There was another praying Indian who, when he had done all the mischief that he could, betrayed his own father into the English hands thereby

44. That is, their principal legislative assembly, before which they expected Mary Rowlandson to stand as she would have had to do before the Massachusetts General Court—the colony's highest legislative and judicial body.

45. For the text of the letter see John Gorham Palfrey, *The History of New England*, 5 vols. (Boston, 1865–1890), III, 188.

to purchase his own life. Another praying Indian was at Sudbury fight,[46] though, as he deserved, he was afterward hanged for it. There was another praying Indian so wicked and cruel as to wear a string about his neck strung with Christians' fingers.[47] Another praying Indian, when they went to Sudbury fight, went with them and his squaw also with him with her papoose at her back.

Before they went to that fight, they got a company together to powwow; the manner was as followeth. There was one that kneeled upon a deerskin with the company round him in a ring, who kneeled, and striking upon the ground with their hands and with sticks, and muttering or humming with their mouths; besides him who kneeled in the ring, there also stood one with a gun in his hand. Then he on the deerskin made a speech, and all manifested assent to it, and so they did many times together. Then they bade him with the gun go out of the ring, which he did, but when he was out, they called him in again. But he seemed to make a stand; then they called the more earnestly till he returned again. Then they all sang. Then they gave him two guns, in either hand one. And so he on the deerskin began again, and at the end of every sentence in his speaking, they all assented, humming or muttering with their mouths and striking upon the ground with their hands. Then they bade him with the two guns go out of the ring again, which he did a little way. Then they called him in again, but he made a stand; so they called him with greater earnestness, but he stood reeling and wavering as if he knew not whether he should stand or fall or which way to go. Then they called him with exceeding great vehemency, all of them, one and another. After a little while he turned in, staggering as he went, with his arms stretched out, in either hand a gun. As soon as he came in, they all sang and rejoiced exceedingly awhile. And then he upon the deerskin made another speech unto which they all assented in a rejoicing manner, and so they ended their business and forthwith went to Sudbury fight.[48]

To my thinking they went without any scruple but that they should

46. Battle of April 18, 1676, in which more than thirty English troops were killed in ambush.

47. Algonquian Indians often made necklaces of animal bones. In wartime they sometimes substituted the bones of their slain enemies.

48. Rowlandson's description of Indian preparations for war is unusually thorough; few Europeans had the opportunity to observe such ceremonies. On Indian warfare in general see Wood, *New England's Prospect*, 102–103; and Williams, *Key into the Language*, 233–239.

prosper and gain the victory. And they went out not so rejoicing, but they came home with as great a victory, for they said they had killed two captains and almost an hundred men. One Englishman they brought along with them; and he said it was too true for they had made sad work at Sudbury, as indeed it proved. Yet they came home without that rejoicing and triumphing over their victory which they were wont to show at other times but rather like dogs (as they say) which have lost their ears. Yet I could not perceive that it was for their own loss of men. They said they had not lost but above five or six, and I missed none except in one wigwam. When they went, they acted as if the devil had told them that they should gain the victory, and now they acted as if the devil had told them they should have a fall. Whither it were so or no, I cannot tell, but so it proved for quickly they began to fall and so held on that summer till they came to utter ruin.

They came home on a Sabbath day, and the powwow that kneeled upon the deerskin came home (I may say without abuse) as black as the devil. When my master came home, he came to me and bid me make a shirt for his papoose of a Holland lace pillowbeer.[49] About that time there came an Indian to me and bid me come to his wigwam at night, and he would give me some pork and groundnuts, which I did. And as I was eating, another Indian said to me, "He seems to be your good friend, but he killed two Englishmen at Sudbury, and there lie their clothes behind you." I looked behind me, and there I saw bloody clothes with bullet holes in them, yet the Lord suffered not this wretch to do me any hurt. Yea, instead of that, he many times refreshed me; five or six times did he and his squaw refresh my feeble carcass. If I went to their wigwam at any time, they would always give me something, and yet they were strangers that I never saw before. Another squaw gave me a piece of fresh pork and a little salt with it and lent me her pan to fry it in, and I cannot but remember what a sweet, pleasant and delightful relish that bit had to me to this day. So little do we prize common mercies when we have them to the full.

The Twentieth Remove

It was their usual manner to remove when they had done any mischief, lest they should be found out, and so they did at this time. We went about

49. That is, pillowcases made of Dutch lace.

three or four miles,[50] and there they built a great wigwam big enough to hold a hundred Indians, which they did in preparation to a great day of dancing. They would say now amongst themselves that the governor would be so angry for his loss at Sudbury that he would send no more about the captives, which made me grieve and tremble. My sister [Hannah] being not far from the place where we now were, and hearing that I was here, desired her master to let her come and see me, and he was willing to it and would go with her. But she, being ready before him, told him she would go before and was come within a mile or two of the place. Then he overtook her and began to rant as if he had been mad and made her go back again in the rain so that I never saw her till I saw her in Charlestown. But the Lord requited many of their ill doings, for this Indian, her master, was hanged afterward at Boston.

The Indians now began to come from all quarters, against their merry dancing day. Among some of them came one Goodwife Kettle.[51] I told her my heart was so heavy that it was ready to break. "So is mine, too," said she. But yet [she] said, "I hope we shall hear some good news shortly." I could hear how earnestly my sister desired to see me, and I as earnestly desired to see her and yet neither of us could get an opportunity. My daughter was also now about a mile off, and I had not seen her in nine or ten weeks as I had not seen my sister since our first taking. I earnestly desired them to let me go and see them; yea, I entreated, begged, and persuaded them but to let me see my daughter, and yet so hardhearted were they that they would not suffer it. They made use of their tyrannical power whilst they had it, but through the Lord's wonderful mercy their time was now but short.

On a Sabbath day, the sun being about an hour high in the afternoon, came Mr. John Hoar (the council permitting him and his own forward spirit inclining him) together with the two forementioned Indians, Tom and Peter, with their third letter from the council. When they came near, I was abroad; though I saw them not, they presently called me in and bade me sit down and not stir. Then they catched up their guns and away they ran as if an enemy had been at hand, and the guns went off apace. I manifested some great trouble, and they asked me what was the matter. I told them I thought they had killed the Englishman (for they had in the meantime informed me that an Englishman was come). They said, "No." They shot over his horse and under, and before his horse, and they pushed him

50. Near the southern end of Lake Wachusett, in Princeton.
51. Elizabeth Ward Kettle of Lancaster.

this way and that way at their pleasure, showing what they could do. Then they let them come to their wigwams. I begged of them to let me see the Englishman, but they would not; but there was I fain to sit their pleasure. When they had talked their fill with him, they suffered me to go to him. We asked each other of our welfare, and how my husband did and all my friends. He told me they were all well and would be glad to see me. Amongst other things which my husband sent me, there came a pound of tobacco which I sold for nine shillings in money, for many of the Indians for want of tobacco smoked hemlock and ground ivy. It was a great mistake in any who thought I sent for tobacco, for through the favor of God that desire was overcome.

I now asked them whether I should go home with Mr. Hoar. They answered, "No," one and another of them. And it being night, we lay down with that answer. In the morning Mr. Hoar invited the sagamores to dinner, but when we went to get it ready, we found that they had stolen the greatest part of the provision Mr. Hoar had brought out of his bags in the night. And we may see the wonderful power of God in that one passage in that when there was such a great number of the Indians together and so greedy of a little good food and no English there but Mr. Hoar and myself that there they did not knock us in the head and take what he had, there being not only some provision but also trading cloth, a part of the twenty pounds agreed upon. But instead of doing us any mischief, they seemed to be ashamed of the fact and said it were some *matchit* [bad] Indian that did it. Oh, that we could believe that there is nothing too hard for God! God showed His power over the heathen in this as He did over the hungry lions when Daniel was cast into the den. Mr. Hoar called them betime to dinner, but they ate very little, they being so busy in dressing themselves and getting ready for their dance, which was carried on by eight of them— four men and four squaws, my master and mistress being two. He was dressed in his Holland shirt with great laces sewed at the tail of it; he had his silver buttons, his white stockings, his garters were hung round with shillings, and he had girdles of wampum upon his head and shoulders. She had a kersey coat and [was] covered with girdles of wampum from the loins upward; her arms from her elbows to her hands were covered with bracelets; there were handfuls of necklaces about her neck and several sorts of jewels in her ears. She had fine red stockings and white shoes, her hair powdered and face painted red that was always before black. And all the dancers were after the same manner. There were two other singing and knocking on a kettle for their music. They kept hopping up and down one after another with a kettle of water in the midst, standing warm upon some embers, to drink of when they were dry. They held on till it was almost night, throwing out wampum to the standersby.

At night I asked them again if I should go home. They all as one said no except my husband would come for me. When we were lain down, my master went out of the wigwam, and by and by sent in an Indian called James the Printer[52] who told Mr. Hoar that my master would let me go home tomorrow if he would let him have one pint of liquors. Then Mr. Hoar called his own Indians, Tom and Peter, and bid them go and see whether he would promise it before them three, and if he would, he should have it, which he did, and he had it. Then Philip, smelling the business, called me to him and asked me what I would give him to tell me some good news and speak a good word for me. I told him I could not tell what to give him. I would anything I had and asked him what he would have. He said two coats and twenty shillings in money and half a bushel of seed corn and some tobacco. I thanked him for his love, but I knew the good news as well as the crafty fox.

My master, after he had had his drink, quickly came ranting into the wigwam again and called for Mr. Hoar, drinking to him and saying he was a good man. And then again he would say, "Hang [the] rogue." Being almost drunk, he would drink to him, and yet presently say he should be hanged. Then he called for me. I trembled to hear him, yet I was fain to go to him, and he drank to me, showing no incivility. He was the first Indian I saw drunk all the while that I was amongst them. At last his squaw ran out, and he after her round the wigwam with his money jingling at his knees, but she escaped him. But having an old squaw, he ran to her, and so through the Lord's mercy, we were no more troubled that night.

Yet I had not a comfortable night's rest, for I think I can say I did not sleep for three nights together. The night before the letter came from the council I could not rest, I was so full of fears and troubles, God many times leaving us most in the dark when deliverance is nearest. Yea, at this time I could not rest night nor day. The next night I was overjoyed, Mr. Hoar being come and that with such good tidings. The third night I was even swallowed up with the thoughts of things, *viz.* that ever I should go home again and that I must go, leaving my children behind me in the wilderness so that sleep was now almost departed from mine eyes.

On Tuesday morning they called their General Court (as they call it) to consult and determine whether I should go home or no. And they all as

---

52. A praying Indian who in 1650s and 1660s had helped John Eliot to print the Bible in an Algonquian dialect.

one man did seemingly consent to it that I should go home except Philip who would not come among them.[53]

But before I go any further, I would take leave to mention a few remarkable passages of providence which I took special notice of in my afflicted time.

1. Of the fair opportunity lost in the long march a little after the fort fight when our English army was so numerous and in pursuit of the enemy and so near as to take several and destroy them, and the enemy in such distress for food that our men might track them by their rooting in the earth for groundnuts while they were flying for their lives. I say that then our army should want provision and be forced to leave their pursuit and return homeward. And the very next week the enemy came upon our town like bears bereft of their whelps or so many ravenous wolves, rending us and our lambs to death. But what shall I say? God seemed to leave His people to themselves and order all things for His own holy ends. "Shall there be evil in the city and the Lord hath not done it? They are not grieved for the affliction of Joseph, therefore shall they go captive with the first that go captive." It is the Lord's doing, and it should be marvelous in our eyes.

2. I cannot but remember how the Indians derided the slowness and dullness of the English army in its setting out. For after the desolations at Lancaster and Medfield, as I went along with them, they asked me when I thought the English would come after them. I told them I could not tell. It may be they will come in May, said they. Thus did they scoff at us, as if the English would be a quarter of a year getting ready.

3. Which also I have hinted before when the English army with new supplies were sent forth to pursue after the enemy, and they, understanding it, fled before them till they came to Baquaug River where they forthwith went over safely, that that river should be impassable to the English. I can but admire to see the wonderful[54] providence of God in preserving the heathen for further affliction to our poor country. They could go in great numbers over, but the English must stop. God had an overruling hand in all those things.

4. It was thought if their corn were cut down they would starve and die with hunger, and all their corn that could be found was destroyed, and they driven from that little they had in store into the woods in the midst of

53. Philip may have shunned the meeting to avoid a unanimous, and therefore binding, decision.

54. Here and elsewhere in the narrative, Rowlandson uses "wonderful" in the obsolete sense of "full of wonder."

winter. And yet how to admiration did the Lord preserve them for His holy ends and the destruction of many still amongst the English! Strangely did the Lord provide for them that I did not see (all the time I was among them) one man, woman, or child die with hunger. Though many times they would eat that that a hog or dog would hardly touch, yet by that God strengthened them to be a scourge to His people.

The chief and commonest food was groundnuts. They eat also nuts and acorns, artichokes, lily roots, groundbeans, and several other weeds and roots that I know not.

They would pick up old bones and cut them to pieces at the joints, and if they were full of worms and maggots, they would scald them over the fire to make the vermin come out and then boil them and drink up the liquor and then beat the great ends of them in a mortar and so eat them. They would eat horses' guts and ears, and all sorts of wild birds which they could catch; also bear, venison, beaver, tortoise, frogs, squirrels, dogs, skunks, rattlesnakes, yea, the very bark of trees, besides all sorts of creatures and provision which they plundered from the English. I can but stand in admiration to see the wonderful power of God in providing for such a vast number of our enemies in the wilderness where there was nothing to be seen but from hand to mouth. Many times in a morning the generality of them would eat up all they had and yet have some further supply against they wanted. It is said, Psal. 81:13, 14, "Oh, that My people had hearkened to Me, and Israel had walked in My ways; I should soon have subdued their enemies and turned My hand against their adversaries." But now our perverse and evil carriages in the sight of the Lord have so offended Him that instead of turning His hand against them the Lord feeds and nourishes them up to be a scourge to the whole land.

5. Another thing that I would observe is the strange providence of God in turning things about when the Indians [were] at the highest and the English at the lowest. I was with the enemy eleven weeks and five days, and not one weeks passed without the fury of the enemy and some desolation by fire and sword upon one place or other. They mourned (with their black faces) for their own losses, yet triumphed and rejoiced in their inhuman and many times devilish cruelty to the English. They would boast much of their victories, saying that in two hours' time they had destroyed such a captain and his company at such a place, and such a captain and his company in such a place, and such a captain and his company in such a place, and boast how many towns they had destroyed; and then scoff and say they had done them a good turn to send them to heaven so soon. Again they would say this summer that they would knock all the rogues in

the head, or drive them into the sea, or make them fly the country, thinking surely Agag-like, "The bitterness of death is past." Now the heathen begins to think all is their own, and the poor Christians' hopes to fail (as to man), and now their eyes are more to God, and their hearts sigh heavenward and to say in good earnest, "Help Lord, or we perish." When the Lord had brought His people to this that they saw no help in anything but Himself, then He takes the quarrel into His own hand, and though they [the Indians] had made a pit in their own imaginations as deep as hell for the Christians that summer, yet the Lord hurled themselves into it. And the Lord had not so many ways before to preserve them, but now He hath as many to destroy them.

But to return again to my going home where we may see a remarkable change of providence. At first they were all against it except my husband would come for me, but afterwards they assented to it and seemed much to rejoice in it. Some asked me to send them some bread, others some tobacco, others shaking me by the hand, offering me a hood and scarf to ride in, not one moving hand or tongue against it. Thus hath the Lord answered my poor desire and the many earnest requests of others put up unto God for me. In my travels an Indian came to me and told me if I were willing, he and his squaw would run away and go home along with me. I told him no. I was not willing to run away but desired to wait God's time that I might go home quietly and without fear. And now God hath granted me my desire. O, the wonderful power of God that I have seen and the experience that I have had! I have been in the midst of those roaring lions and savage bears that feared neither God nor man nor the devil, by night and day, alone and in company, sleeping all sorts together, and yet not one of them ever offered me the least abuse of unchastity to me in word or action.[55] Though some are ready to say I speak it for my own credit, I speak it in the presence of God and to His glory. God's power is as great now and as sufficient to save as when He preserved Daniel in the lion's den or the three children in the fiery furnace. I may well say as his Psal. 107:12, "Oh, give thanks unto the Lord for He is good, for His mercy endureth forever." Let the redeemed of the Lord say so whom He hath redeemed from the hand of the enemy, especially that I should come away in the midst of so many hundreds of enemies quietly and peaceably and not a dog moving his tongue.

55. Despite occasional accusations by Puritan spokesmen that the Indians sexually abused their female captives, the evidence is overwhelming that they did not. Algonquian social and military mores forbade it.

So I took my leave of them, and in coming along my heart melted into tears more than all the while I was with them, and I was almost swallowed up with the thoughts that ever I should go home again. About the sun going down, Mr. Hoar, myself, and the two Indians came to Lancaster, and a solemn sight it was to me. There had I lived many comfortable years amongst my relations and neighbors, and now not one Christian to be seen nor one house left standing. We went on to a farmhouse that was yet standing where we lay all night, and a comfortable lodging we had though nothing but straw to lie on. The Lord preserved us in safety that night and raised us up again in the morning and carried us along that before noon we came to Concord. Now was I full of joy and yet not without sorrow—joy to see such a lovely sight, so many Christians together and some of them my neighbors. There I met with my brother [Josiah White] and my brother-in-law [Henry Kerley] who asked me if I knew where his wife was. Poor heart! He had helped to bury her and knew it not, she being shot down [when] the house was partly burned so that those who were at Boston at the desolation of the town and came back afterward and buried the dead did not know her. Yet I was not without sorrow to think how many were looking and longing and my own children amongst the rest to enjoy that deliverance that I had now received, and I did not know whether ever I should see them again.

Being recruited with food and raiment, we went to Boston that day where I met with my dear husband, but the thoughts of our dear children, one being dead and the other we could not tell where, abated our comfort each to other. I was not before so much hemmed in with the merciless and cruel heathen but now as much with pitiful, tenderhearted, and compassionate Christians. In that poor and distressed and beggarly condition I was received in, I was kindly entertained in several houses; so much love I received from several (some of whom I knew and others I knew not) that I am not capable to declare it. But the Lord knows them all by name. The Lord reward them sevenfold into their bosoms of His spirituals for their temporals.

The twenty pounds, the price of my redemption, was raised by some Boston gentlemen and Mrs. Usher,[56] whose bounty and religious charity I would not forget to make mention of. Then Mr. Thomas Shepard of Charlestown[57] received us into his house where we continued eleven weeks, and a father and mother they were to us. And many more tender-

56. Wife of Boston bookseller and selectman Hezekiah Usher.

57. Son of Rev. Thomas Shepard of Cambridge, a major figure among first generation New England Puritans.

71

hearted friends we met with in that place. We were now in the midst of love, yet not without much and frequent heaviness of heart for our poor children and other relations who were still in affliction. The week following after my coming in, the governor and council sent forth to the Indians again, and that not without success, for they brought in my sister and Goodwife Kettle.

Their not knowing where our children were was a sore trial to us still, and yet we were not without secret hopes that we should see them again. That which was dead lay heavier upon my spirit than those which were alive and amongst the heathen, thinking how it suffered with its wounds and I was no way able to relieve it, and how it was buried by the heathen in the wilderness from among all Christians. We were hurried up and down in our thoughts; sometime we should hear a report that they were gone this way, and sometimes that, and that they were come in in this place or that. We kept inquiring and listening to hear concerning them but no certain news as yet. About this time the council had ordered a day of public thanksgiving,[58] though I thought I had still cause of mourning, and, being unsettled in our minds, we thought we would ride toward the eastward to see if we could hear anything concerning our children. And as we were riding along (God is the wise disposer of all things) between Ipswich and Rowly we met with Mr. William Hubbard,[59] who told us that our son Joseph was come in to Major Waldren's,[60] and another with him which was my sister's son. I asked him how he knew it. He said the major himself told him so.

So along we went till we came to Newbury, and, their minister being absent, they desired my husband to preach the thanksgiving for them, but he was not willing to stay there that night but would go over to Salisbury to hear further and come again in the morning, which he did and preached there that day. At night when he had done, one came and told him that his daughter was come in at Providence. Here was mercy on both hands. Now hath God fulfilled that precious scripture which was such a comfort to me in my distressed condition. When my heart was ready to sink into the earth (my children being gone I could not tell whither), and my knees trembled under me, and I was walking through the valley of the shadow of

58. A broadside issued on June 20, 1676, proclaimed a day of public thanksgiving on June 29 to praise God that "in the midst of his judgements he hath remembered mercy."

59. Minister at Ipswich, Massachusetts, and author of *A Narrative of the Troubles with the Indians* (Boston, 1677), and other works.

60. Richard Waldron of Dover, New Hampshire. See note 18 to John Gyles's narrative and note 24 to John Williams's narrative below.

death, then the Lord brought and now has fulfilled that reviving word unto me. Thus saith the Lord, "Refrain thy voice from weeping, and thine eyes from tears, for thy work shall be rewarded," saith the Lord, "and they shall come again from the land of the enemy."

Now we were between them, the one on the east and the other on the west. Our son being nearest, we went to him first to Portsmouth where we met with him and with the major also who told us he had done what he could but could not redeem him under seven pounds, which the good people thereabouts were pleased to pay. The Lord reward the major and all the rest, though unknown to me, for their labor of love. My sister's son was redeemed for four pounds, which the council gave order for the payment of. Having now received one of our children, we hastened toward the other; going back through Newbury, my husband preached there on the Sabbath day, for which they rewarded him manyfold.

On Monday we came to Charlestown where we heard that the governor of Rhode Island[61] had sent over for our daughter [Mary] to take care of her, being now within his jurisdiction, which should not pass without our acknowledgments. But she being nearer Rehoboth than Rhode Island, Mr. Newman[62] went over and took care of her and brought her to his own house. And the goodness of God was admirable to us in our low estate in that he raised up [com]passionate friends on every side to us when we had nothing to recompense any for their love. The Indians were now gone that way that it was apprehended dangerous to go to her, but the carts which carried provision to the English army, being guarded, brought her with them to Dorchester where we received her safe. Blessed be the Lord for it, for great is His power, and He can do whatsoever seemeth Him good.

Her coming in was after this manner. She was traveling one day with the Indians with her basket at her back; the company of Indians were got before her and gone out of sight, all except one squaw. She followed the squaw till night, and then both of them lay down, having nothing over them but the heavens and under them but the earth. Thus she traveled three days together, not knowing whither she was going, having nothing to eat or drink but water and green hirtleberries. At last they came into Providence where she was kindly entertained by several of that town. The Indians often said that I should never have her under twenty pounds. But now the Lord hath brought her in upon free cost and given her to me the second time. The Lord make us a blessing indeed each to others. Now

61. William Coddington.
62. Rev. Noah Newman of Rehoboth, Massachusetts.

have I seen that scripture also fulfilled, Deut. 30:4, 7: "If any of thine be driven out to the outmost parts of heaven, from thence will the Lord thy God gather thee, and from thence will He fetch thee. And the Lord thy God will put all these curses upon thine enemies, and on them which hate thee which persecuted thee." Thus hath the Lord brought me and mine out of that horrible pit and hath set us in the midst of tenderhearted and compassionate Christians. It is the desire of my soul that we may walk worthy of the mercies received and which we are receiving.

Our family being now gathered together (those of us that were living), the South Church in Boston hired an house for us. Then we removed from Mr. Shepard's, those cordial friends, and went to Boston where we continued about three-quarters of a year. Still the Lord went along with us and provided graciously for us. I thought it somewhat strange to set up housekeeping with bare walls, but as Solomon says, "Money answers all things," and that we had through the benevolence of Christian friends, some in this town and some in that and others, and some from England, that in a little time we might look and see the house furnished with love. The Lord hath been exceeding good to us in our low estate in that when we had neither house nor home nor other necessaries, the Lord so moved the hearts of these and those towards us that we wanted neither food nor raiment for ourselves or ours, Prov. 18:24, "There is a friend which sticketh closer than a brother." And how many such friends have we found and now living amongst? And truly such a friend have we found him to be unto us in whose house we lived, *viz.* Mr. James Whitcomb, a friend unto us near hand and afar off.

I can remember the time when I used to sleep quietly without workings in my thoughts whole nights together, but now it is other ways with me. When all are fast about me and no eye open but His who ever waketh, my thoughts are upon things past, upon the awful dispensation of the Lord towards us, upon His wonderful power and might in carrying of us through so many difficulties in returning us in safety and suffering none to hurt us. I remember in the night season how the other day I was in the midst of thousands of enemies and nothing but death before me. It [was] then hard work to persuade myself that ever I should be satisfied with bread again. But now we are fed with the finest of the wheat, and, as I may say, with honey out of the rock. Instead of the husk, we have the fatted calf. The thoughts of these things in the particulars of them, and of the love and goodness of God towards us, make it true of me what David said of himself, Psal. 6:5 [actually 6:6]. "I watered my couch with my tears." Oh, the wonderful power of God that mine eyes have seen, affording matter

74

enough for my thoughts to run in that when others are sleeping mine eyes are weeping!

I have seen the extreme vanity of this world. One hour I have been in health and wealth, wanting nothing, but the next hour in sickness and wounds and death, having nothing but sorrow and affliction. Before I knew what affliction meant, I was ready sometimes to wish for it. When I lived in prosperity, having the comforts of the world about me, my relations by me, my heart cheerful, and taking little care for anything, and yet seeing many whom I preferred before myself under many trials and afflictions, in sickness, weakness, poverty, losses, crosses, and cares of the world, I should be sometimes jealous lest I should have my portion in this life, and that scripture would come to mind, Heb. 12:6, "For whom the Lord loveth he chasteneth and scourgeth every son whom He receiveth." But now I see the Lord had His time to scourge and chasten me. The portion of some is to have their afflictions by drops, now one drop and then another, but the dregs of the cup, the wine of astonishment, like a sweeping rain that leaveth no food, did the Lord prepare to be my portion. Affliction I wanted and affliction I had, full measure (I thought) pressed down and running over. Yet I see when God calls a person to anything and through never so many difficulties, yet He is fully able to carry them through and make them see and say they have been gainers thereby. And I hope I can say in some measure, as David did, "It is good for me that I have been afflicted."

The Lord hath showed me the vanity of these outward things. That they are the vanity of vanities and vexation of spirit, that they are but a shadow, a blast, a bubble, and things of no continuance. That we must rely on God himself and our whole dependence must be upon Him. If trouble from smaller matters begin to arise in me, I have something at hand to check myself with and say, why am I troubled? It was but the other day that if I had had the world I would have given it for my freedom or to have been a servant to a Christian. I have learned to look beyond present and smaller troubles and to be quieted under them, as Moses said, Exod. 14:13, "Stand still and see the salvation of the Lord."

FINIS

The central portion of John Foster's map of New England, printed in 1677, the year of Quentin Stockwell's capture at Deerfield. Courtesy of the American Antiquarian Society.

"QUENTIN STOCKWELL'S RELATION
OF HIS CAPTIVITY AND REDEMPTION"
· REPORTED BY INCREASE MATHER ·

The formal hostilities of King Philip's War ended in the fall of 1676 with Philip's death at the hands of a Christian Indian and the capitulation of most of his supporters. Scattered battles and sieges continued, however, especially along New England's northern rim. There refugee Indians from southern and central New England, reinforced by local tribes, posed a formidable threat to the Puritan frontier. The Indians were numerous and well-armed, and they could attack with relative impunity. The outer ring of colonial settlements in Massachusetts, New Hampshire, and Maine (at that time a section of Massachusetts) knew too well the horrors of forest warfare.

Deerfield, Massachusetts, was a prime target. Situated near the Connecticut River above the more heavily settled Northampton area, Deerfield was especially vulnerable to raids from the north and west. Between 1677 and 1712 the Indians took at least 125 captives from that harassed town. Two of the narratives in this anthology come from Deerfield victims—Quentin Stockwell, captured in 1677, and John Williams, taken prisoner in 1704.

In September 1677, about fifty Indians launched a surprise attack on several Connecticut Valley towns, suddenly ending almost six months of peace in that area. They destroyed Hatfield, Massachusetts, and carried off seventeen prisoners in a daylight assault while most of the men were away. That evening the Indians struck Deerfield, which had been destroyed two years before and was inhabited only by some men and boys who were rebuilding the town; the Indians took another twenty-four captives, including Stockwell. The raiders were rumored to be Mohawks from New York colony, for some had recently been in the vicinity, but they more likely were remnants of Philip's forces who had taken refuge in Canada.

Little is known about Quentin Stockwell, the author of this narrative, beyond what he tells below. He subsequently lived in Branford, Connecticut, and Suffield, Massachusetts. He survived until at least 1709. Stockwell's story was first published in Increase Mather's *An Essay for the Recording of Illustrious Providences* (Boston, 1684), 39–58, in which the Boston minister presented "proofs" of God's special concern for New England. The version that follows is based on Mather's text. His introduction to the narrative reads: "A Worthy Person hath sent me the Account which one lately belonging to *Deerfield,* (his name is *Quintin Stockwell,*) hath drawn up respecting his own Captivity and Redemption, with the more notable Occurrences of Divine Providence attending him in his distress, which I shall therefore here insert in the Words by himself expressed: He Relateth as followes."

In the year 1677, September 19, between sunset and dark, the Indians came upon us; I and another man being together, we ran away at the outcry the Indians made, shouting and shooting at some other of the English that were hard by. We took [to] a swamp that was at hand for our refuge; the enemy, espying us so near them, ran after us and shot many guns at us. Three guns were discharged upon me, the enemy being within three rod of me, besides many other before that. Being in this swamp that was miry, I slumped in and fell down; whereupon one of the enemy stepped to me with his hatchet lift up to knock me on the head, supposing that I had been wounded and so unfit for any other travel. I (as it happened) had a pistol by me which, though uncharged, I presented to the Indian who presently stepped back and told me if I would yield I should have no hurt. He said (which was not true) that they had destroyed all Hatfield and that the woods were full of Indians.[1] Whereupon I yielded myself and so fell into the enemies' hands and by three of them was led away unto the place whence first I began to make my flight; where two other Indians came running to us, and the one lifting up the butt end of his gun to knock me on the head, the other with his hand put by the blow and said I was his friend.

I was now by my own house which the Indians burned last year and I was bound to build up again, and there I had some hopes to escape from

1. A dozen or more colonists were killed in the September 19 attack on Hatfield. Of the seventeen captives taken, three were adults and fourteen were children. These, as Stockwell notes, were subsequently combined with the captives from Deerfield.

them. There was an horse just by which they bid me take. I did so but made no attempt to escape thereby, because the enemy was near and the beast was slow and dull. Then was I in hopes they would send me to take my own horses, which they did, but they were so frightened that I could not come near to them. And so [I] fell still into the enemies' hands, who now took me and bound me and led me away. And soon was I brought into the company of captives that were that day brought away from Hatfield which were about a mile off, and here methoughts was matter of joy and sorrow both, to see the company—some company in this condition being some refreshing though little help anyways. Then were we pinioned and led away in the night over the mountains in dark and hideous ways about four miles further before we took up our place for rest, which was in a dismal place of wood on the east side of that mountain. We were kept bound all that night. The Indians kept waking, and we had little mind to sleep in this night's travel. The Indians dispersed and, as they went, made strange noises as of wolves and owls and other wild beasts to the end that they might not lose one another, and if followed they might not be discovered by the English.

About the break of day we marched again and got over the great river at Pecomptuck River['s] mouth,[2] and there rested about two hours. There the Indians marked out upon trays the number of their captives and slain as their manner is. Here was I again in great danger. A quarrel arose about me, whose captive I was, for three took me. I thought I must be killed to end the controversy; so when they put it to me whose I was, I said three Indians took me. So they agreed to have all a share in me, and I had now three masters and he was my chief master who laid hands on me first. And thus was I fallen into the hands of the very worst of all the company, as Ashpelon, the Indian captain, told me, which captain was all along very kind to me and a great comfort to the English.

In this place they gave us some victuals which they had brought from the English. This morning also they sent ten men forth to town to bring away what they could find; some provision, some corn out of the meadow, they brought to us upon horses which they had there taken. From hence we went up about the falls where we crossed that river again, and, whilst I was going, I fell right down lame of my old wounds that I had in the war, and, whilst I was thinking I should therefore be killed by the Indians and what death I should die, my pain was suddenly gone and I was much en-

2. That is, the Pocumtuck or Deerfield River, at its junction with the "great" Connecticut River.

couraged again. We had about eleven horses in that company which the Indians made to carry burdens and to carry women.

It was afternoon when we now crossed that river. We traveled up that river till night and then took up our lodging in a dismal place and were staked down and spread out on our backs. And so we lay all night, yea so we lay many nights. They told me their law was that we should lie so nine nights, and by that time it was thought we should be out of our knowledge. The manner of staking down was thus: our arms and legs stretched out were staked fast down and a cord about our necks so that we could stir no ways. The first night of staking down, being much tired, I slept as comfortably as ever.

The next day we went up the river and crossed it and at night lay in Squakheag Meadows.[3] Our provision was soon spent, and while we lay in those meadows, the Indians went an-hunting, and the English army came out after us. Then the Indians moved again, dividing themselves and the captives into many companies that the English might not follow their track. At night, having crossed the river, we met again at the place appointed. The next day we crossed the river again on [the] Squakheag side, and there we took up our quarters for a long time. I suppose this might be about thirty miles above Squakheag, and here were the Indians quite out of all fear of the English but in great fear of the Mohawks.[4] Here they built a long wigwam.[5]

Here they had a great dance (as they call it) and concluded to burn three of us and had got bark to do it with, and (as I understood afterwards) I was one that was to be burned, Sergeant Plimpton[6] another, and Benjamin Wait['s] wife[7] the third. Though I knew not which was to be burned, yet I perceived some were designed thereunto, so much I understood of their language. That night I could not sleep for fear of the next day's work. The Indians, being weary with that dance, lay down to sleep and slept soundly. The English were all loose; then I went out and brought in wood and mended the fire and made a noise on purpose, but none awakened. I thought if any of the English would wake we might kill them all

3. Northfield, Massachusetts.

4. The Mohawks of the Iroquois Confederacy had long been enemies of the New England tribes.

5. One of the several varieties of Indian shelters. For a contemporary description of such shelters see Thomas Morton, *New English Canaan* (Amsterdam, 1637; repr. New York, 1972), 24–26.

6. John Plimpton of Deerfield, subsequently killed by Indians in 1704.

7. Martha Leonard Wait (or Waite) of Hatfield. Benjamin Wait helped to arrange the release of his wife and her fellow captives. He was killed by the Indians in 1704.

sleeping. I removed out of the way all the guns and hatchets, but my heart failing me, I put all things where they were again.[8] The next day when we were to be burned, our master and some others spake for us, and the evil was prevented in this place. And hereabouts we lay three weeks together.

Here I had a shirt brought to me to make, and one Indian said it should be made this way, a second another way, a third his way.[9] I told them I would make it that way that my chief master said whereupon one Indian struck me on the face with his fist. I suddenly rose up in anger ready to strike again. Upon this happened a great hubbub, and the Indians and English came about me; I was fain to humble myself to my master, so that matter was put up.

Before I came to this place, my three masters were gone a-hunting. I was left with another Indian, all the company being upon a march. I was left with this Indian who fell sick so that I was fain to carry his gun and hatchet and had opportunity and had thought to have dispatched him and run away, but did not for that the English captives had promised the contrary to one another, because if one should run away that would provoke the Indians and endanger the rest that could not run away. Whilst we were here, Benjamin Stebbins,[10] going with some Indians to Wachuset Hills,[11] made his escape from them. And when the news of his escape came, we were all presently called in and bound. One of the Indians, a captain among them and always our great friend, met me coming in and told me Stebbins was run away, and the Indians spake of burning us, some of only burning and biting off our fingers by and by. He said there would be a court, and all would speak their minds, but he would speak last and would say that the Indian that let Stebbins run away was only in fault and so no hurt should be done us; fear not. So it proved accordingly.

Whilst we lingered hereabout, provision grew scarce; one bear's foot must serve five of us a whole day. We began to eat horseflesh and eat up seven in all. Three were left alive and were not killed. Whilst we had been here, some of the Indians had been down and fallen upon Hadley [Massachusetts] and were taken by the English, agreed with and let go again, and were to meet the English upon such a plain, there to make further terms. Ashpalon was much for it, but Wachuset sachems, when they came, were much against it and were for this: that we [the Indians] should meet the

8. Compare Stockwell's decision with Hannah Dustan's, whose narrative appears as chapter 6 of this volume.

9. See note 24 to Rowlandson's narrative.

10. Benjamin (or Benoni) Stebbins of Northampton, Massachusetts, was taken at Deerfield along with Stockwell. Stebbins was killed in the Indian raid on Deerfield in 1704.

11. Several miles west of Lancaster, Massachusetts.

English, indeed, but there fall upon them and fight them and take them. Then Ashpalon spake to us English not to speak a word more to further that matter, for mischief would come of it. When those Indians came from Wachuset, there came with them squaws and children, about four score, who reported that the English had taken Uncas[12] and all his men and sent them beyond seas. They were much enraged at this and asked us if it were true. We said no; then was Ashpalon angry and said he would no more believe Englishmen. They examined us everyone apart; then they dealt worse by us for a season than before.

Still provision was scarce. We came at length to a place called Squaw-maug River;[13] there we hoped for salmon, but we came too late. This place I account to be above two hundred miles above Deerfield; then we parted into two companies, some went one way and some went another way. And we went over a mighty mountain.[14] We were eight days a-going over it and traveled very hard, and every day we had either snow or rain. We noted that on this mountain all the water run[s] northward. Here also we wanted provision but at length met again on the other side of the mountain, *viz.* on the north side of this mountain at a river that runs into the lake;[15] and we were then half a day's journey off the lake.

We stayed here a great while to make canoes to go over the lake. Here I was frozen, and here again we were like to starve. All the Indians went a-hunting but could get nothing. [Several] days they powwowed[16] but got nothing; then they desired the English to pray and confessed they could do nothing. They would have us pray and see what the Englishman's God could do. I prayed; so did Sergeant Plimpton in another place. The Indians reverently attended morning and night; next day they got bears. Then they would needs have us desire a blessing, return thanks at meals. After awhile they grew weary of it and the sachem did forbid us.[17]

When I was frozen they were very cruel towards me because I could

12. Uncas, chief sachem of the Mohegan tribe for several decades, supported the English against King Philip. The rumor described here by Stockwell was untrue.

13. In northern New England, near the Canadian border.

14. One of the Green Mountains in present-day Vermont, an area then claimed by New York and New Hampshire.

15. Probably Lake Champlain.

16. "Powwow" was a general term for Indian religious ceremonies or parleys and for Indian priests or healers. See William Wood, *New England's Prospect,* ed. Alden T. Vaughan (Amherst, Mass., 1977), 100–102, 120; and Daniel Gookin, *Historical Collections of the Indians in New England* (Boston, 1792 [written in 1670s]; repr. New York, 1972), 14.

17. The Indians often resorted to English religious practices if their own did not produce the desired results.

not do as at other times. When we came to the lake we were again sadly put to it for provision; we were fain to eat touchwood fried in bear's grease. At last we found a company of raccoons, and then we made a feast, and the manner was that we must eat all.[18] I perceived there would be too much for one time so one Indian that sat next to me bid me slip away some to him under his coat, and he would hide it for me till another time; this Indian, as soon as he had got my meat, stood up and made a speech to the rest and discovered me so that the Indians were very angry and cut me another piece and gave me raccoon grease to drink, which made me sick and vomit. I told them I had enough so that ever after that they would give me none but still tell me I had raccoon enough. So I suffered much and, being frozen, was full of pain and could sleep but a little yet must do my work.

When they went upon the lake, and as they came to the lake, they light of [on] a moose and killed it and stayed there till they had eaten it all up. And entering upon the lake, there arose a great storm; we thought we should all be cast away, but at last we got to an island and there went to powwowing. The powwow said that Benjamin Wait and another man was coming and that storm was raised to cast them away. This afterward appeared to be true, though then I believed them not. Upon this island we lay still several days and then set out again, but a storm took us so that we lay to and fro upon certain islands about three weeks. We had no provision but raccoons, so that the Indians themselves thought they should be starved. They gave me nothing so that I was sundry days without any provision.

We went on upon the lake, upon that isle, about a day's journey. We had a little sled upon which we drew our load. Before noon I tired, and just then the Indians met with some Frenchmen. Then one of the Indians that took me came to me and called me all manner of bad names and threw me down upon my back. I told him I could not do any more; then he said he must kill me. I thought he was about it, for he pulled out his knife and cut out my pockets and wrapped them about my face, helped me up, took my sled and went away. And [he] gave me a bit of biscuit as big as a walnut which he had of the Frenchman and told me he would give me a pipe of

18. The Indians could get by on amazingly little food by English standards, but occasionally they indulged in gluttonous feasts. Colonial writers criticized the Indians for such shortsighted extravagance; on the other hand, the same writers almost always praised the Indians' health and hardiness. The Indian custom of feasting, especially when traveling, made good sense; it would have been difficult to cure and transport the surplus, and new sources of food could usually be found when necessary.

tobacco. When my sled was gone, I could run after him, but at last I could not run but went a foot-pace; then the Indians were soon out of sight. I followed as well as I could; I had many falls upon the ice. At last I was so spent I had not strength enough to rise again, but I crept to a tree that lay along and got upon it, and there I lay.

It was now night and very sharp weather. I counted no other but that I must die there. Whilest I was thinking of death, an Indian hallooed, and I answered him; he came to me and called me bad names and told me if I could not go he must knock me on the head. I told him he must then so do; he saw how I had wallowed in that snow but could not rise. Then he took his coat and wrapped me in it and went back and sent two Indians with a sled. One said he must knock me on the head, the other said no, they would carry me away and burn me. Then they bid me stir my instep to see if that were frozen. I did so; when they saw that, they said that was *wurregen* [*wunnegen*, a good thing]. There was a surgeon at the French that could cure me. Then they took me upon the sled and carried me to the fire, and they then made much of me, pulled off my wet [clothes] and wrapped me in dry clothes, made me a good bed. They had killed an otter and gave me some of the broth and a bit of the flesh. Here I slept till towards day and then was able to get up and put on my clothes; one of the Indians awakened and, seeing me go, shouted as rejoicing at it.

As soon as it was light, I and Samuel Russel[19] went before on the ice upon a river.[20] They said I must go where I could on foot else I should freeze. Samuel Russel slipped into the river with one foot. The Indians called him back and dried his stockings and then sent us away and an Indian with us to pilot us. And we went four or five miles before they overtook us. I was then pretty well spent; Samuel Russel was (he said) faint and wondered how I could live, for he had (he said) ten meals to my one. Then I was laid on the sled, and they ran away with me on the ice; the rest and Samuel Russel came softly after. Samuel Russel I never saw more nor know what became of him.[21] They got but halfway, and we got through to Chambly about midnight.

Six miles from Chambly (a French town) the river was open, and when I came to travail in that part of the ice I soon tired, and two Indians ran away to town, and only one was left. He would carry me a few rods, and then I would go as many, and that trade we drove and so were long a-going six miles. This Indian now was kind and told me that if he did not

19. Eight-year-old Samuel Russell of Hatfield, son of Philip and Elizabeth Russell.
20. The Richelieu River in Canada.
21. He was killed by the Indians.

carry me I would die, and so I should have done sure enough. And he said I must tell the English how he helped me.

When we came to the first house there was no inhabitant. The Indian [was] spent, [we were] both discouraged; he said we must now both die. At last he left me alone and got to another house, and thence came some French and Indians and brought me in. The French were kind and put my hands and feet in cold water and gave me a dram of brandy and a little hasty pudding and milk. When I tasted victuals, I was hungry and could not have forborne it but that I could not get it. Now and then they would give me a little as they thought best for me. I lay by the fire with the Indians that night but could not sleep for pain. Next morning the Indians and French fell out about me because the French, as the Indian said, loved the English better than the Indians.[22]

The French presently turned the Indians out of doors and kept me. They were very kind and careful and gave me a little something now and then. While I was here, all the men in that town came to see me. At this house I was three or four days and then invited to another and after that to another. At this place I was about thirteen days and received much civility from a young man, a bachelor, who invited me to his house, with whom I was for the most part. He was so kind as to lodge me in the bed with himself; he gave me a shirt and would have bought me but could not for the Indians asked a hundred pounds for me. We were then to go to a place called Sorel, and that young man would go with me because the Indians should not hurt me. This man carried me on the ice one day's journey, for I could not now go at all. Then there was so much water on the ice we could go no further. So the Frenchman left me and provisions for me; here we stayed two nights and then traveled again, for then the ice was strong. And in two days more I came to Sorel.

The first house we came to was late in the night; here again the people were kind. Next day, being in much pain, I asked the Indians to carry me to the surgeon as they had promised, at which they were wroth. And one of them took up his gun to knock me, but the Frenchman would not suffer it but set upon him and kicked him out of doors. Then we went away from thence to a place two or three miles off where the Indians had wigwams. When I came to these wigwams some of the Indians knew me and seemed to pity me. While I was here, which was three or four days, the French

22. Despite frequent hostility between French and English settlers, their similar religious and cultural backgrounds often provided a common bond against the Indians. The French often rescued Englishmen from Indian captivity, as the narratives in this volume amply illustrate.

came to see me, and, it being Christmastime, they brought cakes and other provisions with them and gave to me so that I had no want. The Indians tried to cure me but could not;[23] then I asked for the surgeon, at which one of the Indians in anger struck me on the face with his fist. A Frenchman being by, the Frenchman spake to him. I knew not what he said and [he] went his way. By and by came the captain of the place into the wigwam with about twelve armed men and asked where the Indian was that struck the Englishman, and took him and told him he should go to the bilboes and then be hanged. The Indians were much terrified at this, as appeared by their countenances and trembling. I would have gone too, but the Frenchman bid me not fear; the Indians durst not hurt me.

When that Indian was gone, I had two masters still. I asked them to carry me to that captain that I might speak for the Indian. They answered [that] I was a fool. Did I think the Frenchmen were like to the English to say one thing and do another? They were men of their words, but I prevailed with them to help me thither, and I spake to the captain by an interpreter and told him I desired him to set the Indian free and told him what he had done for me. He told me he was a rogue and should be hanged. Then I spake more privately, alleging this reason: because all the English captives were not come in, if he were hanged, it might fare the worse with them. Then the captain said that was to be considered. Then he set him at liberty upon this condition, that he should never strike me more and every day bring me to his house to eat victuals. I perceived that the common people did not like what the Indians had done and did to the English.

When the Indian was set free, he came to me and took me about the middle and said I was his brother. I had saved his life once, and he had saved mine (he said) thrice. Then he called for brandy and made me drink and had me away to the wigwams again. When I came there, the Indians came to me one by one to shake hands with me, saying *wurregen netop* [*wunnegen nētop*, good, or welcome, friend], and were very kind, thinking no other but that I saved the Indian's life. The next day he carried me to that captain's house and set me down; they gave me victuals and wine, and, being left there awhile by the Indians, I showed the captain my fin-

23. For seventeenth-century accounts, largely unflattering, of Algonquian medical practices, see Wood, *New England's Prospect*, 93f., 101; Gookin, *Historical Collections*, 14; Morton, *New English Canaan*, 36; and Roger Williams, *A Key into the Language of America*, ed. John J. Teunissen and Evelyn J. Hinz (Detroit, 1973), 242–246. A general study of Indian medicine is Virgil J. Vogel, *American Indian Medicine* (Norman, Okla., 1970). Contemporary European medical practices were, of course, extremely primitive, although as Stockwell relates, a French physician eventually cured his frostbitten hands.

gers which, when he and his wife saw, he and his wife ran away from the sight and bid me lap it up again and sent for the surgeon who, when he came, said he could cure me and took it in hand and dressed it. The Indians towards night came for me; I told them I could not go with them. They were displeased, called me rogue, and went away.

That night I was full of pain; the French did fear that I would die. Five men did watch with me and strove to keep me cheery, for I was sometimes ready to faint. Oftentimes they gave me a little brandy. The next day the surgeon came again and dressed me, and so he did all the while I was among the French.

I came in at Christmas and went thence May second. Being thus in the captain's house, I was kept there till Ben Waite came, and my Indian master, being in want of money, pawned me to the captain for fourteen beavers or the worth of them at such a day. If he did not pay, he must lose his pawn or else sell me for twenty-one beavers, but he could not get beaver and so I was sold.

[Increase Mather's addendum]

But by being thus sold he was in God's good time set at liberty and returned to his friends in New England again.[24] Thus far is this poor captive's relation concerning the changes of Providence which passed over him.

There is one remarkable passage more affirmed by him. For he saith that in their travels they came to a place where was a great wigwam (i.e., Indian house) at both ends was an image; here the Indians in the wartime were wont to powwow (i.e., invocate the devil) and so did they come down to Hatfield, one of the images told them they should destroy a town; the other said no, half a town. This god (said that Indian) speaks true, the other was not good, he told them lies. No doubt but others are capable of declaring many passages of Divine Providence no less worthy to be recorded than these last recited, but inasmuch as they have not been brought to my hands, I proceed to another relation.

---

24. Massachusetts raised a public fund of £340 to ransom the Hatfield and Deerfield survivors. All but three who were slain by the Indians—John Plimpton, Samuel Russell, and Mary Foote—were redeemed, as were two children born in captivity.

THREE

One of the "Four Kings of Canada" (actually Iroquois chiefs) who visited Queen Anne in 1710 and gained fame in England and America—as John Gyles noted in his narrative. Courtesy of the New-York Historical Society, New York City.

Published in 1736 *Period of Great Awakening*

· JOHN GYLES ·
"MEMOIRS OF ODD ADVENTURES,
STRANGE DELIVERANCES, ETC."

Sporadic raids disturbed New England's northern border throughout the late 1670s and 1680s, but they seldom involved many combatants or casualties. That situation changed in 1689 when Europe became embroiled in the long and costly War of the League of Augsburg, which pitted England and the Dutch Republic against Louis XIV's France. The war's American phase—called King William's War in mocking honor of England's monarch—inaugurated a century of international and interracial struggle along the New England frontier. For a decade after the outbreak of the war, scattered but intense hostilities plagued the northern tier of Puritan provinces as Indian allies of the French, often accompanied by a few French soldiers, sought to outmaneuver the English militia. Once again, frontier towns bore the brunt.

On August 2, 1689, the remote outpost at Pemaquid, Maine, fell to French and Indian forces. They took about twenty captives, including Thomas Gyles, his wife, and four of their children. John Gyles was then about ten years old. After six years among the Eastern Indians and almost three years among the French—by far the longest captivity among the Puritan narrators—he was released and reunited with the surviving members of his family. Gyles almost immediately put his unusual experiences to work: for many years he served Massachusetts as an interpreter and negotiator among the French and Indians. He also held lieutenant's and captain's commissions for duty on the Maine frontier. In 1717, when Judge Samuel Sewall, Boston's distinguished jurist and diarist, journeyed to the Kennebec River to help negotiate a treaty with the Eastern Indians, he reported that he "dispatched Capt. Gyles with a Letter to the Govr in a Birch Canoe." Gyles continued to hold diplomatic and military positions until shortly before his death in late 1754 or early 1755.

The following text is based on the first edition of *Memoirs of Odd Adventures, Strange Deliverances, etc. in the Captivity of John Gyles, Esq., Commander of the Garrison on St. George's River* (Boston, 1736). (A nine-

teenth-century version edited by Samuel G. Drake has often been reprinted, but it is not faithful to the original.) The title page of the first edition asserts that the *Memoirs* were "written by himself," but according to
R. W. G. Vail, an annotation on the copy of the historian Jeremy Belknap
(1744–1798) observes that it was "Said to be *really* written & embellished by Joseph Seccombe, Chaplain of the Garrison at St. George's, afterwards minister of Kingston in N. Hampshire." Even if Gyles did not
actually compose all of the narrative, he was primarily responsible for one
of the most diverse accounts of New England captivity: part horror story,
part ethnography, part natural history, and part sermon. Gyles's narrative
is reproduced here in its entirety except for marginal notes that merely
summarize adjacent paragraphs and a brief appendix that sketches his later
career.

Forgetful youth! but know the power above
With ease can save each object of his love;
Wide as his will extends his boundless grace,
Nor tossed by time nor circumscribed by place.
Happier his lot who many sorrows past,
Long laboring gains his natal shore at last
Than who so speedy hastes to end his life
By some stern ruffian.

—Homer's *Odyssey*

Introduction

These private memoirs were collected from my minutes at the earnest request of my second consort for the use of our family, that we might have a
memento ever ready at hand to excite in ourselves gratitude and thankfulness to God and in our offspring a due sense of their dependence on the
Sovereign of the universe from the precariousness and vicissitudes of all
sublunary enjoyments. In this state and for this end, they have laid by me
for some years. [They] at length falling into the hands of some for whose
judgment I had a value, I was pressed for a copy for the public. And
others, desiring of me to extract particulars from thence which the multi-
plicity and urgency of my affairs would not admit, I have now determined
to suffer their publication. I have made scarce any addition to this manual
except in the chapter of creatures which I was urged to have made much
larger and might have greatly enlarged, but I feared it would grow beyond

its proportion.[1] I have been likewise advised to give a particular account of my father which I am not very fond of, having no dependence on the virtues or honors of my ancestors to recommend me to the favor of God or men; nevertheless, because some think it is a respect due to the memory of my parents, whose name I was obliged to mention in the following story and a satisfaction which their posterity might justly expect from me, I shall give some account [of him], though as brief as possible.

The flourishing state of New England (before the unhappy Eastern wars)[2] drew my father hither, whose first settlement was on Kennebeck River at a place called Merrymeeting Bay, where he dwelt for some years till, on the death of my grandparents, he, with his family, returned to England to settle his affairs. This done, he came over with design to have returned to his farm, but on his arrival at Boston the Eastern Indians had begun their hostilities. He therefore began a settlement on Long Island. The air of that place not so well agreeing with his constitution, and the Indians being peaceable, he again proposed to resettle his lands in Merrymeeting Bay, but, finding that place deserted and that plantations were going on at Pemmaquid, he purchased several tracts of land of the inhabitants there. Upon his highness the Duke of York's resuming a claim to those parts, he also took out patents upon that claim, and, when Pemmaquid was set off by the name of the county of Cornwall in the province of New York, he was commissioned chief justice of the same by Governor Duncan.[3] He was a strict sabbatizer and met with considerable difficulty in the discharge of his office from the immoralities of a people who had long

1. This passage suggests that Gyles wrote the initial draft of his memoirs many years after his release from captivity, perhaps when he was in his late forties or early fifties. In 1736, in his mid-fifties, he revised it for publication. Gyles's "second consort" was Hannah Heath, whom he married in 1722 after the death of his first wife, Ruth True.

2. The wars along the New England frontier that began in 1676, in the aftermath of King Philip's War, and lasted intermittently into the eighteenth century. "Eastern Indians" was a term loosely applied in the seventeenth century to the Abenaki tribes in Maine and New Hampshire. The Abenaki were part of the broader Algonquian ethnic group, but unlike the agricultural tribes in southern New England, they subsisted primarily on hunting and gathering. The Eastern or Abenaki Indians are described in William Wood, *New England's Prospect,* ed. Alden T. Vaughan (Amherst, Mass., 1977), 79–80; John R. Swanton, *The Indian Tribes of North America* (Washington D.C., 1952), 13–15; Frederick Webb Hodge, ed., *Handbook of American Indians North of Mexico,* 2 vols. (Washington, D.C., 1907), I, 2–6; and *Handbook of North American Indians,* XV, *Northeast,* ed. Bruce G. Trigger (Washington, D.C., 1978), 137–159.

3. James Stuart, subsequently King James II, claimed the province of Maine along with the territory England conquered from the Dutch in 1664. Thomas Dongan was governor of New York, and hence of Maine, from 1683 to 1688.

lived lawless. He laid out no inconsiderable income which he had annually from England on the place and at last lost his life there, as hereafter related.

I am not insensible of the truth of an assertion of Sir Roger L'Estrange that "Books and dishes have this common fate: there never was any one of either of them that pleased all palates," and am fully of his opinion in this: "It is as little to be wished for as expected, for an universal applause is at least two thirds of a scandal."[4] To conclude with the knight, "Though I made this composition principally for my family, yet, if any man has a mind to take part with me, he has free leave and [is] welcome, but let him carry this consideration along with him, that he is a very unmannerly guest that presses upon another man's table and then quarrels with his dinner."

CHAPTER I

Containing the Occurrences of the First Year

SECTION I. *Of the Taking the Family of Thomas Gyles, Esq.*

On the second day of August, *Anno Christi* 1689, in the morning, my honored father, Thomas Gyles, Esq., went with some laborers, my two elder brothers, and myself to one of his farms which lay on the river about three miles above Fort Charles,[5] adjoining Pemmaquid Falls, there to gather in his English harvest[6] and labored securely till noon. But after we had dined, our people went to their labor, some in one field to their English hay, the others to another field of English corn, except my father, the youngest of my two brothers, and myself, who tarried near the farmhouse in which we had dined till about one of the clock, when we heard the report of several great guns from the fort. Upon the hearing of them, my father said that he hoped it was a signal of good news and that the Great Council had sent back the soldiers to cover the inhabitants, for, on report of the [Glorious] Revolution, they had deserted. But to our great surprise about thirty or forty Indians discharged a volley of shot at us from behind

4. Sir Roger L'Estrange was a seventeenth-century English author.
5. [Gyles's note.] Fort Charles stood on the spot where Frederick's Fort was, not long since, founded by the Hon. Colonel Dunbar. The township adjoining thereto was called Jamestown in honor to the Duke of York. In this town, within a quarter of a mile of the fort, was the dwelling-house of Thomas Gyles, Esq., from which he went out that unhappy morning.
6. That is, to harvest his English crops, as distinct from Indian corn or maize. "English corn," in the following sentence, was wheat.

96

a rising ground near our barn.[7] The yelling of the Indians, the whistling of
their shot, and the voice of my father, whom I heard cry out, "What now!
What now!" so terrified me, though he seemed to be handling a gun, that
I endeavored to make my escape. My brother ran one way and I another,
and, looking over my shoulder, I saw a stout fellow, painted, pursuing me
with a gun and a cutlass glittering in his hand which I expected every moment in my brains. I presently fell down and the Indian took me by the left
hand, offered me no abuse, but seized my arms, lift[ed] me up, and pointed
to the place where the people were at work about the hay and led me that
way. As we passed, we crossed my father who looked very pale and bloody
and walked very slowly. When we came to the place, I saw two men shot
down on the flats and one or two more knocked on the head with hatchets,
crying out, "O Lord!" etc. There the Indians brought two captives, one
man and my brother James, he that endeavored to escape by running from
the house when I did.[8]

After they had done what mischief they could, [they] sat down, making
us sit with them and after some time arose, pointing us to go eastward.
They marched about a quarter of a mile and then made a halt and brought
my father to us and made proposals to him by old Moxus, who told him
that they were strange Indians who shot him and that he was sorry for it.[9]
My father replied that he was a dying man and wanted no favor of them
but to pray with his children which, being granted, he recommended us to
the protection and blessing of God Almighty; then [he] gave us the best
advice and took his leave for this life, hoping in God that we should meet
in a better. He parted with a cheerful voice but looked very pale by reason
of his great loss of blood which boiled out of his shoes. The Indians led
him aside. I heard the blows of the hatchet, but neither shriek nor groan.
(I afterwards heard that he had five or seven shotholes through his waistcoat or jacket and that the Indians covered him with some boughs.)

7. [Gyles.] The Indians have a custom of uttering a most horrid howl when they discharge guns, designing thereby to terrify those whom they fight against.

8. [Gyles.] He was about fourteen years of age. The eldest brother, whose name was
Thomas, wonderfully escaped by land to the Barbican (a point of land on the west side of
the river opposite to the fort) where several fishing vessels lay; he got on board one of them
and came to sail that night.

9. "Old Moxus" was an Indian from the Pemaquid region. The "strange Indians" who
attacked Pemaquid were from other parts of Maine or eastern Canada; at least some of
them were Maliseets from present-day New Brunswick, a tribe of the Abenaki Confederacy. For an excellent modern discussion of the Maliseets see Trigger, ed., *Handbook of
North American Indians*, XV, *Northeast*, 123–136.

SECTION II. *Of Their Taking Pemmaquid Town and Fort*

The Indians led us, their captives, on the east side of the river toward the fort, and, when we came within a mile and [a] half of the fort and town and could see the fort, we saw firing and smoke on all sides. Here we made a short stop and then moved within or near the distance of three-quarters of a mile from the fort into a thick swamp. There I saw my mother and my two little sisters and many other captives who were taken from the town. My mother asked me of my father; I told her that he was killed but could say no more for grief. She burst into tears, and the Indians moved me a little farther off and seized me to a tree.

The Indians came to New Harbor and sent spies several days to observe how and where the people were employed, etc., who found that the men were generally at work at noon and left about their houses only women and children. Therefore the Indians divided themselves into several parties, some ambushing the way between the fort and the houses, as likewise between them and the distant fields, and then alarming the farthest off first, they killed and took the people as they moved towards the town and fort at their pleasure so that very few escaped to the fort. Mr. Pateshall[10] was taken and killed as he lay with his sloop near the Barbican.

On the first stir about the fort my youngest brother was at play near the same and ran in, and so by God's goodness was preserved. Captain Weems[11] with great courage and resolution defended the weak old fort two days till that he was much wounded and the best of his men killed, and then beat up a parley. And the conditions were:

1. That they, the Indians, should give him Mr. Pateshall's sloop.

2. That they should not molest him in carrying off the few people that had got into the fort and three captives that they had taken.

3. That the English should carry off in their hands what they could from the fort.

On these conditions the fort was surrendered, and Captain Weems went off. And soon after, the Indians set on fire the fort and houses, which made a terrible blast and was a melancholy sight to us poor captives who were sad spectators.

10. Captain Richard Pattishall of Boston.

11. James Weems surrendered a small contingent of New England troops to an overwhelmingly superior Abenaki force, reputedly under an agreement that his men would be free and unmolested. Instead, most were immediately killed or captured.

98

JOHN GYLES

SECTION III. *Of the Transportation of the Captives to Penobscot, the Nearest Indian Village Eastward of Pemmaquid*

After the Indians had thus laid waste Pemmaquid, they moved us all to New Harbor.[12] And when we turned our backs on the town, my heart was ready to break. I saw my mother; she spake to me, but I could not answer her. That night we tarried at New Harbor, and the next day went in their canoes for Penobscot. About noon, the canoe which my mother and that which I was in came side by side, whether accidental[ly] or by my mother's desire I cannot say. She asked me how I did. I think I said, "Pretty well," though my heart was full of grief. Then she said, "Oh my child! How joyful and pleasant it would be if we were going to old England to see your uncle Chalker and other friends there. Poor babe! We are going into the wilderness, the Lord knows where." She burst into tears and the canoes parted. That night following, the Indians with their captives lodged on an island.

A few days after we arrived at Penobscot Fort where I again saw my mother, my brother and sisters, and many other captives. I think we tarried here eight days and in that time the Jesuit had a great mind to buy me.[13] My Indian master made a visit to the Jesuit and carried me with him.[14] I saw the Jesuit show him pieces of gold and understood afterward that he tendered them for me. The Jesuit gave me a biscuit which I put into my pocket and dare not eat but buried it under a log, fearing that he had put something in it to make me love him, for I was very young and had heard much of the Papists torturing the Protestants, etc., so that I hated the sight of a Jesuit. When my mother heard the talk of my being sold to a Jesuit, she said to me, "Oh my dear child! If it were God's will, I had rather follow you to your grave, or never see you more in this world than you should be sold to a Jesuit, for a Jesuit will ruin you, body and

12. [Gyles.] New Harbor is about two miles east of Pemmaquid, a small harbor much used by fishermen. Before the war there were about twelve houses, but the rumor of war disposed them to secure themselves by forsaking their habitations.

13. Several French missionaries lived among the Algonquian Indians in Maine. Gyles here refers to Father Louis Pierre Thury (c. 1644–1699), who had been assigned to the Abenaki and later was superior of the mission in Acadia. According to the nineteenth-century historian of Canada, Francis Parkman (*Frontenac and New France under Louise XIV* [Boston, 1877; new ed., 1903], 392), Fr. Thury was no innocent bystander; he was largely responsible for inciting the Indians to battle. It is doubtful, however, that the priest approved the violation of surrender terms. For Thury's account of the raid see H. R. Casgrain, *Les Sulpiciens* . . . (Quebec, 1897).

14. [Gyles.] The Indian that takes and will keep a captive is accounted his master and the captive his property till he give or sell him to another.

99

soul." And it pleased God to grant her request, for she never saw me more, though she and my two little sisters were, after several years' captivity, redeemed; she died before I returned. And my brother who was taken with me was, after several years' captivity, most barbarously tortured to death by the Indians.

SECTION IV. *Of the Occurrences in My Passing from Penobscot to St. John's, Where the Next Eastern Tribe Have Their Rendezvous*

My Indian master carried me up Penobscot River to a village called Madawamkee [Mattawamkeag] which stands on a point of land between the main river and a branch which heads to the east of it. At home I had ever seen strangers treated with the utmost civility, and, being a stranger, I expected some kind treatment here. But [I] soon found myself deceived, for I presently saw a number of squaws got together in a circle, dancing and yelling. And an old grimace-squaw took me by the hand and led me to the ring where the other squaws seized me by the hair of my head and by my hands and feet like so many furies, but my Indian master presently laid down a pledge and released me. A captive among the Indians is exposed to all manners of abuse and to the utmost tortures unless his master or some of his master's relations lay down a ransom such as a bag of corn, or a blanket, or such like, by which they may redeem them from their cruelties for that dance so that he shall not be touched by any.

The next day we went up that eastern branch of Penobscot River many leagues, carried over land to a large pond, and from one pond to another till in a few days we went down a river[15] which vents itself into St. John's River. But before we came to the mouth of this river, we carried over a long carrying place[16] to Medoctack Fort, which stands on a bank of St. John's River. My Indian master went before and left me with an old Indian and two or three squaws. The old man often said (which was all the English he could speak), "By and by, come to a great town and fort," so that I comforted myself in thinking how finely I should be refreshed, etc., when I came to this great town.

15. [Gyles.] Medocktack River. [The Meductic or Eel River.]

16. [Gyles.] A carrying place is a path or track in which they pass from one river or part of a river or pond to another; 'tis so called because the Indians are obliged to carry their baggage over them.

SECTION V. *Of My Treatment at My Arrival at Medoctack on St. John's River*

After some miles' travel we came in sight of a large cornfield and soon after of the fort, to my great surprise, for two or three squaws met us, took off my pack, and led me to a large hut or wigwam where thirty or forty Indians were dancing and yelling round five or six poor captives who had been taken some months before from Quochecho[17] at the same time when Major Waldein [Waldron] was most barbarously butchered by them.[18]

I was whirled in among them, and we looked on each other with a sorrowful countenance. And presently one of them was seized by each hand and foot by four Indians who swung him up and let his back with force fall on the hard ground, till they had danced (as they call it) round the whole wigwam which was thirty or forth feet in length. But when they torture a boy, they take him up between two. This is one of their customs of torturing captives. Another is to take up a person by the middle with his head

17. Dover, New Hampshire.

18. [Gyles.] Major Waldein was taken in the beginning of April on the night after a Sabbath [June 27, 1689]. I have heard the Indians say at a feast that there being a truce for some days, they contrived to send in two squaws to take notice of the numbers, lodgings, and other circumstances of the people in his garrison and, if they could obtain leave to lodge there, to open the gates and whistle. (They said the gates had no locks but were fastened with pins and that they kept no watch there.) The squaws had a favorable season to prosecute their projection, for it was dull weather when they came and begged leave to lodge in the garrison. They told the major that a great number of Indians were not far from them with considerable quantities of beaver, who would trade with him the next day, etc. Some of the people were very much against their lodging in the garrison, but the major said, "Let the poor creatures lodge by the fire." The squaws went into every apartment and observed the numbers in each and when the people were all asleep, rose and opened the gates and gave the signal, and the other Indians came to them, and, having received an account of the state of the garrison, they divided according to the number of people in each apartment and soon took and killed them all. The major lodged within an inner room, and, when the Indians broke in upon him, he cried out, "What now! What now!" jumped out of bed in his shirt and drave them out with his sword through two or three doors. And as he was returning to his apartment, an Indian came behind him and knocked him on the head with his hatchet, stunned him, and hauled him out, and set him upon a long table in his hall and bid him judge Indians again. Then they cut and stabbed him, and he cried out, "O Lord! O Lord!" They bid him order his book of accounts to be brought and cross out all the Indian debts (for he had traded much with the Indians), and after they had tortured him to death, they burned the garrison and drew off. This narration I heard from their mouths at a general meeting and have reason to think it true. And it should be a warning to all persons who have the care of garrisons, for the greatest losses we meet with are for want of due caution and circumspection. [The Indians were taking revenge on Waldron for his slaughter, under the guise of truce, of a large body of Indians in 1676.]

downwards and jolt him round till one would think his bowels would shake out of his mouth. Sometimes they will take a captive by the hair of the head and stoop him forward and strike him on the back and shoulder till the blood gush out of his mouth and nose. Sometimes an old shriveled squaw will take up a shovel of hot embers and throw them into a captive's bosom, and, if he cry out, the other Indians will laugh and shout and say, "What a brave action our old grandmother has done!"[19] Sometimes they torture them with whips, etc.

The Indians looked on me with a fierce countenance, signifying that it would be my turn next. They champed cornstalks and threw them in my hat which was in my hand. I smiled on them though my heart ached. I looked on one and another but could not perceive that any eye pitied me. Presently came a squaw and a little girl and laid down a bag of corn in the ring; the little girl took me by the hand, making signs for me to go out of the circle with them, but, knowing their custom, I supposed that they designed to kill me and would not go out with them. Then a grave Indian came and gave me a short pipe and said in English, "Smoke it." Then [he] took me by the hand and led me out, but my heart ached, thinking myself near my end, but he carried me to a French hut about a mile from the Indian fort. The Frenchman was not at home, but his wife who was a squaw had some discourse with my Indian friend which I did not understand. We tarried about two hours and returned to the village where they gave me some victuals. Not long after I saw one of my fellow captives who gave me a melancholy account of their sufferings after I left them, etc.

SECTION VI

After some weeks had passed, we left the village and went up St. John's River about ten miles to a branch called Medockscenecasis where there was one wigwam. At our arrival an old squaw saluted me with a yell, taking me by the hair and one hand, but I was so rude as to break her hold and quit myself. She gave me a filthy grin, and the Indians set up a laugh; so it passed over. Here we lived upon fish, wild grapes, roots, etc., which was hard living to me.

19. Active participation by Indian women in torture ceremonies was often noted by European commentators in New England and elsewhere. On the other hand, women often saved captives by adopting them as replacements for slain kin. No thorough study of Algonquian torture practices has been made; on the neighboring Iroquois see Anthony F. C. Wallace, *The Death and Rebirth of the Seneca* (New York, 1969), 102–107. On northeastern Indians in general see Nathaniel Knowles, "The Torture of Captives by the Indians of Eastern North America," *American Philosophical Society Proceedings*, 82 (1940), 151–225.

SECTION VII. *The First Winter's Hunting*

When the winter came on, we went up the river till the ice came down and run thick in the river and then, according to the Indian custom, laid up our canoes till the spring. And then [we] traveled sometimes on the ice and sometimes on the land till we came to a river that was open and not fordable, where we made a raft and passed over, bag and baggage.[20] I met with no abuse from them in this winter's hunting though I was put to great hardships in carrying burdens and for want of food, for they underwent the same difficulty and would often encourage me, saying in broken English, "By-by, great deal moose." But they could not answer any question that I asked them. So that knowing nothing of their customs and way of life, though I thought it tedious to be constantly moving from place to place, yet it might be in some respects an advantage, for it ran still in my mind that we were traveling to some settlement. And when my burden was over-heavy, and the Indians left me behind and the still evening came on, I fancied I could see through the bushes and hear the people of some great town, which hope might be some support to me in the day, though I found not the town at night.

Thus we had been hunting three hundred miles from the sea and knew no man within fifty or sixty miles of us. We were eight or ten in number and had but two Indian men with guns on whom we wholly depended for food, and if any disaster had happened, we must all have perished. And sometimes we had no manner of sustenance for three or four days, but God wonderfully provides for all creatures! In one of those fasts God's Providence was remarkable. Our two Indian men, in hunting, started a moose,[21] there being a shallow crusted snow on the ground, but the moose discovered them and ran with great force into a swamp. The Indians went round the swamp, and finding no tract, returned at night to the wigwam and told what had happened. The next morning they followed him on the track and soon found the moose lying on the snow, for, crossing the roots

20. [Gyles.] For the Indians carry their house and household stuff on their backs in the winter, and to these they add in the summer their vessels and furniture, provisions, etc.

21. [Gyles.] A moose is a fine lofty creature about eight feet high with a long head and nose like a horse, with horns very large and strong (some of them are above six feet from the extremity of one horn to the other) shaped and shed every year like the horns of a deer; likewise their feet are cloven like deer's feet. Their hind legs are long and forelegs short like a rabbit. They resemble a rabbit also in the length of their ears and shortness of their tail. The female have two dugs like a mare, though they sometimes bring three young ones at a foaling. They foal but once a year and at one season, *viz.* when the trees put out leaves for them. There are a sort of moose that have a mane like a horse.

of a large tree that had been blown up by the roots, having ice underneath, the moose in his furious flight broke through and hitched one of his hind legs in among the roots so fast that by striving to get it out, he pulled the thigh bone out of the socket at the hip. Thus extraordinarily were we provided for in our great strait. Sometimes they would take a bear, which go into dens in the fall of the year without any sort of food, and lie there without any [food] four or five months, never going out till the spring of the year, in which time they neither lose nor gain in flesh; if they went into their dens fat, they will come out so, or if they went in lean, they will come out lean. I have seen some that have come out with four whelps and both old and young very fat,[22] and then we feasted. And an old squaw and captive, if any present, must stand without the wigwam, shaking their hands and body as in a dance, and singing, *"Wegage oh nelo woh,"* which if Englished would be "Fat is my eating." This is to signify their thankfulness in feasting times. And when this was spent, we fasted till further success.

The way of their preserving meat is by stripping off the flesh from the bones and drying them over a smoke by which 'tis kept sound months or years without salt.

We moved still further up the country after moose when our store was out so that by spring we had got to the northward of the Lady Mountains.[23] And when the spring came on and the rivers broke up, we moved back to the head of St. John's River, and there made canoes of moosehides, sewing three or four together and pitching the seams with charcoal beaten and mixed with balsam. Then we went down the river to a place called Madawescok [Madawaska]; there an old man lived and kept a sort of tradinghouse where we tarried several days and went farther down the river till we came to the greatest falls in these parts, called Checanekepeag, where we carried a little way over the land, and, putting off our canoes, we went downstream still. And as we passed down by the mouth of any large branches, we saw Indians, but when any dance was proposed, I was bought off. At length we arrived at the place where we left our birch canoes in the fall and put our baggage into them and went in them down to the fort.

22. [Gyles.] Guillim in his heraldry mentions it as the opinion of some naturalists that they bring forth an unformed embryo and lick their litter into shape—a gross mistake! I have seen their fetus of all sizes taken out of the matrix by the Indians, and they are as much and as well shaped as the young of any animal.
23. Near the St. Lawrence River, north of Chaleur Bay.

SECTION VIII. *Of the Manner of the St. John's Indians Living in the Summer*

There we planted corn and, after planting, went a-fishing and to look for and dig roots till the corn was fit to weed. And after weeding, [we] took a second tour on the same errand and returned to hill our corn. And after hilling, we went some distance from the fort and field up the river to take salmon and other fish and dry them for food till corn was filled with the milk, some of which we dried then, the other as it ripened. And when we had gathered our corn and dried it,[24] we put some into Indian barns, i.e., holes in the ground lined and covered with bark and then with dirt. The rest we carried up the river upon our next winter hunting. Thus God wonderfully favored me and carried me through the first year of my captivity.

CHAPTER II
Of the Abusive and Barbarous Treatment Which Several Captives Met With from the Indians, etc.

SECTION I. *Of My Brother's Torture*

When any great number of Indians meet, or when any captives have been lately taken, or when any captives desert and are retaken, the Indians have a dance and at these dances torture the unhappy people who fall into their hands. My unfortunate brother [James], who was taken with me, after about three years' captivity deserted with an Englishman who was taken from Casco Bay and was retaken by the Indians at New Harbor and carried back to Penobscot Fort, where they were both tortured at a stake by fire for some time; then their noses and ears were cut off and they made to eat them, after which they were burned to death at the stake. The Indians at the same time declar[ed] that they would serve all deserters in the same manner. Thus they divert themselves in their dances!

SECTION II. *Of Their Barbarity to James Alexander, etc.*

On the second spring of my captivity my Indian master and his squaw went to Canada but sent me down the river with several Indians to the fort

24. [Gyles.] When the corn is in the milk, they gather a large kettle full and boil it on the ears till it's pretty hard and then take it up and shell it of[f] the cob with clam shells and dry it on bark in the sun. And when it's thoroughly dried, a kernel is no bigger than a pea and would keep years, and boiled again it swells as large and tastes incomparably sweeter than other corn.

in order to plant corn. The day before we came to the planting field, we met two young Indian men who seemed to be in great haste. After they had passed us, I understood that they were going with an express to Canada and that there was an English vessel at the mouth of the river. I, not perfect in the language nor knowing that English vessels traded with them in time of war, supposed a peace was concluded on and that the captives would be released and was so transported with the fancy that I slept but little, if at all, that night. Early the next morning we came to the village where the ecstasy ended, for I no sooner landed but three or four Indians dragged me to the great wigwam where they were yelling and dancing round James Alexander, a Jersey man who was taken from Falmouth in Casco Bay. This was occasioned by two families of Cape Sable Indians[25] who, having lost some friends by a number of English fishermen, came some hundred of miles to revenge themselves on the poor captives! They soon came to me and tossed me about till I was almost breathless and then threw me into the ring to my fellow captive and took him out again and repeated their barbarities to him. And then I was hauled out again by three Indians by the hair of my head and held down by it till one beat me on the back and shoulders so long that my breath was almost beat out of my body. And then others put a tomahawk into my hand and ordered me get up and dance and sing Indian, which I performed with the greatest reluctance and in the act seemed resolute to purchase my death by killing two or three of those monsters of cruelty, thinking it impossible to survive their bloody treatment.

But it was impressed on my mind, " 'Tis not in their power to take away your life," so I desisted. Then those Cape Sable Indians came to me again like bears bereaved of their whelps saying, "Shall we who have lost relations by the English suffer an English voice to be heard among us?" etc. Then they beat me again with the axe. Then I repented that I had not sent two or three of them out of the world before me, for I thought that I had much rather die than suffer any longer. They left me the second time, and the other Indians put the tomahawk[26] into my hand again and compelled me to sing. And then I seemed more resolute than before to destroy

25. Micmac Indians, an Abenaki tribe in southeastern Canada.

26. [Gyles.] The tomahawk is a warlike club, the shape of which may be seen in cuts of Etowohkoam, one of the four Indian chiefs, which cuts are common amongst us. [In 1710, five Iroquois chiefs made a diplomatic excursion to London. John Verelst, a prominent English artist, painted portraits of the four who survived the voyage, and other artists made engravings, mezzotints, and derivative paintings—including one on ivory—from Verelst's portraits. The reproductions sold well in England and America.]

some of them, but a strange and strong impulse that I should return to my own place and people suppressed it as often as such a motion rose in my breast. Not one of the Indians showed the least compassion, but I saw the tears run down plentifully on the cheeks of a Frenchman that sat behind, which did not alleviate the tortures that poor James and I were forced to endure for the most part of this tedious day, for they were continued till the evening and were the most severe that ever I met with in the whole six years that I was captive with the Indians.

After they had thus inhumanely abused us, two Indians took us up and threw us out of the wigwam, and we crawled away on our hands and feet and were scarce able to walk, etc., for several days. Sometime after, they again concluded on a merry dance, when I was at some distance from the wigwam dressing leather, and an Indian was so kind as to tell me that they had got James Alexander and were in search for me. My Indian master and his squaw bid me run as for my life into a swamp and hide and not to discover myself unless they both came to me, for then I might be assured the dance was over. I was now master of their language, and a word or a wink was enough to excite me to take care of one. I ran to the swamp and hid in the thickest place that I could find. I heard halloing and whooping all around me; sometimes they passed very near, and I could hear some threaten and others flatter me, but I was not disposed to dance. And if they had come upon me, I resolved to show them a pair of heels, and they must have had good luck to have caught me. I heard no more of them till about evening (for I think I slept) when they came again, calling, "Chon! Chon!" but John would not trust them. After they were gone, my master and his squaw came where they told me to hide but could not find me, and when I heard them say with some concern that they believed that the other Indians had frightened me into the woods and that I was lost, I came out. And they seemed well pleased and told me that James had had a bad day of it; that as soon as he was released, he ran away into the woods, and they believed he was gone to the Mohawks. James soon returned and gave me a melancholy account of his sufferings, and the Indians' fright concerning the Mohawks passed over.

They often had terrible apprehension of the incursion of the Mohawks.[27] One very hot season a great number gathered together at the village, and, being a very droughty [thirsty] people, they kept James and

27. [Gyles.] These are called also *Maquas,* a most ambitious, haughty, and bloodthirsty people from whom the other Indians take their measures and manners, and their modes and changes of dress, etc.

myself night and day fetching water from a cold spring that ran out of a rocky hill about three-quarters of a mile from the fort. In going thither, we crossed a large interval cornfield and then a descent to a lower interval before we ascended the hill to the spring. James, being almost dead as well as I with this continual fatigue, contrived to fright the Indians; he told me of it but conjured me to secrecy, yet said he knew that I could keep counsel. The next dark night James, going for water, set his kettle on the descent to the lowest interval and ran back to the fort puffing and blowing as in the utmost surprise and told his master that he saw something near the spring that looked like Mohawks (which he said were only stumps, aside). His master, being a most courageous warrior, went with James to make discovery, and when they came to the brow of the hill, James pointed to the stumps and withal touched his kettle with his toe which gave it motion downhill and at every turn of the kettle the bail clattered, upon which James and his master could see a Mohawk in every stump or motion and turned tail to, and he was the best man that could run fastest. This alarmed all the Indians in the village. They, though about thirty or forty in number, packed off bag and baggage, some up the river and others down, and did not return under fifteen days.[28] And the heat of the weather being finally over, our hard service abated for this season. I never heard that the Indians understood the occasion of the fright, but James and I had many a private laugh about it.

SECTION III. *Of John Evans, His Difficulties and Death, etc.*

But my most intimate and dear companion was one John Evans, a young man taken from Quochecho. We, as often as we could, met together and made known our grievances to each other, which seemed to ease our minds. But when it was known by the Indians, we were strictly examined apart and falsely accused that we were contriving to desert, but we were too far from the sea to have any thought of that, and when they found that our story agreed, we received no punishment. An English captive girl about this time (who was taken by Medocawando) would often falsely accuse us of plotting to desert, but we made the truth so plainly appear that she was checked and we released. But the third winter of my captivity he went into the country, and the Indians imposed a heavy burden on him though he was extreme[ly] weak with long fasting. And as he was going off the upland over a place of ice which was very hollow, he broke

28. This episode demonstrates the Algonquians' dread of the Mohawks as well as the Mohawk warriors' long reach from their homeland near Albany, New York.

through, fell down, and cut his knee very much; notwithstanding, he traveled for some time. But the wind and cold were so forceable that they soon overcame him, and he sat or fell down, and all the Indians passed by him. Some of them went back the next day after him or his pack and found him, with a dog in his arms, both froze as stiff as a stake. And all my fellow captives were dispersed and dead, but through infinite and unmerited goodness I was supported under and carried through all difficulties.

CHAPTER III
Of Further Difficulties and Deliverances

SECTION I. *Of a Near Escape from Death by Frost*

One winter as we were moving from place to place, our hunters killed some moose, and, one lying some miles from our wigwams, a young Indian and myself were ordered to fetch part of it. We sat out in the morning when the weather was promising, but it proved a very cold, cloudy day. It was late in the evening [when] we arrived at the place where the moose lay so that we had no time to provide materials for fire or shelter. At the same time a storm came on very thick of snow and continued till the next morning. We made a small fire with what little rubbish we could find around us, which, with the heat of our bodies, melted the snow upon us as fast as it fell and filled our clothes with water. Nevertheless, early in the morning we took our loads of mooseflesh and set out in order to return to our wigwams. We had not traveled far before my moosekin coat (which was the only garment that I had on my back, and the hair in most places worn off) was froze stiff round my knees like a hoop, as likewise my snowshoes and shoeclouts to my feet. Thus I marched the whole day without fire or food.

At first I was in great pain; then my flesh numbed, and I felt at times extremely sick and thought I could not travel one foot further but wonderfully revived again. After long traveling I felt very drowsy and had thoughts of sitting down which, had I done, without doubt I had fallen on my final sleep as my dear companion Evans had done before, for my Indian companion, being better clothed, had left me long before. But again my spirits revived as much as if I had received the richest cordial. Some hours after sunset I recovered the wigwam and crawled in with my snowshoes on. The Indians cried out, "The captive is froze to death!" They took off my pack, and where that lay against my back was the only place that was not frozen. The Indians cut off my shoes and stripped the clouts from my feet, which were as void of feeling as any frozen flesh could be. But I had not sat long by the fire before the blood began to circulate, and my feet to my ankles turned black and swelled with bloody blisters and were inexpressibly painful. The Indians said one to another, "His feet will rot, and he'll die!" Nevertheless, I slept well at night.

Soon after the skin came off my feet from my ankles whole, like a shoe, and left my toes naked without a nail and the ends of my great toe bones bare which, in little time, turned black so that I was obliged to cut the first joint off with my knife. The Indians gave me rags to bind up my feet and advised me to apply fir balsam, but, withal, said that they believed it was not worthwhile to use means, for I should certainly die. But by the use of my elbows and a stick in each hand I shoved myself on my bottom over the snow from one tree to another till I got some fir balsam, then burned it in a clamshell till it was of a consistence like salve. And [I] applied it to my feet and ankles, and by the divine blessing within a week I could go about upon my heels with my staff. And through God's goodness we had provision enough so that we did not remove under ten or fifteen days. And then the Indians made two little hoops, something in the form of a snowshoe, and seized them to my feet. And I followed them in their track on my heels from place to place, sometimes half-leg deep in snow and water, which gave me the most acute pain imaginable, but I was forced to walk or die. But within a year my feet were entirely well, and the nails came on my great toes so that a very critical eye could scare perceive any part missing or that they had been froze at all.

SECTION 11. *By the Fall of a Scaffold on My Head*

In a time of great scarcity of provisions the Indians chased a large moose into the river and killed him and brought the flesh to the village and laid it on a scaffold in a large wigwam in order to make a feast. I was very officious in supplying them with wood and water, which pleased them so well that they now and then gave me a piece of flesh half-boiled or roasted which I did eat with eagerness, and I doubt without great thankfulness to the Divine Being who so extraordinarily fed me. At length the scaffold broke and one large piece fell and knocked me on the head (the Indians said that I lay stunned a considerable time); the first I was sensible of was a murmuring noise in my ears, then my sight gradually returned with an extreme pain in my head which was very much bruised, and it was long before I recovered, the weather being very hot.

SECTION III. ... *from Drowning by the Oversetting of a Canoe*

I was once with an Indian fishing for sturgeon. The Indian darting one, his feet slipped and turned the canoe bottoms upwards with me under it holding fast the crossbar (for I could not swim) with my face to the bottom of the canoe. But I turned myself and brought my breast to bear on the crossbar, expecting every minute that the Indian would have towed me to the bank, but he had other fish to fry. Thus I continued a quarter of an hour without want of breath, sounding for the bottom, till the current drove me on a rocky point where I could reach bottom; there I stopped and turned up my canoe. I looked for the Indian, and he was half a mile distant up the river. I went to him and asked why he did not tow me to the bank, seeing he knew that I could not swim. He said he knew that I was under the canoe for there were no bubbles anywhere to be seen and that I should drive on the point; therefore he took care of his fine sturgeon which was eight or ten feet long.

SECTION IV. *Another Instance of Preservation from Drowning*

Fishing for salmon at the fall of about fifteen feet of water, there being a deep hole at the foot of the fall, the Indians went into the water to wash themselves and asked me to go in with them. I told them that I could not swim. They bid me strip (which was done) and dive across the deepest place, and if I fell short of the other side, they said they would help me. But instead of diving across the narrowest, I was crawling on the bottom into the deepest place. But not seeing me rise and knowing whereabouts I was by the bubbling of the water, a young girl dove into the water and seizing me by the hair of my head drew me out. Otherwise I had perished in the water.[29]

SECTION V. *Of My Preservation from Being Murdered*

While at the Indian village I had been cutting wood and was binding it up with an Indian rope in order to carry it to the wigwam, when a stout, ill-natured young fellow about twenty years of age threw me backward, sat on my breast, and, pulling out his knife, said that he would kill me, for he had never yet killed an English person. I told him that he might go to war and that would be more manly than to kill a poor captive who was doing

---

29. [Gyles.] Though both male and female may be in the water at a time, they have each of them more or less of their clothes on and behave with the utmost chastity and modesty.

their drudgery for them. Notwithstanding all that I could say, he began to cut and stab me on my breast. I seized him by the hair and tumbled him from off me on his back, and followed him with my fist and knee so that he presently said he had enough. But when I saw the blood run and felt the smart, I [was] at him again and bid him get up and not lie there like a dog, told him of his former abuses offered to me and other poor captives and that if ever he offered the like to me again I would pay him double. I sent him before me, took up my burden of wood, and came to the Indians and told them the whole truth, and they commended me. And I don't remember that ever he offered me the least abuse afterward though he was big enough to have dispatched two of me. I pray God I may never be forgetful of His wonderful goodness, and that these instances may excite others in their adversities to make their addresses to the Almighty and put their confidence in Him in the use of proper means.

CHAPTER IV

*Of Remarkable Events of Providence
in the Deaths of Several Barbarous Indians*

SECTION I. *The Deaths of Those Savage Cape Sable Indians Mentioned Ch. II, Sect. II*

The priest of this river was of the order St. Francis, a gentleman of a humane, generous disposition.[30] In his sermons he most severely reprehended the Indians for their barbarities to the captives. He would often tell them that, excepting their errors in religion, the English were a better people than themselves and that God would remarkably punish such cruel wretches and had begun to execute His vengeance upon such. He gave an account of the retaliations of Providence to those murderous Cape Sable Indians abovementioned, one of whom ran a splinter into his foot which festered and rotted his flesh till it killed him. Another ran a fishbone into her hand or arm, and she rotted to death notwithstanding all means that were used. In some such manner they all died so that not one of those two families lived to return home. Were it not for this remark of the priest, I should not, perhaps, have made the observation.

---

30. Father Simon de la Place (1657–1699), a Récollet missionary among the Maliseet tribe.

SECTION II. *Of a Barbarous Old Squaw*

There was an old squaw who ever endeavored to outdo all others in cruelty to captives. Wherever she came into a wigwam where any poor, naked, starved captives were sitting near the fire, if they were grown persons, she would privately take up a shovel of hot coals and throw them into their bosom, or young ones she would take by the hand or leg and drag them through the fire, etc. The Indians, according to their custom, left their village in the fall of the year and dispersed themselves for hunting, and after the first or second removal, they all strangely forgot that old squaw and her grandson about twelve years of age. They were found dead in the place where they were left some months afterward and no further notice taken of them. This was very much observed by the priest and seemed strange to all that heard it, for the Indians were generally very careful not to leave their old or young.

SECTION III. *Of a Plague among Them*

In the latter part of summer or beginning of autumn, the Indians were frequently frightened by the appearance of strange Indians passing up and down this river in canoes. And about that time the next year died more than one hundred persons of old and young, all or most of those that saw those strange Indians. The priest said that it was a sort of plague. A person seeming in perfect health would bleed at the mouth and nose, turn blue in spots, and die in two or three hours.[31] (It was very tedious to me, who was forced to move from place to place this cold season. The Indians applied red ochre to my sores which by God's blessing cured me.) The Indians all scattered, it being at the worst as winter came on, and the blow was so great that the Indians did not settle or plant at the village while I was on the river, and I know not whether they have to this day.

Before they thus deserted the village when they came in from hunting, they would be drunk and fight for several days and nights together, till they had spent most of their skins in wine and brandy which was brought to the village by a Frenchman called Monsieur Sigenioncor.

31. Calvin Martin, an authority on Native American epidemiology, interprets these symptoms as probably scurvy, possibly tularemia (personal communication).

CHAPTER V
*Of Their Familiarity with
and Frights from the Devil, etc.*

SECTION I. *Of Their Powwowing*

The Indians are very often surprised with the appearance of ghosts and demons and sometimes encouraged by the devil, for they go to him for success in hunting, etc. I was once hunting with Indians who were not brought over to the Romish faith, and after several days they proposed to inquire, according to their custom, what success they should have. They accordingly prepared many hot stones and laid them in a heap and made a small hut covered with skins and mats, and then in a dark night two of the powwows went into this hot house with a large vessel of water which at times they poured on those hot rocks which raised a thick steam so that a third Indian was obliged to stand without and lift up a mat to give it vent when they were almost suffocated. There was an old squaw who was kind to captives and never joined with them in their powwowing to whom I manifested an earnest desire to see their management. She told me that if they knew of my being there, they would kill me, and that when she was a girl she had known young persons to be taken away by an hairy man, and, therefore, she would not advise me to go lest the hairy man should carry me away. I told her that I was not afraid of that hairy man, nor could he hurt me, if she would not discover me to the powwows. At length she promised that she would not but charged me to be careful of myself. I went within three or four feet of the hot house, for it was very dark, and heard strange noises and yellings such as I never heard before. At times the Indian who tended without would lift up the mat and steam rose up which looked like fire in the dark. I lay there two or three hours but saw none of their hairy men or demons. And when I found that they had finished their ceremony, I went to the wigwam and told the squaw what had passed, who was glad that I returned without hurt and never discovered what I had done. After some time inquiry was made what success we were like to have in our hunting. The powwows said that they had very likely signs of success but no real visible appearance as at other times. A few days after we moved up the river and had pretty good success.[32]

One afternoon as I was in a canoe with one of the powwows, the dog barked and presently a moose passed by within a few rods of us so that the

32. This account, like Rowlandson's of the war dance, is a rare eyewitness report of a ceremony seldom observed by Europeans.

114

waves which he made by wading rolled over our canoe. The Indian shot at him, but the moose took very little notice of it and went into the woods to the southward. The fellow said, "I'll try if I can't fetch you back for all your haste." The evening following we built our two wigwams on a sandy point on the upper end of an island in the river northwest of the place where the moose went into the woods, and the Indian powwowed the greatest part of the night following, and in the morning we had the fair track of a moose round our wigwams, though we did not see or taste of it. I am of the opinion that the devil was permitted to humor those unhappy wretches sometimes in some things.[33]

SECTION II. *An Instance of the Devil's Frighting the Indians*

An Indian being some miles from his wigwam and the weather being warm, he supposed the hedgehogs would come out of their den; he way-laid the mouth of it till late at night (see chapter six, section three). They not coming out as usual, he was going home but had not passed far before he saw a light like a blaze at a little distance before him, and darting his spear at it, it disappeared; then on the bank of the river he heard a loud laughter with a noise like a rattling in a man's throat. The Indian railed at the demon whom he supposed made the noise, calling it a rotten spirit of no substance, etc. He continued to hear the noise and see the light till he came into the wigwam, which he entered in his hunting habit, with snow-shoes all on, so frightened that it was some time before he could speak to relate what had happened.

SECTION III. *Two Indian Fables*

That it may further appear how much they were deluded or under the in-fluence of Satan, read two stories which were related and believed by the Indians.

The first [is] of a boy who was carried away by a large bird called a *gul-loua,* who buildeth her nest on a high rock or mountain. A boy was hunt-ing with his bow and arrow at the foot of a rocky mountain when the *gul-loua* came diving through the air, grasped the boy in her talons, and though he was eight or ten years of age, she soared aloft and laid him in her nest, a prey of her young, where the boy lay constantly on his face but would look sometimes under his arms and saw two young ones with much fish and flesh in the nest and the old bird constantly bringing more, so that

33. Gyles's description of powwows mirrors William Wood's earlier definition of a powwow as a "conjurer or wizard." *New England's Prospect,* 120.

the young ones not touching him, the old one clawed him up and set him where she found him, who returned and related the odd event to his friends. As I have, in a canoe, passed near the mountain, the Indians have said to me, "There is the nest of the great bird that carried the boy away." And there seemed to be a great number of sticks put together in form of a nest on the top of the mountain. At another time they said, "There is the bird, but he is now as a boy to a giant to what he was in former days." The bird which they pointed to was a large speckled bird like an eagle though somewhat larger.[34]

The other notion is that a young Indian in his hunting was belated and lost his way, and on a sudden he was introduced to a large wigwam full of dried eels which proved to be a beaver's house in which he lived till the spring of the year when he was turned out of the house and set upon a beaver dam and went home and related the affair to his friends at large.

CHAPTER VI

A Description of Several Creatures Commonly Taken by the Indians on St. John's River[35]

SECTION I. *Of the Beaver*

The beaver has a very thick strong neck; his foreteeth, which are two in the upper and two in the under jaw, are concave and sharp like a carpenter's gouge. Their side teeth are like a sheep's, for they chew the cud. Their legs are short, the claws something longer than in other creatures; the nails on the toes of their hind feet are flat like an ape's but joined together by membrane as those of waterfowl, their tails broad and flat like the broad end of a paddle. Near their tails they have four bottles, two of which contain oil, the others gum; the necks of these meet in one common orifice. The latter of these contain the proper castorum and not the testi-

34. [Gyles.]   When from the mountain tops, with hideous cry
And clattering wings, the hungry harpies fly,
They snatched——
——And whether gods or birds obscene they were,
Our vows for pardon and for peace prefer.
—Dryden's *Virgil*

35. Gyles's extensive treatment of New England fauna is unusual in a captivity narrative and is perhaps partly explained by the long lapse between Gyles's release and the writing of his story. Moreover, his employment as a hunter during his years among the French and his subsequent career as an interpreter made him a true frontiersman, in contrast to other Puritan captives.

cles as some have fancied, for the testicles are distinct and separate from these in the males only, but the castorum and oil bottles are common to male and female. With this oil and gum they preen themselves so that when they come out of the water it runs off them as it doth off a fowl. They have four teats which are on their breasts so that they hug up their young and suckle them as women do their infants. They have generally two and sometimes four in a litter. I have seen seven or five in the matrix, but the Indians think it a strange thing to find so many in a litter, and they assert that when it so happens the dam kills all above four.

They are the most laborious creatures that I have met with. I have known them to build dams across rivers which were thirty or forty perch wide[36] with wood and mud so as to [over]flow many acres of land. In the deepest part of a pond so raised, they build their houses round in the figure of an Indian wigwam, eight or ten feet in height and six or eight feet diameter on the floor, which is made descending to the water, the parts near the center about four and near the circumference between ten and twenty inches above the water. These floors are covered with strippings of wood like shavings; on these they sleep with their tails in the water, and if the freshets rise they have the advantage of rising on their floor to the highest part. They feed on the leaves and bark of trees and pond lily roots. In the fall of the year they lay in their provision for the approaching winter. Cutting down trees great and small, with one end in their mouths they drag their branches near to their house and sink many cords of it. (They will cut down trees of a fathom in circumference.) They have doors to go down to the wood under the ice; and, in case the freshets rise, break down, and carry off their store of wood, they often starve. They have a note for conversing, calling, and warning each other when at work or feeding, and while they are at labor they keep out a guard who upon the first approach of an enemy so strikes the water with its tail that he may be heard half a mile, which so alarms the rest that they are all silent, quit their labor, and are to be seen no more for that time. And if the male or female die, the surviving seeks a mate and conducts him or her to their house and carry on affairs as above.[37]

36. A perch equals a rod; hence the dams Gyles describes were roughly sixty to sixty-five feet wide.

37. Gyles's account of the beaver is exceptionally detailed, even more so than William Wood's (*New England Prospect*, 47–48, which does, however, provide some information that Gyles does not), and considerably more extensive than that of the early naturalist John Josselyn in *New England's Rarities Discovered in Birds, Beasts, Fishes, Serpents, and Plants of that Country* (London, 1672; repr. *American Antiquarian Society Transactions and Collections*, 4 [1860], 130–238.)

SECTION II. *Of the Wolverine*

The wolverine is a very fierce and mischievous creature about the bigness of a middling dog, having short legs, broad feet, and very sharp claws and, in my opinion, may be reckoned a species of cats. They will climb trees and wait for moose and other creatures who feed below and, when opportunity presents, jump and strike their claws in them so fast that they will hang on them till they have gnawed the main nerve of the neck asunder and the creature dies. I have known many moose killed thus. I was once traveling a little way behind several Indians and heard them laughing very merrily. When I came to them, they showed me the track of a moose and how a wolverine had climbed a tree and where he had jumped off upon the moose, and the moose had given several large leaps; and happening to come under a branch of a tree, [it] had broke the wolverine's hold and torn him off, and by his track in the snow he went off another way with short steps, as if he had been stunned with the blow. The Indians who impute such accidents to the cunning of the creature were wonderfully pleased that the moose should thus outwit the mischievous wolverine.

These wolverines go into wigwams which have been left for any time, scatter the things abroad, and most filthily pollute them with ordure. I have heard the Indians say that they have hauled guns from under their heads while they were asleep and left them so defiled. An Indian told me that having left his wigwam with sundry things on the scaffold among which was a birch flask with several pounds of powder in it, at their return they were much surprised and grieved for a light snow had fallen and a wolverine visits their wigwam, mounts the scaffold, and [sets] to plundering, heaves down bag and baggage. The powder happened to fall into the fire which filled the wolferine's eyes and threw him and the wigwam some rods. At length they found the blind creature rambling backward and forward, had the satisfaction of kicking and beating him about, which in great measure made up their loss, and then they could contentedly pick up their utensils and rig out their wigwam.[38]

SECTION III. *Of the Hedgehog or Urchin*

Our hedgehog or urchin is about the bigness of a hog of six months old. His back and sides and tail are full of sharp quills so that if any creature approach they will contract themselves to a globular form. If a creature

38. Wolverines did not inhabit New England; thus Gyles's description is rare among New England authors. Europeans often called this member of the weasel family "the Indian devil" because of its penchant for mischief.

attack them, those quills are so sharp and loose in their skins that they fix in the mouth of the adversary and leave their own skin. They will strike with great force with their tails so that whatever falls under the lash of them are certainly filled with their prickles. But that they shoot their quills as some assert they do is a great mistake, as to the American and I believe as to the African hedgehog or porcupine also; as to the former I have taken them at all seasons of the year (see chapter five, section two).

SECTION IV. *Of the Tortoise*

It is needless to describe the freshwater tortoise, whose form is so well known in all parts, but their way of propagating their species is not so universally known. I have observed that sort whose shell is about fourteen or sixteen inches wide. In their coition or treading they may be heard half a mile, making a noise like a woman washing her linen with a batting staff. They lay their eggs in the sand near some deep, still water about a foot beneath the surface of the sand. They are very curious in covering them with the sand so that there is not the least mixture of it amongst them nor the least rising of sand on the beach where they lie. I have often searched for them with the Indians by thrusting a stick into the sand at random and brought up some part of an egg clinging to it and, uncovering the place, have found near one hundred and fifty in one nest. Both their eggs and flesh are good eating when boiled, etc. I have observed a difference as to the length of time which they are hatching, which is between twenty and thirty days, some sooner than others. Whether this difference ought to be imputed to the various quality or site of the sand in which they lay (as to its cold or heat, etc.), I leave to the conjecture of the virtuosi. As soon as they were hatched, they broke through the sand and betook themselves to the water, as far as I could discover, without any further care or help of the old ones.

SECTION V. *Of the Salmon*

Of the salmon I shall only note that they come from the sea early in the spring to the fresh rivers and with great pains ascend the falls till they come to the heads of the rivers where the water runs riffling over a coarse gravel near some pond or deep still water. There they work holes to lodge in and in the night resort to them by two and two, the male with his female; thus lying together, the female ejects a spawn like a pea, the male a sperm like milk which sink among the gravel. I have often been fishing for them with a torch in the night when the water hath been so shoal that they have lain with their backs and tails above the water. And if our spear missed its stroke, the fish darted at would flutter and alarm the whole shoal (though it consisted of a vast multitude) which immediately repaired to the deep water and returned not in plenty for several nights. When the leaf falls they have done spawning and return to the sea.

CHAPTER VII
Of Their Feasting, etc.

SECTION I. *Of Their Feasting before They Go out to War*

When the Indians determine for war or are entering upon a particular expedition, they kill a number of their dogs, burn off their hair, and cut them into pieces, leaving only one dog's head whole. The rest of the flesh they boil and make a fine feast of it, after which the dog's head that was left whole is scorched till the nose and lips have shrunk from the teeth and left them bare and grinning. This done, they fasten it on a stick, and the Indian who is proposed to be chief in the expedition takes the head into his hand and sings a warlike song, in which he mentions the town they design to attack and the principal man in it, threatening that in a few days he will carry that man's head and scalp in his hand in the same manner. When the chief hath sung, he so places the dog's head as to grin at him whom he supposeth will go his second, who, if he accepts, takes the head in his hand and sings, but if he refuse to go he turns the teeth to another, and thus from one to another till they have enlisted their company.[39]

The Indians imagine that dogs' flesh makes them bold and courageous. I have seen an Indian split a dog's head with a hatchet and take out the brains hot and eat them raw with the blood running down his jaws.

SECTION II. *Of Their Mourning for the Dead, and Feast after It*

When a relation dies, in a still evening a squaw will walk on the highest land near her abode and with a loud, mournful voice exclaim, *"Oh hawe, hawe, hawe,"* with a long mournful tone to each *hawe* for a long time together. After the mourning season is over, the relations of the deceased make a feast to wipe off tears, and they may marry freely. If the deceased were a squaw, the relations consult together and choose a squaw (doubtless a widow) and send her to the widower, and if he like her, he takes her to

___

39. Different tribal customs are reflected in the contrast between this ceremony and the one described by Rowlandson.

be his wife; if not, he sends her back, and the relations choose and send till they find one that he approveth of.

SECTION III. *A Further Account of Their Marriages*

If a young fellow determines to marry, his relations and the Jesuit advise him to a girl, and the young fellow goes into the wigwam where she is and looks on her. And if he likes her, he tosseth a chip or stick into her lap which she takes and with a reserved side look views the person who sent it, yet handleth the chip with admiration as though she wondered from whence it came. If she likes him, she throws the chip to him with a modest smile, and then nothing is wanting but a ceremony with the Jesuit to consummate the marriage. But if the young squaw dislike the fellow, she with a surly countenance throws the chip aside, and he comes no more there.

If parents have a daughter marriageable,[40] they seek a husband for her who is a good hunter. And if he have a gun and ammunition, a canoe, spear and hatchet, a *monoodah*,[41] and crooked knife, a looking-glass and paint, a pipe, tobacco and knot-bowl to toss a kind of dice in, he is accounted a gentleman of a plentiful fortune. (By their sort of dice they lose much time, playing whole days and nights together, and sometimes their whole estate, though this is accounted a great vice by the old men.) Whatever the new-married man procures the first year belongs to his wife's parents. (If the pair have a child with a year and nine months, they are thought to be very forward, libidinous persons.)

SECTION IV. *A Digression Containing an Account of a Rape Committed by a Demon*

There is an old story told among the Indians of a family who had a daughter that was accounted a finished beauty and adorned with the precious jewel of an Indian education, so formed by nature and polished by art that they could not find for her a suitable consort. At length, while they resided on the head of Penobscot River under the white hills called the Teddon, this fine creature was missing, and her parents could have no account of her. After much time spent, pains and tears showered in quest of her, they saw her diverting herself with a beautiful youth whose hair, like hers, flowed down below his waist, swimming, washing, etc., in the water, but

---

40. [Gyles.] A virgin who has been educated to make *monoodahs* and birch dishes, to lace snowshoes, and make Indian shoes, to string wampum belts, sew birch canoes, and boil the kettle is esteemed as a lady of fine accomplishments.

41. [Gyles.] A *monoodah* is an Indian bag.

the youth vanished upon their approach.[42] This beautiful person, whom they imagined to be one of those kind spirits who inhabit the Teddon, they looked upon him as their son-in-law, so that (according to custom) they called upon him for moose, bear, or whatever creature they desired, and if they did but go to the waterside and signify their desire, the creature which they would have came swimming to them.

I have heard an Indian say that he [the spirit] lived by the river at the foot of the Teddon, and in his wigwam; seeing the top of it through the hole left in the top of the wigwam for the passing of smoke, he was tempted to travel to it. Accordingly, he set out early on a summer's morning and labored hard in ascending the hill all day, and the top seemed as distant from the place where he lodged at night as from the wigwam whence he began his journey, and concluding that spirits were there, never dare make a second attempt.

I have been credibly informed that several others have failed in the same attempt, particularly that three young men toured the Teddon three days and a half and then began to be strangely disordered and delirious, and when their imagination was clear and they could recollect where they were and had been, they found themselves returned one day's journey. How they came down so far they can't guess, unless the genie of the place conveyed them. These white hills at the head of the Penobscot River are by the Indians said to be much higher than those called Agiockochook above Saco.

SECTION V. *Of Common Feasts*

But to return to an Indian feast, of which you may request a bill of fare before you go, and if you dislike it, stay at home. The ingredients are fish, flesh, or Indian corn and beans boiled together, or hasty pudding made of pounded corn. Whenever and as often as these are plenty, an Indian boils four or five large kettles full and sends a messenger to each wigwam door who exclaims, *"Kuh menscoorehah,"* i.e., "I come to conduct you to a

42. [Gyles.] Where now, in his divinest form arrayed,
In his true shape he captivates the maid;
Who gazes on him and with wondering eyes
Beholds the new majestic figure rise,
His glowing features, and celestial light,
And all the god discovered to her sight.
—*Europa's Rape*

122

feast." The man within demands whether he must take a spoon or a knife in his dish, which he always carries with him. They appoint two or three young men to mess it out to each man his portion according to the number of his family at home, which is done with the utmost exactness.[43] When they have done eating, a young fellow stands without the door and cries aloud, *"Mensecommook,"* "Come and fetch!" Immediately each squaw goes to her husband and takes what he has left, which she carries home and eats with the children. For neither married women nor any youth under twenty years of age are allowed to be present, but old widow squaws and captive men may sit by the door. The Indian men continue in the wigwam, some relating their warlike exploits, others something comical, others give a narrative of their hunting. The seniors give maxims of prudence and grave counsels to the young men, though every one's speech be agreeable to the run of his own fancy, yet they confine themselves to rule and but one speaks at a time. After every man has told his story, one rises up, sings a feast song, and others succeed alternately as the company see fit.

SECTION VI. *Their Extraordinary Ways of Getting Fire and Boiling Their Food*

Necessity is the mother of invention. If an Indian has lost his fire-work, he can presently take two sticks, the one harder than the other (the drier the better), and in the softest make a hollow or socket to which they'll fit one end of the hardest stick. Then holding the softest wood firm between their knees, they fix the end of the hard stick made fit into the socket and whirl it round in their hand like a drill, and it takes fire in a few minutes.

If they have lost left their kettle, 'tis but putting the victuals into a birch dish, leaving a vacancy in the middle, filling it with water, and putting in hot stones alternately. And they will thus thoroughly boil the toughest neck of beef.

43. [Gyles.]   What lord of old would bid his cook prepare
                     Mangoes, potargo, champignons, caviar?
                     Or would our thrum-capped ancestors find fault
                     For want of sugar tongs or spoons for salt?
                     Where everything that every soldier got,
                     Fowl, bacon, cabbage, mutton, and what not,
                     Was all thrown into bank, and went to pot.
                                 —*Art of Cookery*

CHAPTER VIII
Of My Three Years' Captivity with the French

SECTION I. *Of a Contention among the Indians, Which Caused Them to Sell Me to the French*

When about six years of my doleful captivity had passed, my second Indian master died, whose squaw and my first Indian master disputed whose slave I should be, and some malicious persons advised them to end the quarrel by putting a period to my life. But honest Father Simon, the priest of the river, told them that it would be a heinous crime and advised them to sell me to the French. There came annually one or two men-of-war to supply the fort, which was on the river about thirty-four leagues from the sea.[44] The Indians, having advice of the arrival of a man-of-war at the mouth of the river, they, about thirty or forty in number, went aboard, for the gentlemen from France made a present to them every year and set forth the riches and victories of their monarch, etc. At this time they presented a bag or two of flour with some prunes as ingredients for a feast. I, who was dressed up in an old greasy blanket without cap, hat, or shirt (for I had no shirt for the six years but that which was on my back when I was taken), was invited into the great cabin where many well-rigged gentlemen were sitting who would fain have had a full view of me. I endeavored to hide myself behind the hangings, for I was much ashamed, thinking of my former wearing clothes and of my living with people who could rig as well as the best of them.[45] My master asked me whether I chose to be sold aboard the man-of-war or to the inhabitants. I replied with tears, "I should be glad if you would sell me to the English from whom you took me, but if I must be sold to the French, I choose to be sold to the lowest on the river or nearest inhabitant to the sea," about twenty-five leagues from the mouth of the river. For I thought that if I were sold to the gentlemen aboard the man-of-war, I should never return to the English. This was the first sight I had of salt water in my captivity and the first time that I had tasted salt or bread.

SECTION II. *Of My Being Sold to the French*

My master presently went ashore, and after a few days all the Indians went up the river. And when we came to the house which I mentioned to

44. Probably the fort at Meductic, the main Maliseet village on the St. John's River.
45. This episode reveals how thoroughly Gyles still adhered to the European notion of clothing as a sign of civility. Nakedness implied savagery or wildness.

my master, he went ashore with me and tarried all night. The master of the house spoke kindly to me in Indian, for I could not then speak one word of French. Madam also looked pleasant[ly] on me and gave me some bread. The next day I was sent six leagues further up the river to another French house. My master and the friar tarried with Monsieur Dechouffour,[46] the gentleman who had entertained us the night before. Not long after Father Simon came and said, "Now you are one of us, for you are sold to that gentleman by whom you were entertained the other night." I replied, "Sold! To a Frenchman!" I could say no more, went into the woods alone, and wept till I could scarce see or stand. The word *sold*, and that to a people of that persuasion which my dear mother so detested, and in her last words manifested so great fears of my falling into! The thoughts of these almost broke my heart. When I had given vent to my passions, I rubbed my eyes, endeavoring to hide my grief, but Father Simon, perceiving that my eyes were swollen, called me aside and bid me not to grieve, for the gentleman to whom I was sold was of a good humor, that he had formerly bought two captives of the Indians who both went home to Boston. This in some measure revived me. But he added that he did not suppose that I would ever incline to go to the English, for the French way of worship was much to be preferred; also, that he should pass that way in about ten days, and if I did not like to live with the French better than with the Indians, he would buy me again.

On the day following, Father Simon and my Indian master went up the river six and thirty leagues to their chief village, and I went down the river six leagues with two Frenchmen to my new master, who kindly received me and in a few days madam[47] made me an osnaburg shirt and French cap, and a coat out of one of my master's old coats. Then I threw away my greasy blanket and Indian flap and looked as smart as ———. And I never more saw the old friar, the Indian village, or my Indian master till about fourteen years after. I saw my Indian master at Port Royal, whither I was sent by the government with a flag of truce for exchanging prisoners. And again, about twenty-four years since, he came from St. John's to George's to see me, where I made him very welcome.[48]

46. Louis Damours, Sieur de Chaffours (1655–1708), Canadian fur trader and soldier. He was later (from 1703 to 1706) a captive of the English in Boston.

47. Marguerite Guyon de Chaffours.

48. This is a rare instance of temporary Indian captivity producing a lasting interracial friendship.

SECTION III. *Of My Employment among the French*

My French master held a great trade with the Indians which suited me very well, I being thorough in the languages of the tribes at Cape Sable's and St. John's. I had not lived long with this gentleman before he committed to me the keys of his store, etc., and my whole employment was trading and hunting, in which I acted faithfully for my master and never knowingly wronged him to the value of one farthing. They spake to me so frequently in Indian that it was some time before I was perfect in the French tongue. Monsieur generally had his goods from the man-of-war which came there annually from France.

In the year 1696, two [French] men-of-war came to the mouth of the river, which had taken the *Newport,* Capt. Paxton commander, and brought him with them. They made the Indians some presents and invited them to join in an expedition to Pemmaquid, which invitation they accepted and soon after arrived there. And Capt. Chubb[49] delivered the fort without much dispute to Monsieur Debervel [D'Iberville], as I heard the gentleman say whom I lived with who was there present.[50]

Early in the spring I was sent with three Frenchmen to the mouth of the river for provision which came from Port Royal. We carried over land from the river to a large bay where we were driven on an island by a northeast storm and were kept there seven days without any sustenance, for we expected a quick passage and carried nothing with us, the wind

49. [Gyles.] The Reverend Dr. Mather says wittily (as he said everything), "This Chubb found opportunity in a pretty chubbish manner to kill the famous *Edgeremet* and *Ahenquid,* a couple of principal Indians, with one or two other Indians, on a Lord's day, the sixteenth of February 1695. If there were any unfair dealings in this action of Chubb, there will be another February not far off wherein the avenger of blood will take their satisfaction." *History of N.E.* B. 7. p. 79. [Gyles here quotes, somewhat inaccurately, from Cotton Mather's *Magnalia Christi America* (London, 1702), Bk. VII, 89. Parkman (*Frontenac and New France,* 398) condemns Capt. Pascho Chubb of Andover, Massachusetts, for treacherously slaying the Indians—another instance of English troops practicing the very barbarities they attributed to Indians.]

50. [Gyles.] Our last quoted author says on the fourth or fifth of August, Chubb, with an unaccountable baseness, did surrender the brave fort of Pemmaquid into their hands.
> Unthinking men no sort of scruples make,
> And some are bad, only for mischief's sake;
> But even the best are guilty by mistake.

[When Chubb was threatened with the butchery of his entire garrison if he did not surrender, he relinquished Fort Pemaquid on condition that his men be sent safely to Boston in exchange for French and Indian prisoners. On his arrival in Boston, Chubb was arrested for cowardice. He was later released and returned to his home in Andover where some Abenaki Indians killed him the next year—in apparent revenge for his earlier treachery.]

continuing boisterous so that we could not return back, and the ice prevented our going forward. After seven days the ice broke up and we went forward, though we were so weak that we could scarce hear each other speak. And the people at the mouth of the river were surprised to see us so feeble and advised us to be cautious and abstemious in eating. By this time I knew as much of fasting as they and dieted on broth and recovered very well, as also one of the others, but the other two would not be advised, and I never saw any persons in greater torment than they were till they obtained a passage [of the bowels], on which they recovered.

S E C T I O N I V. *Of the Friar's Transaction while I Was among Them*

A friar who lived in the family invited me to confession, but I excused myself as well as I could. One evening he took me into his apartment, in the dark, and advised me to confess to him what sins I had committed. I told him that I could not remember a thousandth part of them, they were so numerous. Then he bid me remember and relate as many as I could, and he would pardon them, signifying that he had a bag to put them in. I told him I did not believe that it was in the power of any but God to pardon sin. He asked me whether I had read the Bible. I told him that I had when I was a little boy, so long since that I had forgot most of it. Then he told me that he did not pardon my sins, but when he knew them he prayed God to pardon them when, perhaps, I was at my sports and plays. He wished me well and hoped that I should be better advised and said he should call for me in a little time. Thus he dismissed and never called me to confession more.

The gentleman whom I lived with had a fine field of wheat which great numbers of black birds visited and destroyed much of. But the French said a Jesuit would come and banish them, who came at length and all things were prepared, *viz.* a basin of what they call holy water, a staff with a little brush to sprinkle withal, and the Jesuit's white robe which he put on. I asked several prisoners who had lately been taken by privateers and brought hither, *viz.* Mr. Woodberry, Cocks, and Morgan, whether they would go and see the ceremony. Mr. Woodberry asked me whether I designed to go. I told him that I did. He said that I was then as bad a papist as they and a damned fool. I told him that I believed as little of it as they did, but I inclined to see the ceremony that I might rehearse it to the English. They entered the field and walked through the wheat in procession, a young lad going before the Jesuit with a basin of their holy water, then the Jesuit with his brush, dipping it into the basin and sprinkling the field on each side of him, next him a little bell tingling and about thirty men following in order, singing with the Jesuit, *Ora pro nobis* [Pray for us]. At the end of the field they wheeled to the left about and returned. Thus they went through the field of wheat, the birds rising before them and lighting behind them. At their return I said to a French lad [that] the friar hath done no service; he had better take a gun and shoot the birds. The lad left me awhile (I thought to ask the Jesuit what to say) and when he returned he said the sins of the people were so great that the friar could not prevail against those creatures. The same Jesuit as vainly attempted to banish the mosquitoes from Signecto, for the sins of that people were so great also that he could not prevail against them but rather drew more as the French informed me.

SECTION V. *1696. A Party of English Soldiers Attempt the Taking of Fort Vielbon*

Sometime after, Col. Hawthorn [Hathorne] attempted the taking the French fort up this river.[51] We heard of them sometime before they came up the river by the guard which Governor Vielbon[52] had ordered at the river's mouth. Monsieur, the gentleman whom I lived with, was gone to France, and madam advised with me. She desired me to nail a paper on the door of her house[53] containing as follows:

"I entreat the general of the English not to burn my house or barn nor destroy my cattle. I don't suppose that such an army come up this river to destroy a few inhabitants but for the fort above us. I have shown kindness to the English captives as we were capacitated and have bought two captives of the Indians and sent them to Boston and have one now with us, and he shall go also when a convenient opportunity presents and he desires it."

This done, madam said to me, "Little English, we have shown you kindness, and now it lies in your power to serve or disserve us as you know where our goods are hid in the woods and that monsieur is not at home. I could have sent you to the fort and put you under confinement, but my respects to you and assurance of your love to us has disposed me to confide

51. In 1696 Col. John Hathorne (c. 1646–1717), the principal judge in the Salem witchcraft trials, led Massachusetts forces against the fort at Nashwaak (Naxoat) at present-day Frederickton. Curiously, Gyles spells the colonel's name the way his famous descendant, Nathaniel Hawthorne, did by adding a *w;* the nineteenth-century writer added the letter, hoping to dissociate himself from his notorious ancestor.

52. Joseph Robineau de Villebon (1655–1700), governor of Acadia from 1690 to 1700.

53. [Gyles.] The place where our house stood was called Hagimsack, twenty-five leagues from the river's mouth, as before noted.

in you, persuaded you will not hurt us nor our affairs. And now if you will not run away to the English who are coming up the river but serve our interest, I will acquaint monsieur of it on his return from France, which will be very pleasing to him, and I now give my word that you shall have liberty to go to Boston on the first opportunity (if you desire it) or that any other favor in my power shall not be denied you."

I replied, "Madam, it is contrary to the nature of the English to requite evil for good. I shall endeavor to serve you and your interest. I shall not run to the English, but if I am taken by them shall willingly go with them and yet endeavor not to disserve you either in your person or goods."

This said, we embarked and went in a large boat and canoe two or three miles up an eastern branch of the river that comes from a large pond,[54] and in the evening [we] sent down four hands to make discovery. And while they were sitting in the house, the English surrounded it and took one of the four; the other three made their escape in the dark through the English soldiers and came to us and gave a surprising account of affairs. Again madam said to me, "Little English, now you can go from us, but I hope you will remember your word."

I said, "Madam, be not concerned for I will not leave you in this strait."

She said, "I know not what to do with my two poor little babes."

I said, "Madam, the sooner we embark and go over the great pond the better."

Accordingly we embarked and went over the pond. The next day we spake with Indians who were in a canoe and gave us an account that Signecto town was taken and burned. Soon after we heard the great guns at Governor Vielbon's fort,[55] which the English engaged several days, killed one man, and drew off and went down the river, for it was so late in the fall that had they tarried a few days longer in the river they would have been froze in for the winter. Hearing no report of the great guns for several days, I, with two others, went down to our house to make discovery, where we found our young lad who was taken by the English when they went up the river. For the general was so honorable that, on reading the note on our door, he ordered that the house and barn should not be burned nor their cattle or other creatures killed, except one or two and the poultry for their use. And at their return, [he] ordered the young lad to be put ashore. Finding things in this posture, we returned and gave madam an account.

54. Grand Lake.
55. Fort Saint Joseph or Nashwaak.

She acknowledged the many favors which the English had shown her with gratitude and treated me with great civility. The next spring monsieur arrived from France in the man-of-war, who thanked me for my care of his affairs and said that he would endeavor to fulfill what madam had promised to me.

SECTION VI. *Of My Release and Return to My Friends*

And accordingly in the year 1698, the peace being proclaimed, and a sloop come to the mouth of the river with a ransom for one Michael Cooms,[56] I put monsieur in mind of his word. I told him that there was now an opportunity for me to go and see the English. He advised me to tarry and told me that he would do for me as for his own, etc. I thanked him for his kindness but rather chose to go to Boston, for I hoped I had some relations yet alive. Then he advised me to go up to the fort and take my leave of the governor, which I did and he spake very kindly, etc. Some days after I took my leave of madam; monsieur went down to the mouth of the river with me to see me safe aboard and asked the master, Mr. Starkee, a Scotchman, whether I must pay for my passage; if so, he would pay it himself rather than I should have it to pay at my arrival in Boston but gave me not a penny. The master told him that there was nothing to pay, and that if the owner should make any demand he would pay it himself rather than a poor prisoner should suffer, for he was glad to see any English person come out of captivity.

On the 20th of June, I took my leave of monsieur, and the sloop came to sail for Boston where we arrived on the 28th of the same, at night. In the morning after my arrival a youth came on board and asked many questions relating to my captivity and at length gave me to understand that he was my little brother who was at play with some other children, and upon hearing the guns and seeing the Indians run, made their escape to the fort and went off with the captain and people, and that my elder brother who made his escape from the farm whence I was taken and our two little sisters were alive and that our mother had been dead some years, etc., as above related. Then we went ashore and saw our elder brother, etc.

On the second of August, 1689, I was taken, and on the 28th of June, 1698, arrived at Boston, so that I was absent eight years, ten months, and twenty-six days.[57] In all which time, though I underwent extreme difficul-

56. Perhaps the son of Michael and Joan Combs (Cooms, Coombs) of Salem. If so, he was then approximately thirty years old.

57. In the first edition (1736), Gyles's dates for his capture, release, arrival in Boston,

ties, yet I saw much of the goodness of God. May the most powerful and beneficent Being accept this public testimony of it, and bless my experiences to excite others to confide in His all-sufficiency, through the infinite merits of Jesus Christ.

and total time in captivity were apparently muddled, for the erratum, p. [44], gives corrected dates. So does the copy of Gyles's *Memoirs* in the Massachusetts Historical Society that is believed to have been owned by his daughter (the flyleaf inscription reads "Mary Gyles Her Book 1736"), which contains handwritten changes; most of them are grammatical or stylistic improvements. The present edition incorporates the first edition's erratum—on the assumption that they reflect Gyles's preferences—but not the other changes in Mary Gyles's copy.

FOUR

Cotton Mather, leading Puritan clergyman of the third generation and the fore-most publicist of New England captivities. Etching based on Peter Pelham's oil portrait. Courtesy of the American Antiquarian Society.

· COTTON MATHER ·
"NEW ASSAULTS FROM THE INDIANS" AND
"THE CONDITION OF THE CAPTIVES"

Cotton Mather (1663–1728) wrote voluminously, more than four hundred and fifty titles, about almost everything—theology, history, biography, medicine, morals, and education, to name only some of his varied interests. His most famous and influential work appeared early in his career. *Magnalia Christi Americana: or, the Ecclesiastical History of New England* (London, 1702) demonstrated Mather's usual flamboyance and pedantry but also his unparalleled fund of knowledge and grandeur of purpose. Mather's over-arching goal—difficult to discern in the following selections—was to demonstrate "the *Wonders* of the Christian religion, flying from the depravations of Europe to the American strand . . . and the wonderful displays of [God's] infinite power, wisdom, goodness, and faithfulness, wherein His Divine Providence hath irradiated an Indian wilderness." To achieve that purpose, Mather offered a hodgepodge of narrative history, biographical sketches, anecdotes, and much, much else, including the Indian captivities printed below. In sum, *Magnalia Christi Americana* was a treasure trove of the Puritan mind: a history of New England from 1620 to 1698 as seen through the eyes of its most illustrious character.

Mather's lifelong interest in the conversion of Indians prompted him to publish several tracts for their supposed edification, including his bilingual *Epistle to the Christian Indians, giving them a Short Account, of What [the] English Desire Them to Know and to Do in Order to Their Happiness* (1700). He also served many years as a commissioner of Indian affairs for the New England Company, an English corporation devoted to Christianizing and "civilizing" the Indians. Mather's commitment to such activities did not prevent him from reviling the Indians with undisguised scorn at times, especially when describing their wartime atrocities. (He usually kept silent about Puritan atrocities.) The accounts of captivity and Indian cruelty presented here had appeared in shorter form a few years earlier in Mather's *Decennium Luctuosum: An History of Remarkable Occurrences in the Long War, which New-England hath had with the Indian Salvages, from the Year 1688, to . . . 1698 . . .* (Boston, 1699), and they reflect the hatred toward Indians engendered by a decade of war. The following text is based on the version included in the first edition of *Magnalia Christi Americana* (London, 1702), Bk VII, 68–71, in which Mather related the experiences of several men and women seized on the New Hampshire and Maine frontiers.

In 1690, shortly after the outbreak of King William's War, the governor-general of Canada, Louis de Baude, Comte de Frontenac, sent three war parties against English outposts. The first, launched from Montreal, sacked Schenectady, New York, in February 1690; the second traveled overland from Trois Rivières to attack Salmon Falls, New Hampshire, in mid-March; the third, based at Quebec, assaulted the Maine frontier in early May. François Hertel led the second contingent. After raiding the New Hampshire towns he moved east to join the attack on Maine. Frontenac had recently lowered the bounty on English scalps and raised it on captives; partly for that reason, perhaps, his forces took an unusually large number of captives, most of them women and children.

ARTICLE VI

New Assaults from the Indians with Some Remarkables of Captives Taken in Those Assaults

The sun and the war be again returning! The year 1690 must begin very inauspiciously. In February the French with Indians made a descent from Canada upon a Dutch town called Schenectady, twenty miles above Albany, under the government of New York.[1] And in that surprising incursion they killed about sixty persons, whereof one was their minister, and carried about half as many into captivity, but the people there, assisted by the Maquas [Mohawks], pursued them and recovered some of their captives from them. Upon the advice of this mischief in the west, order was dispatched unto Major [Charles] Frost in the east that the towns there should stand upon their guard. The major did his duty, but they did not

1. For a detailed account of the raid see Francis Parkman, *Frontenac and New France under Louis XIV* (Boston, 1877; repr. 1903), 222–229. Mather calls Schenectady a Dutch town because it had been founded while the Dutch Republic controlled New Netherland, and in the 1690s the town still contained a preponderance of Dutch inhabitants. England seized New Netherland in 1664 during an Anglo-Dutch war and renamed it New York.

136

theirs. They dreamed that while the deep snow of the winter continued, they were safe enough, but this proved as vain as a dream of a dry summer.

On March 18 [1690] the French with Indians, being half one [and] half the other, half Indianized French and half Frenchified Indians, commanded by Monsieur Artel and Hoop-Hood,[2] fell suddenly upon Salmon Falls [New Hampshire], destroying the best part of the town with fire and sword. Near thirty persons were slain and more than fifty were led into what the reader will by and by call the worst captivity in the world. It would be a long story to tell what a particular share in this calamity fell to the family of one Clement Short. This honest man with his pious wife and three children were killed and six or seven of their children were made prisoners, the most of which arrived safe to Canada through a thousand hardships and the most of these were with more than a thousand mercies afterwards redeemed from Canada unto their English friends again.[3] But my readers will be so reasonable as to excuse me if I do not mention the fate of every family that hath suffered a share in the calamity of this grievous war, for 'tis impossible that I should know all that hath happened, and it would be improper for me to write all that I know. And very little is the advantage of having a name standing upon record only among unhappy sufferers.

About seven score English went out after them and came up with them.[4] Nevertheless, through the disadvantages of their feet by the snow, they could make no hand on it. Four or five of ours were killed and as many of the enemy, but the night put an end unto the action. Ours took one prisoner, a Frenchman, who confessed that they came from Canada where both French and Indians were in pay at ten livres per month, and he particularly declared the state of Canada. This prisoner met with such kind usage from us that he became a freeman of Christ and embraced and professed the Protestant religion. But of the prisoners which the enemy took from us there were two which immediately met with a very different fate.

Three Indians hotly pursued one Thomas Toogood, and one of them overtaking him while the rest perceiving it stayed behind the hill, he yielded himself a prisoner. While the savage was getting strings to bind

2. François Hertel's party consisted of about twenty-five French and as many Indians, mostly Abenaki led by Chief Hopehood or Wohawa. Mather was inconsistent in his spelling of the chief's name.

3. Among the captured children was Mercy Short, who later played a prominent role in the Salem witchcraft frenzy.

4. English militia caught up with Hertel's retreating war party at Wooster River.

him, he held his gun under his arm which, Toogood observing, suddenly plucked it from his friend stark naught, threatening and protesting that he would shoot him down if he made any noise and so away he ran with it unto Quochecho.[5]

If my reader be inclined now to smile when he thinks how simple poor Isgrim looked returning to his mates behind the hill without either gun or prey or anything but strings to remember him of his own deserts, the smiles will all be presently turned into tears. The Indians had now made a prisoner of one Robert Rogers, and, being on their journey, they came to an hill where this man, being through his corpulency (for which he was usually nicknamed Robin Pork) and an insupportable and intolerable burden laid upon his back, not so able to travel as the rest, he absconded. The wretches, missing him, immediately went in pursuit of him, and it was not long before they found his burden cast in the way and the track of his going out of the way which they followed until they found him hidden in a hollow tree. They took him out, they stripped him, they beat him, and pricked him, and pushed him forward with their swords until they were got back to the hill. And, it being almost night, they fastened him to a tree with his hands behind him and made themselves a supper, singing, dancing, roaring, and uttering many signs of joy but with joy little enough to the poor creature who foresaw what all this tended unto. They then cut a parcel of wood, and, bringing it into a plain place, they cut off the top of a small red oak tree, leaving the trunk for a stake whereto they bound their sacrifice. They first made a great fire near this tree of death, and, bringing him unto it, they bid him take his leave of his friends which he did in a doleful manner; no pen, though made of a harpy's quill, were able to describe the dolor of it! They then allowed him a little time to make his prayers unto heaven, which he did with an extreme fervency and agony. Whereupon they bound him to the stake and brought the rest of the prisoners with their arms tied each to other so setting them round the fire.

This being done, they went behind the fire and thrust it forwards upon the man with much laughter and shouting, and when the fire had burned some while upon him even till he was near stifled, they pulled it again from him. They danced about him, and at every turn they did with their knives cut collops of his flesh from his naked limbs and throw them with his blood into his face. When he was dead, they set his body down upon the glowing coals and left him tied with his back to the stake where the English army

5. Present-day Dover, New Hampshire; usually spelled Cocheco.

soon after found him. He was left for us to put out the fire with our tears! Reader, who should be the father of these myrmidons?

ARTICLE VII

The Condition of the Captives that from Time to Time Fell into the Hands of the Indians, with Some Very Remarkable Accidents

We have had some occasion, and shall have more, to mention captives falling into the hands of the Indians. We will here without anything worthy to be called a digression a little stand still and with mournful hearts look upon the condition of the captives in those cruel hands. Their condition truly might be expressed in the terms of the ancient Lamentations (thus by some translated) Lam. 4:3, "The daughter of my people is in the hands of the cruel that are like the ostrich in the wilderness." Truly the dark places of New England where the Indians had their unapproachable kennels were habitations of cruelty, and no words can sufficiently describe the cruelty undergone by our captives in those habitations. The cold, and heat, and hunger, and weariness, and mockings, and scourgings, and insolencies endured by the captives would enough deserve the name of cruelty, but there was this also added unto the rest: that they must ever now and then have their friends made a sacrifice of devils before their eyes but be afraid of dropping a tear from those eyes lest it should upon that provocation be next their own turn to be so barbarously sacrificed. Indeed, some few of the captives did very happily escape from their barbarous oppressors by a flight wisely managed. And many more of them were bought by the French who treated them with a civility ever to be acknowledged until care was taken to fetch them home. Nevertheless, many scores of them died among the Indians, and what usage they had may be gathered from the following relations which I have obtained from credible witnesses.

RELATION I

James Key, son to John Key of Quochecho, was a child of about five years of age taken captive by the Indians at Salmon Falls,[6] and that hellish fellow, Hope-Hood, once a servant of a Christian master in Boston, was be-

6. John Key and three of his children—John Jr., James, and Abigail—were captured. The father and his namesake were redeemed in 1695. Abigail, about eleven years old when captured, was converted to Catholicism five years later and renamed Margueritte. In 1705 she married a French soldier and remained in Canada the rest of her life.

come the master of this little Christian. This child, lamenting with tears the want of parents, his master threatened him with death if he did not refrain his tears, but these threatenings could not extinguish the natural affections of a child. Wherefore upon his next lamentations this monster stripped him stark naked and lashed both his hands round a tree and scourged him so that from the crown of the head unto the sole of his foot he was all over bloody and swollen. And when he was tired with laying on his blows on the forlorn infant, he would lay him on the ground with taunts, remembering him of his parents. In this misery the poor creature lay horribly roaring for divers days together while his master, gratified with the music, lay contriving of new torments wherewith to martyr him. It was not long before the child had a sore eye which his master said proceeded from his weeping on the forbidden accounts. Whereupon, laying hold on the head of the child with his left hand, with the thumb of his right he forced the ball of his eye quite out, therewithal telling him that when he heard him cry again he would serve the other so too and leave him never an eye to weep withal. About nine or ten days after, this wretch had occasion to remove with his family about thirty miles further, and when they had gone about six miles of the thirty, the child, being tired and faint, sat him down to rest, at which this horrid fellow, being provoked, he buried the blade of his hatchet in the brains of the child and then chopped the breathless body to pieces before the rest of the company and threw it into the river. But for the sake of these and other such truculent things done by Hope-Hood, I am resolved that in the course of our story I will watch to see what becomes of that hideous *loup-garou* [werewolf], if he come to his end (as I am apt to think he will) before the story.

RELATION II

Mehetable Goodwin,[7] being a captive among the Indians, had with her a child about five months old which through hunger and hardship, she being unable to nourish it, often made most grievous ejaculations. Her Indian master told her that if the child were not quiet he would soon dispose of it, which caused her to use all possible means that his *Netop-ship*[8] might not be offended and sometimes carry it from the fire out of his hearing, where she sat up to the waist in snow and frost for several hours until it was lulled to sleep. She thus for several days preserved the life of her babe until he

7. Mehitable, or Hetty, Goodwin, wife of Thomas Goodwin and daughter of Lt. Roger Plaisted and Olive Coleman Plaisted. Her father had been killed in King Philip's War.

8. *Netop* meant "friend" in Algonquian (Massachusetts dialect). It is here used sarcastically.

saw cause to travel with his own cubs further afield. And then lest he should be retarded in his travel, he violently snatched the babe out of its mother's arms and before her face knocked out its brains and stripped it of the few rags it had hitherto enjoyed and ordered her the task to go wash the bloody clothes. Returning from this melancholy task, she found the infant hanging by the neck in a forked bough of a tree. She desired leave to lay it in the earth, but he said it was better as it was, for now the wild beasts would not come at it (I am sure they had been at it!), and she might have the comfort of seeing it again if ever they came that way.

The journey now before them was like to be very long, even as far as Canada, where his purpose was to make merchandise of his captive, and glad was the captive of such happy tidings. But the desperate length of the way and want of food and grief of mind wherewith she now encountered caused her within a few days to faint under her difficulties. When at length she sat down for some repose with many prayers and tears unto God for the salvation of her soul, she found herself unable to rise until she espied her furious executioner coming towards her with fire in his eyes, the devil in his heart, and his hatchet in his hand ready to bestow a mercy-stroke of death upon her. But then this miserable creature got on her knees and, with weeping and wailing and all expressions of agony and entreaty, pre-vailed on him to spare her life a little, and she did not question but God would enable her to walk a little faster. The merciless tyrant was prevailed withal to spare her this time. Nevertheless, her former weakness quickly returning upon her, he was just going to murder her, but a couple of In-dians, just at that instant coming in, suddenly called upon him to hold his hand whereat such an horror surprised his guilty soul that he ran away. But hearing them call his name, he returned and then permitted these his friends to ransom his prisoner from him.

After this, being seated by a riverside, they heard several guns go off on the other side, which they concluded was from a party of Albany Indians[9] who were enemies unto these, whereupon this bold blade would needs go in a canoe to discover what they were. They fired upon him and shot through him and several of his friends before the discovery could be made unto satisfaction. But some days after this, divers of his friends gathered a party to revenge his death on their supposed enemies, with whom they joined battle and fought several hours until their supposed enemies did really put them to the rout.

Among the captives which they left in their fight was this poor Good-

9. Mohawks.

141

win who was overjoyed in seeing herself thus at liberty. But the joy did not last long, for these Indians were of the same sort with the other and had been by their own friends thus through a strange mistake set upon. However, this crew proved more favorable to her than the former and went away silently with their booty, being loath to have any noise made of their foul mistake. And yet a few days after such another mistake happened, for meeting with another party of Indians which they imagined in the English interests, they furiously engaged each other, and many were killed and wounded on either side. But they proved a party of the French Indians who took this poor Goodwin and presented her to the French captain by whom she was carried unto Canada where she continued five years and then was brought safe back into New England.[10]

RELATION III

Mary Plaisted, the wife of Mr. James Plaisted, was made a captive by the Indians about three weeks after her delivery of a male child.[11] They then took her with her infant off her bed and forced her to travel in this her weakness the best part of a day without any respect of pity. At night the cold ground in the open air was her lodging, and for many a day she had no nourishment but a little water with a little bearflesh, which rendered her so feeble that she with her infant were not far from totally starved. Upon her cries to God there was at length some supply sent in by her master's taking a moose, the broth whereof recovered her. But she must now travel many days through woods and swamps and rocks, and over mountains and frost and snow, until she could stir no farther. Sitting down to rest, she was not able to rise until her diabolical master helped her up,

10. Mehitable Goodwin was baptized a Catholic at Quebec in 1693 and renamed Marie Esther; at the time she was a servant of Mademoiselle de Nauguiere (or de la Naudiere), widow of Frontenac's Captain of the Guard. The conversion apparently was feigned or temporary, for Goodwin was redeemed in 1695, reunited with her family, and lived the rest of her life in Maine. See Emma Lewis Coleman, *New England Captives Carried to Canada,* 2 vols. (Portland, Me., 1925), 185–186.

11. Mary Rishworth Plaisted, daughter of Rev. John Plaisted of Wells, Maine. Although she was only thirty-two at the time of her capture, James Plaisted was her fourth husband; at least two of his predecessors had died quite young. In 1692 Mary Plaisted and two daughters by a previous marriage, eleven-year-old Mary Sayward and seven-year-old Esther Sayward, were captured at York, Maine, by Acadian Indians. Mary Plaisted was baptized by French Catholics at Montreal in 1693 but was redeemed in 1695; she returned to her family and the Congregational church. The two daughters, however, remained in Canada. The elder became a nun and was eventually the head of a mission school for girls; the younger married a Canadian merchant. For more information on the three captives see Coleman, *New England Captives,* I, 236–243.

which, when he did, he took her child from her and carried it unto a river where, stripping it of the few rags it had, he took it by the heels and against a tree dashed out its brains and then flung it into the river. So he returned unto the miserable mother, telling her she was now eased of her burden and must walk faster than she did before!

RELATION IV

Mary Ferguson,[12] taken captive by the Indians at Salmon Falls, declares that another maid of about fifteen or sixteen years of age taken at the same time had a great burden imposed on her. Being over-borne with her burden, she burst out into tears, telling her Indian master that she could go no further. Whereupon he immediately took off her burden and, leading her aside into the bushes, he cut off her head, and, scalping it, he ran about laughing and bragging what an act he had now done, and, showing the scalp unto the rest, he told them they should all be served so if they were not patient.

In fine, when the children of the English captives cried at anytime so that they were not presently quieted, the manner of the Indians was to dash out their brains against a tree.

And very often when the Indians were on or near the water, they took the small children and held them under water till they had near drowned them and then gave them unto their distressed mothers to quiet them.

And the Indians in their frolics would whip and beat the small children until they set them into grievous outcries and then throw them to their amazed mothers for them to quiet them again as well as they could.

This was Indian captivity!

Reader, a modern traveler assures us that at the Villa Ludovisia, not far from Rome, there is to be seen the body of a petrified man and that he himself saw by a piece of the man's leg, broken for satisfaction, both the bone and the stone crusted over it. All that I will say is that if thou canst read these passages without relenting bowels,[13] thou thyself art as really petrified as the man at Villa Ludovisia.

12. In 1692 Mary Ferguson was captured somewhere in the Piscataqua region of Maine (the record is unclear on the exact time and place), along with several other settlers. She was redeemed in 1695. The "maid of about fifteen or sixteen years of age" who fell victim to the Indian's wrath is unidentified.

13. The bowels, according to seventeenth-century natural philosophers, were the seat of tenderness and compassion. "Bowels" had several meanings; it often referred to the insides of the body in general or specifically to the heart. Mather seems to use it in the latter sense.

PURITANS AMONG THE INDIANS

Nescio tu quibus es, lector, lecturus ocellis;
Hoc scio quod siccis scribere non potui.

[I know not, reader, whether you will read this record with dry or tearful eyes; I only know I could not write it without tears in mine.]

attributed
Good things to God
But bad things to
Indians

it — upon her evils
to God ↗ supplies
to be sent.
to

FIVE

Magnalia Christi Americana :

OR, THE

𝕰𝖈𝖈𝖑𝖊𝖘𝖎𝖆𝖘𝖙𝖎𝖈𝖆𝖑 𝕳𝖎𝖘𝖙𝖔𝖗𝖞

OF

NEW-ENGLAND,

FROM

Its First Planting in the Year 1620. unto the Year of our LORD, 1698.

In Seven BOOKS.

I. Antiquities : In Seven Chapters. With an Appendix.
II. Containing the Lives of the Governours, and Names of the Magistrates of *New-England :* In Thirteen Chapters. With an Appendix.
III. The Lives of Sixty Famous Divines, by whose Ministry the Churches of *New-England* have been Planted and Continued.
IV. An Account of the University of *Cambridge* in *New-England* ; in Two Parts. The First contains the Laws, the Benefactors, and Viciffitudes of *Harvard College* ; with Remarks upon it. The Second Part contains the Lives of some Eminent Persons Educated in it.
V. Acts and Monuments of the Faith and Order in the Churches of *New-England,* passed in their Synods ; with Historical Remarks upon those Venerable Affemblies ; and a great Variety of Church-Cases occurring, and refolved by the Synods of thofe Churches : In Four Parts.
VI. A Faithful Record of many Illustrious, Wonderful Providences, both of Mercies and Judgments, on divers Perfons in *New-England :* In Eight Chapters.
VII. *The Wars of the Lord.* Being an History of the Manifold Afflictions and Disturbances of the Churches in *New-England,* from their Various Adverfaries, and the Wonderful Methods and Mercies of God in their Deliverance : In Six Chapters : To which is fubjoined, An Appendix of Remarkable Occurrences which *New-England* had in the Wars with the *Indian* Salvages, from the Year 1688, to the Year 1698.

By the Reverend and Learned *COTTON MATHER,* M. A. And Paftor of the North Church in *Bofton, New-England.*

LONDON:

Printed for *Thomas Parkhurft,* at the *Bible* and *Three Crowns* in *Cheapfide.* MDCCII.

Title page of Cotton Mather's *Magnalia Christi Americana,* which recounts several Puritan captivities including Hannah Swarton's "Notable Deliverances." By permission of the Houghton Library, Harvard University.

"A NARRATIVE OF HANNAH SWARTON CONTAINING WONDERFUL PASSAGES RELATING TO HER CAPTIVITY AND DELIVERANCE" · RELATED BY COTTON MATHER ·

The third of the three French and Indian war parties launched by Governor Frontenac in early 1690 assaulted Casco Bay and vicinity that spring. Le Sieur de Portneuf's expedition consisted of about fifty Frenchmen and perhaps twice that many Abenaki warriors; it was joined in Maine by a contingent of Penobscots and by François Hertel's forces. The total may have reached four or five hundred. Between May 16 and 20 this combined army attacked four small forts and the larger Fort Loyal, whose garrison had recently been depleted to enlarge Massachusetts Governor William Phips's campaign against Port Royal. Remaining in Fort Loyal under Captain Sylvanus Davis were about seventy-five men, mostly local militia, and perhaps two hundred noncombatants who took refuge when the advanced French and Indian units, according to Captain Davis's account of the war, "killed sundry cattle, came into houses and threatened to knock the people on the head, and at several times gave out reports, that they would make war upon the English; and that they were animated so to do by the French." The colonists accordingly seized about twenty Indians who, Davis claimed, "had been bloody, murderous rogues in the first [King Philip's] Indian war, being the chief ringleaders and most fittest and capable to do the mischief, . . . in order for their examination, and to bring in the rest to a treaty." While the prisoners were incarcerated at Falmouth, other Indians raided English settlements and took several captives. Sir Edmund Andros, governor of the Dominion of New England—a brief experiment in imperial consolidation that joined the New England colonies and New York under one administration—ordered all of the Indians released, even if no English captives were offered in return.

When the main assault came in 1690, Davis's forces resisted for five days. With most of his men killed or wounded and all the houses outside

147

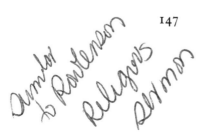

the fort in ashes, Davis surrendered on promise of safe passage of the survivors to the nearest English town. According to Davis, the Indians instead slaughtered most of the garrison and carried the rest to Canada. There Davis complained to Governor Frontenac, who appeared to be annoyed at his soldiers' breach of faith but insisted that the English were mere rebels against their king: William and Mary had recently acceded to the English throne, and the deposed James II had taken refuge in France. In 1692 Captain Benjamin Church arrived at deserted Casco and buried the remains of the victims.

Hannah Swarton was among the captives. She and her family had recently migrated to Casco Bay from Beverly, Massachusetts. More directly than most New England narrators, Swarton interpreted her ordeal as God's punishment for her own shortcomings; she belatedly concluded that her remove from an orderly, pious town to a frontier settlement with little civil government and no church had been for worldly rather than godly ends. "I must justifie the Lord in all that has befallen me," she ruefully admitted, "and [I] acknowledged that he hath punish'd me less than my Iniquities deserved." Yet Mrs. Swarton's punishment was indeed severe. She remained a captive for five and a half years; her husband and one child were killed; and two other children were never redeemed.

Among the captivity narratives Cotton Mather included in his various publications, Swarton's was the most extensive. He first published "A Narrative of Hannah Swarton, containing Wonderful Passages, relating to her Captivity and her Deliverance" in *Humiliations Followed with Deliverances* (Boston, 1697), and in an expanded version in *Magnalia Christi Americana* (London, 1702), Bk. VI, 10–14. The following text is based on Mather's second version. There is no way of knowing how much Mather altered Swarton's original account—no copy of it survives—but the abundant and precise biblical quotations suggest a clerical hand. So too, perhaps, does the unusual emphasis on captivity as a punishment for rejecting civil and ecclesiastical society.

I was taken by the Indians when Casco Fort was taken (May 1690), my husband being slain and four children taken with me.[1] The eldest of my sons they killed about two months after I was taken, and the rest scattered

1. John Swarton was a veteran of English military service in Flanders and later of colonial service under Benjamin Church along the Maine frontier. Originally from the island of Jersey, he settled in North Yarmouth in the late 1680s.

from me. I was now left a widow and as bereaved of my children though I had them alive, yet it was very seldom that I could see them, and I had not liberty to discourse with them without danger either of my own life or theirs; for our consoling each other's condition and showing natural affection was so displeasing to our Indian rulers unto whose share we fell, that they would threaten to kill us if we cried each to other or discoursed much together. So that my condition was like what the Lord threatened the Jews in Ezek. 24:22, 23. We durst not mourn or weep in the sight of our enemies, lest we lost our own lives. For the first times, while the enemy feasted on our English provisions, I might have had some with them, but then I was so filled with sorrow and tears that I had little stomach to eat. And when my stomach was come, our English food was spent. The Indians wanted themselves and we more, so that then I was pined with want. We had no corn or bread but sometimes groundnuts, acorns, purslain, hogweed, weeds, roots, and sometimes dogs' flesh but not sufficient to satisfy hunger with these, having but little at a time. We had no success at hunting save that one bear was killed, which I had part of, and a very small part of a turtle I had another time. And once an Indian gave me a piece of moose's liver, which was a sweet morsel to me, and fish if we could catch it.

Thus I continued with them, hurried up and down the wilderness from May 20 [1690] till the middle of February [1691], carrying continually a great burden in our travels, and I must go their pace or else be killed presently. And yet [I] was pinched with cold for want of clothing, being put by them into an Indian dress with a slight blanket, no stockings, and but one pair of Indian shoes, and of their leather stockings for the winter. My feet were pricked with sharp stones and prickly bushes sometimes and other times pinched with snow, cold, and ice that I traveled upon, ready to be frozen and faint for want of food, so that many times I thought I could go no further but must lie down and, if they would kill me, let them kill me. Yet then the Lord did so renew my strength that I went on still further as my master would have me and held out with them. Though many English were taken and I was brought to some of them at times while we were about Casco Bay and Kennebeck River, yet at Norridgewock[2] we were separated and no English were in our company but one John York[3]

2. Norridgewock was a Catholic Indian mission at the junction of Sandy River and Kennebec River where the town of Madison now stands. English occupation of the area began in 1773.

3. John York was a resident and trustee of North Yarmouth, Maine, who had sought refuge at Casco in 1690.

and myself who were both almost starved for want and yet told that if we could not hold up to travel with them they would kill us. And accordingly, John York growing weak by his wants, they killed him and threatened me with the like.

One time my Indian mistress and I were left alone while the rest went to look for eels, and they left us no food from Sabbath-day morning till the next Saturday, save that we had a bladder (of moose I think) which was well filled with maggots; and we boiled it and drank the broth, but the bladder was so tough we could not eat it. On the Saturday I was sent by my mistress to that part of the island most likely to see some canoe and there to make fire and smoke to invite some Indians, if I could spy any, to come to relieve us, and I espied a canoe and by signs invited them to come to shore. It proved to be some squaws who, understanding our wants, one of them gave me a roasted eel which I ate and it seemed unto me the most savory food I ever tasted before. Sometimes we lived on wortle berries, sometimes on a kind of wild cherry which grew on bushes, which I was sent to gather once in so bitter a cold season that I was not able to bring my fingers together to hold them fast. Yet under all these hardships the Lord kept me from any sickness or such weakness as to disenable me from traveling when they put us upon it.

My Indian mistress was one that had been bred by the English at Black Point[4] and now married to a Canada Indian and turned papist. And she would say that had the English been as careful to instruct her in our religion as the French were to instruct her in theirs, she might have been of our religion. And she would say that God delivered us into their hands to punish us for our sins.[5] And this I knew was true as to myself. And as I desired to consider of all my sins for which the Lord did punish me, so this lay very heavy upon my spirit many a time that I had left the public worship and ordinances of God where I formerly lived (*viz.* at Beverley) to remove to the north part of Casco Bay where there was no church or

4. Black Point was included in the town of Scarborough, Maine, beginning in 1658, although the original name persisted. For a brief description of Maine in the 1660s see John Josselyn, *An Account of Two Voyages to New-England* in *Massachusetts Historical Society Collections,* 3rd ser., 3 (1833), 343–352.

5. Apparently most New Englanders concurred in this assessment. See the report of the "Reforming Synod" of 1679–1680 in Williston Walker, ed., *Creeds and Platforms of Congregationalism* (New York, 1893; repr. Boston, 1960), 423–437, for an example of Puritan self-accusation. The belief that Indian raids, along with natural calamities and other misfortunes, were signs of God's wrath upon His chosen people remained common throughout the Puritan era. Of course Swarton's Indian mistress believed the New Englanders' sins to be their rejection of Catholicism and their wars against the Indians.

minister of the Gospel. And this we did for large accommodations in the world, thereby exposing our children to be bred ignorantly like Indians and ourselves to forget what we had been formerly instructed in, and so we turned our backs upon God's ordinances to get this world's goods. But now God hath stripped me of these things also so that I must justify the Lord in all that has befallen me and acknowledged that He hath punished me less than my iniquities deserved. I was now bereaved of husband, children, friends, neighbors, house, estate, bread, clothes, or lodging suitable, and my very life did hang daily in doubt, being continually in danger of being killed by the Indians, or pined to death with famine, or tired to death with hard traveling, or pinched with cold till I died in the winter season. I was so amazed with many troubles and hurried in my spirit from one exercise to another how to preserve myself in danger and supply myself in the want that was present that I had not time or leisure so composedly to consider of the great concernments of my soul as I should have done, neither had I any Bible, or good book to look into, or Christian friend to be my counselor in these distresses. But I may say the words of God which I had formerly heard or read, many of them came oft into my mind and kept me from perishing in my afflictions. As when they threatened to kill me many times, I often thought of the words of our savior to Pilate, John 19:11, "Thou couldest have no power at all against me except it were given thee from above."

I knew they had no power to kill me but what the Lord gave them, and I had many times hope that the Lord would not suffer them to slay me but deliver me out of their hands and in His time I hoped return me to my country again. When they told me that my eldest son [Samuel] was killed by the Indians, I thought of that in Jer. 33:8, "I will cleanse them from all their iniquities whereby they have sinned against me, and I will pardon all their iniquities." I hoped, though the enemy had barbarously killed his body, yet that the Lord had pardoned his sins and that his soul was safe. When I thought upon my many troubles, I thought of Job's complaint, chapter 14:16, 17, "Thou numberest my steps and watchest over my sin; my transgression is sealed up into a bag, and thou sewest up mine iniquity." This was for my humiliation and put me upon prayer to God for His pardoning mercy in Christ. And I thought upon David's complaint, Psalm 13:1, 2, and used it in my prayers to the Lord: "How long wilt Thou forget me, O Lord, forever? How long wilt Thou hide Thy face from me? How long shall I take counsel in my soul, having sorrow in my heart? How long shall my enemy be exalted over me?" I sometimes bemoaned myself as Job, chapter 19:9, 10, "He hath stripped me of my glory and taken my crown from my head; He hath destroyed me on every side, and I am gone, and my hope hath He removed like a tree." Yet sometimes encouraged from Job 22:27, "Thou shalt make thy prayer to Him, and He shall hear thee, and thou shalt pay thy vows." I made vows to the Lord that I would give up myself to Him if He would accept me in Jesus Christ and pardon my sins, and I desired and endeavored to pay my vows unto the Lord. I prayed to Him, "Remember not against me the sins of my youth," and I besought Him, "Judge me, O God, and plead my cause against an ungodly nation; deliver me from the deceitful and unjust man. Why go I mourning because of the oppression of the enemy?" And by many other scriptures that were brought to my remembrance was I instructed, directed, and comforted.

I traveled over steep and hideous mountains one while, and another while over swamps and thickets of fallen trees lying one, two, three foot from the ground which I have stepped on from one to another, nigh a thousand in a day, carrying a great burden on my back. Yet I dreaded going to Canada for fear lest I should be overcome by them to yield to their religion which I had vowed unto God that I would not do. But the extremity of my sufferings were such that at length I was willing to go to preserve my life. And after many weary journeys through frost and snow, we came to Canada about the middle of February 1690 [1691]. And traveling over the river, my master pitched his wigwam in sight of some French houses westward of us and then sent me to those houses to beg victuals for them, which I did and found the French very kind to me, giving me beef and pork and bread which I had been without near nine months before so that now I found a great change as to diet. But the snow being knee-deep and my legs and hams very sore, I found it very tedious to travel, and my sores bled so that as I traveled I might be tracked by my blood that I left behind me on the snow. I asked leave to stay all night with the French when I went to beg again, which my master consented unto, and sent me eastward to houses which were toward Quebec (though then I knew it not). So, having begged provisions at a French house, and it being near night after I was refreshed myself and had food to carry to the Indians, I signified as well as I could to make the French woman understand that I desired to stay by her fire that night. Whereupon she laid a good bed on the floor and good coverings for me, and there I lodged comfortably.

And the next morning when I had breakfasted with the family and the menkind were gone abroad, as I was about to go to my Indian master the French woman stepped out and left me alone in her house, and I then stayed her return to give her thanks for her kindness. And while I waited, came in two men, and one of them spake to me in English, "I am glad to see you, country-woman!" This was exceedingly reviving to hear the voice of an Englishman, and, upon inquiry, I found he was taken at the Northwest Passage[6] and the other was a French ordinary keeper. After some discourse he asked me to go with him to Quebec, which he told me was about four miles off. I answered [that] my Indian master might kill me for it when I went back. Then, after some discourse in French with his fellow-traveler, he said this Frenchman engaged that if I would go with them he would keep me from returning to the Indians, and I should be ransomed. And my French hostess, being now returned indoors, persuaded me to go with them to Quebec, which I did, and was conveyed unto the house of the Lord Intendant, Monsieur Le Tonant,[7] who was the chief judge and second to the governor. And I was kindly entertained by the lady and had French clothes given me with good diet and lodging and was carried thence unto the hospital where I was physicked and blooded and very courteously provided for. And sometime after my Indian master and mistress coming for me, the Lady Intendant paid a ransom for me, and I became her servant.[8] And I must speak it to the honor of the French, they were exceeding kind to me at first, even as kind as I could expect to find the English so that I wanted nothing for my bodily comfort which they could help me unto.

Here was a great and comfortable change as to my outward man in my freedom from my former hardships and hardhearted oppressors. But here began a greater snare and trouble to my soul and danger to my inward man. For the Lady, my mistress, the nuns, the priests, the friars, and the rest set upon me with all the strength of argument they could from scripture, as they interpreted it, to persuade me to turn papist, which they pressed with very much zeal, love, entreaties, and promises if I would turn

6. The Northwest Passage is not identified. It was probably a trading post on a passage between two lakes or bays in northern New England or southeastern Canada.

7. Swarton (or Mather) is confused about the identity of the intendant, the chief social, economic, and judicial officer of Canada. (The governor-general, by contrast, was primarily responsible for military and administrative matters.) Jean Bochart de Champigny, Sieur de Noroy et de Verneuil, was the intendant of New France from 1686 to 1702. "Monsieur Le Tonant" may simply be a corruption of "Monsieur L'Intendant" or it may refer to Louis-Armand de Lom d'Arce de Lahontan, a principal aide to Governor Frontenac during this period. However, Lahontan was seldom in Quebec during Swarton's captivity, and he was not married at the time. It appears, then, that Swarton was at Bochart de Champigny's house.

8. Probably Marie-Madeleine de Chaspoux, Madame de Champigny.

to them, and with many threatenings and sometimes hard usages because I did not turn to their religion. Yea, sometimes the papists, because I would not turn to them, threatened to send me to France, and there I should be burned because I would not turn to them.

Then was I comforted from that in 2 Cor. 1:8, 9, 10: "We were pressed out of measure above strength insomuch that we despaired even of life, but we had the sentence of death in ourselves that we should not trust in ourselves but in God who raises the dead, who delivered us from so great a death and doth deliver; in whom we trust that He will yet deliver us." I knew God was able to deliver me as He did Paul and as He did the three children out of the fiery furnace. And I believed He would either deliver me from them or fit me for what He called me to suffer for His sake and name. For their praying to angels they brought the history of the angel that was sent to the Virgin Mary in the first of Luke. I answered them from Rev. 19:10 and 22:9. They brought Exod. 17:11 of Israel's prevailing while Moses held up his hands. I told them we must come to God only by Christ, John 6:37, 44. For purgatory they brought Matthew 5:25. I told them to agree with God while here on earth was to agree with our adversary in the way, and if we did not, we should be cast into hell and should not come out until we paid the utmost farthing, which could never be paid. But it's bootless for me, a poor woman, to acquaint the world with what arguments I used if I could now remember them, and many of them are slipped out of my memory.

I shall proceed to relate what trials I met with in these things. I was put upon it either to stand to the religion I was brought up in and believed in my conscience to be true or to turn to another which I believed was not right. And I was kept from turning by that scripture, Matthew 10:32, 33: "Whosoever shall confess me before men, him will I confess before my Father which is in heaven, and whosoever denies me before men, him also will I deny before my Father which is in heaven." I thought that if I should deny the truth and own their religion, I should deny Christ. Yet upon their persuasions I went to see and be present at their worship sometimes but never to receive their sacrament. And once when I was at their worship that scripture, 2 Cor. 6:14 to the end, came into my mind: "What communion hath light with darkness, what concord hath Christ with Belial, what part hath he that believeth with an infidel, and what agreement hath the temple of God with idols? Wherefore come out from among them and be ye separate and touch not the unclean thing, and I will receive you, and I will be a Father unto you, and ye shall be my sons and daughters, saith the Lord Almighty." This scripture was so strong upon my spirit that I thought I was out of my way to be present at the idolatrous worship, and I resolved never to come unto it again. But when the time drew nigh that I was to go again, I was so restless that night that I could not sleep, thinking what I would say to them when they urged me to go again, and what I should do. And so it was in the morning that a Frenchwoman of my acquaintance told me if I would not be of their religion I did but mock at it to go to their worship and bid me that if I would not be of their religion I should go no more. I answered her that I would not be of their religion, and I would go no more to their worship. And accordingly I never went more, and they did not force me to it.

I have had many conflicts in my own spirit, fearing that I was not truly converted unto God in Christ and that I had no saving interest in Christ. I could not be of a false religion to please men, for it was against my conscience. And I was not fit to suffer for the true religion and for Christ. For I then feared I had no interest in Him. I was neither fit to live nor fit to die and brought once to the very pit of despair about what would become of my soul. In this time I had gotten an English Bible and other good books by the help of my fellow captives. I looked over the scripture and settled on the prayer of Jonah and those words, "I said I am cast out of Thy sight, yet will I look again towards Thy holy temple." I resolved I would do as Jonah did. And in the meditation upon this scripture the Lord was pleased by His Spirit to come into my soul and so fill me with ravishing comfort that I cannot express it.

Then came to mind the history of the transfiguring of Christ and Peter's saying, Matthew 17:4, "Lord, it is good for us to be here!" I thought it was good for me to be here, and I was so full of comfort and joy I even wished I could be so always and never sleep or else die in that rapture of joy and never live to sin any more against the Lord. Now I thought God was my God, and my sins were pardoned in Christ, and now I could suffer for Christ, yea, die for Christ, or do anything for Him. My sins had been a burden to me. I desired to see all my sins and to repent of them all with all my heart and of that sin which had been especially a burden to me, namely, that I left the public worship and ordinances of God to go live in a remote place without the public ministry, depriving ourselves and our children of so great a benefit for our souls, and all this for worldly advantages. I found a heart to repent of them all and to lay hold of the blood of Christ to cleanse me from them all.

I found much comfort while I was among the French by the opportunities I had sometimes to read the scriptures and other good books and pray to the Lord in secret and the conference that some of us captives had together about things of God and prayer together sometimes, especially with one that was in the same house with me, Margaret Stilson.[9] Then was the word of God precious to us, and they that feared the Lord spake one to another of it as we had opportunity. And Col. Tyng[10] and Mr. Alden,[11] as they were permitted, did speak to us to confirm and strengthen us in the ways of the Lord. At length the French debarred our coming together for religious conference or other duties. And word was sent us by Mr. Alden that this was one kind of persecution that we must suffer for Christ.

These are some of the scriptures which have been my support and comfort in the affliction of my captivity among the papists. That of Ezek. 16:6–8 I applied unto myself, and I desired to enter into covenant with God and to be His, and I prayed to the Lord and hoped the Lord would return me to my country again [and] that I might enter into covenant with Him among His people and enjoy communion with Him in His churches and public ordinances. Which prayers the Lord hath now heard and graciously answered, praised be His name! The Lord enable me to live suitably to His mercy and to those public and precious privileges which I now enjoy. So, that in Ezek. 11:16, 17 was a great comfort unto me in my captivity, "Although I have cast them far off among the heathen, yet will I be a little sanctuary to them. I will gather you from the people where you have been scattered." I found that God was a little sanctuary to me there and hoped that the Lord would bring me unto the country from whence I had been scattered. And the Lord hath heard the prayer of the destitute and not despised my prayer but granted me the desire of my soul in bringing me to His house and my relations again. I often thought on the history of the man born blind of whom Christ, when His disciples asked whether this man had sinned or his parents, answered [that] neither this

9. Margaret Gould Stilson, wife of James Stilson of Marblehead. He was killed at or near Pemaquid in 1689; she was redeemed in 1695.

10. Edward Tyng, a veteran of King Philip's War, was governor of Annapolis, Nova Scotia, in 1691. The French captured him aboard John Alden's ship (see below), kept him in Quebec for a time, and then carried him prisoner to France where he died in 1694.

11. This John Alden was the grandson of the Pilgrim father. He was captured, along with his father, Capt. John Alden (c. 1623–1702), and held in Quebec while his father was freed to carry messages to Boston. The father commanded a sloop in Massachusetts service and was active throughout the late seventeenth century in efforts to redeem English captives. The two John Aldens were seized by a French frigate in 1691, along with Edward Tyng and John Nelson. John Alden the younger was taken to France along with Tyng and later released; his father was soon after accused of witchcraft in the Salem hysteria of 1692 and incarcerated in the Boston jail for fifteen weeks. He eventually escaped and remained in hiding until the frenzy dissipated.

man nor his parents, but this was that the works of God might be made manifest in him. So, though I had deserved all this, yet I knew not but one reason of God's bringing all these afflictions and miseries upon me and then enabling me to bear them was that the works of God might be made manifest. And in my great distress I was revived by that in Psalms 118:17, 18, "I shall not die but live and declare the works of the Lord. The Lord hath chastened me sore, but He hath not given me over to death."

I had very often a secret persuasion that I should live to declare the works of the Lord. And 2 Chron. 6: 36, 37, 38, 39 was a precious scripture to me in the day of evil. We have read over and prayed over this scripture together and talked together of this scripture, Margaret and I, how the Lord had promised though they were scattered for their sins, yet there should be a return if they did bethink themselves and turn and pray. So we did bethink ourselves in the land where we were carried captive, did turn, did pray, and endeavor to return to God with all our hearts. And, as they were to pray towards the temple, I took it that I should pray towards Christ and accordingly did so and hoped the Lord would hear, and He hath heard from heaven, His dwelling-place, my prayer and supplication and maintained my cause and not rejected me but returned me. And oh, how affectionate was my reading of the 84th Psalm in this condition!

The means of my deliverance were by reason of letters that had passed between the governments of New England and of Canada. Mr. Cary was sent with a vessel to fetch captives from Quebec,[12] and when he came, I, among others with my youngest son [Jasper], had our liberty to come away. And by God's blessing upon us we arrived in safety at Boston in November 1695, our desired haven. And I desire to praise the Lord for His goodness and for His wonderful works to me. Yet still I have left behind two children, a daughter [Mary] of twenty years old at Montreal whom I had not seen in two years before I came away and a son [John] of nineteen years old whom I never saw since we parted the next morning after we were taken.[13] I earnestly request the prayers of my Christian friends that the Lord will deliver them.

What shall I render to the Lord for all His benefits?

---

12. In 1695 Matthew Carey, in *Tryal,* conveyed twenty-two English captives from Quebec to Boston. Twice that many remained in captivity.

13. Detained in Canada when her mother was redeemed in 1695, Mary Swarton underwent instruction in the Catholic faith and later married Jean Lahey, an Irish Canadian. She remained in the vicinity of Montreal for the rest of her life. John Swarton's fate is unknown.

SIX

Hannah Dustan's dramatic escape from captivity, portrayed by the anonymous illustrator of Robert B. Caverly's *Heroism of Hannah Duston* (Boston, 1874). Courtesy of Columbia University Libraries.

· COTTON MATHER ·
"A NARRATIVE OF HANNAH DUSTAN'S NOTABLE DELIVERANCE FROM CAPTIVITY"

In the waning days of King William's War a band of Indians struck at Haverhill, Massachusetts. Apparently the town was ill-prepared, judging from the subsequent charge by the Massachusetts Council that the official responsible for Haverhill's defense "Did not (as he ought): when he had notice of the enemies approach take Care to Draw [the English] into Garrison." Consequently the Indians met little opposition to their early morning assault on March 15, 1697. They burned several houses, killed twenty-seven inhabitants, and carried off thirteen survivors, including Hannah Emerson Dustan (1657–c. 1736).

Despite the brevity of her story, Hannah Dustan's is among the most famous. Her bold and bloody escape earned her legendary honors in New England's annals and, more recently, a place in *Notable American Women* (Cambridge, Mass., 1971), where she is listed among the "heroines." And as Cotton Mather noted at the end of his version of her captivity, she and her companions gained material honors too: a £50 reward from the Massachusetts government and a "very generous token of his favor" from Governor Francis Nicholson of Maryland. Dustan's adventure apparently had few ill effects on her. In 1698 she gave birth to her thirteenth child, and she lived to be nearly eighty yers old.

Cotton Mather first published Dustan's "Narrative of a Notable Deliverance from Captivity" as an appendix to *Humiliations Followed with Deliverances* (Boston, 1697). Ever alert for opportunities to make a theological point, Mather added "an improvement of the foregoing narrative" to warn readers that "a slavery to *devils,* to be in their hands, is worse than to be in the hands of Indians! I beseech you then, by the mercies of God, that you present yourselves unto the Lord Jesus Christ [and] become the sincere servants of that Lord." Mather expanded Dustan's story slightly in *Decennium Luctuosum* (Boston, 1699) where he entitled it "A Notable Exploit; wherein Dux Faemina Facti," and in *Magnalia Christi Americana* (London, 1702), Bk. VII, 90–91. The following text is based on Mather's last version of Dustan's escapade. Mather's editorial hand is evident throughout.

On March 15, 1697, the savages made a descent upon the skirts of Haverhill, murdering and captiving about thirty-nine persons and burning about half a dozen houses. In this broil, one Hannah Dustan, having lain-in about a week, attended with her nurse, Mary Neff, a widow,[1] a body of terrible Indians drew near unto the house where she lay with designs to carry on the bloody devastations. Her husband[2] hastened from his employments abroad unto the relief of his distressed family, and, first bidding seven of his eight children (which were from two to seventeen years of age) to get away as fast as they could unto some garrison in the town, he went in to inform his wife of the horrible distress come upon them. Ere she could get up, the fierce Indians were got so near that utterly despairing to do her any service he ran out after his children, resolving that on the horse which he had with him he would ride away with that which he should in this extremity find his affections to pitch most upon and leave the rest unto the care of the Divine Providence. He overtook his children about forty rod from his door. But then such was the agony of his parental affections that he found it impossible for him to distinguish any one of them from the rest, wherefore he took up a courageous resolution to live and die with them all. A party of Indians came up with him and now, though they fired at him and he fired at them, yet he manfully kept at the rear of his little army of unarmed children while they marched off with the pace of a child of five years old until, by the singular providence of God, he arrived safe with them all unto a place of safety about a mile or two from his house.

But his house must in the meantime have more dismal tragedies acted at it. The nurse, trying to escape with the newborn infant, fell into the hands of the formidable savages, and those furious tawnies, coming into the house, bid poor Dustan to rise immediately. Full of astonishment she did so, and, sitting down in the chimney with an heart full of most fearful ex-

1. Mary Corliss Neff was about fifty years old and a local midwife. Her husband William had been killed in the Indian wars on the Maine frontier.

2. Thomas Dustan. The surname is now commonly spelled Dustin; in the colonial period the second vowel was interchangeably *i, o,* or *a.* Thomas used *a* in a petition to the General Court of Massachusetts, his only recorded signature. He was a farmer and bricklayer.

pectation, she saw the raging dragons rifle all that they could carry away and set the house on fire. About nineteen or twenty Indians now led these away with about half a score other English captives, but ere they had gone many steps they dashed out the brains of the infant against a tree. And several of the other captives, as they began to tire in their sad journey, were soon sent unto their long home. The savages would presently bury their hatchets in their brains and leave their carcasses on the ground for birds and beasts to feed upon. However, Dustan (with her nurse), notwithstanding her present condition, traveled that night about a dozen miles and then kept up with their new masters in a long travel of an hundred and fifty miles, more or less, within a few days ensuing without any sensible damage in their health from the hardships of their travel, their lodging, their diet, and their many other difficulties. These two poor women were now in the hands of those whose tender mercies are cruelties, but the good God who hath all hearts in His own hands, heard the sighs of these prisoners and gave them to find unexpected favor from the master who laid claim unto them.

That Indian family consisted of twelve persons: two stout men, three women, and seven children; and for the shame of many an English family that has the character of prayerless upon it, I must now publish what these poor women assure me. 'Tis this: in obedience to the instructions which the French have given them, they would have prayers in their family no less than thrice every day, in the morning, at noon, and in the evening, nor would they ordinarily let their children eat or sleep without first saying their prayers. Indeed, these idolaters were—like the rest of their whiter brethren—persecutors and would not endure that these poor women should retire to their English prayers if they could hinder them. Nevertheless, the poor women had nothing but fervent prayers to make their lives comfortable or tolerable, and by being daily sent out upon business, they had opportunities together and asunder to do like another Hannah in pouring out their souls before the Lord. Nor did their praying friends among ourselves forbear to pour out supplications for them. Now they could not observe it without some wonder that their Indian master sometimes when he saw them dejected would say unto them, "What need you trouble yourself? If your God will have you delivered, you shall be so." And it seems our God would have it so to be.

This Indian family was now traveling with these two captive women (and an English youth taken from Worcester a year and a half before)[3]

3. Samuel Lenorson (or Leonardson) had been captured near Lake Quinsigamond in Worcester, Massachusetts, in September 1695.

unto a rendezvous of savages which they call a town somewhere beyond Penacook,[4] and they still told these poor women that when they came to this town they must be stripped and scourged and run the gauntlet through the whole army of Indians. They said this was the fashion when the captives first came to a town, and they derided some of the faint-hearted English which they said fainted and swooned away under the torments of this discipline.[5] But on April 30, while they were yet it may be about an hundred and fifty miles from the Indian town, a little before break of day when the whole crew was in a dead sleep (Reader, see if it prove not so!) one of these women took up a resolution to imitate the action of Jael upon Sisera [Judges 4], and, being where she had not her own life secured by any law unto her, she thought she was not forbidden by any law to take away the life of the murderers by whom her child had been butchered. She heartened the nurse and the youth to assist her in this enterprise, and they all furnishing themselves with hatchets for the purpose, they struck such home-blows upon the heads of their sleeping oppressors that ere they could any of them struggle into any effectual resistance at the feet of those poor prisoners, "They bowed, they fell, they lay down; at their feet they bowed, they fell where they bowed; there they fell down dead" [Judges 5:27].

Only one squaw escaped, sorely wounded, from them in the dark, and one boy whom they reserved asleep, intending to bring him away with them, [who] suddenly waked and scuttled away from this desolation. But cutting off the scalps of the ten wretches, they came off and received fifty pounds from the General Assembly of the province as a recompense of their action, besides which they received many presents of congratulation from their more private friends. But none gave them a greater taste of bounty than Colonel [Francis] Nicholson, the governor of Maryland, who, hearing of their action, sent them a very generous token of his favor.[6]

---

4. Near present-day Concord, New Hampshire.

5. Running captives through a gauntlet was usual among many northeastern tribes. See James Axtell, "The White Indians of Colonial America," *William and Mary Quarterly*, 3rd ser., 32 (1975), 55–88, especially 69–72.

6. The prominent Massachusetts judge and diarist Samuel Sewall recorded on April 29 that the "day is signalised by the Atchievment of Hannah Dustun, Mary Neff, and Samuel Lennerson; who kill'd Two men, their Masters, and two women and 6. others, and have brought in Ten Scalps." M. Halsey Thomas, ed., *The Diary of Samuel Sewall, 1674–1729*, 2 vols. (New York, 1973), I, 372.

164

Illustrations from the Reverend Titus Strong's *The Deerfield Captive, an Indian Story* (Greenfield, Mass., 1832), a retelling of John Williams's narrative intended for Sunday schools. Courtesy of the American Antiquarian Society.

·JOHN WILLIAMS·
"THE REDEEMED CAPTIVE
RETURNING TO ZION"

John Williams (1664–1729) was a thorough New Englander. Educated at Roxbury (Massachusetts) Latin School and Harvard College, he taught for a while in neighboring Dorchester, then in 1686 settled in Deerfield as the Congregational minister. Williams's first wife, Eunice, was a member of New England's most prestigious clan: daughter of Eleazar Mather of Northampton, granddaughter of Richard Mather of Dorchester, niece of Increase Mather of Boston (president of Harvard College during Williams's student days), and cousin of Cotton Mather. Not surprisingly, John Williams's narrative is heavily laced with Puritan piety.

After a brief respite from border warfare between 1697 (the Treaty of Ryswick) and 1702 (the outbreak of Queen Anne's War—Europe's War of the Spanish Succession), French and Indian raiding parties again harassed the New England frontier. Despite Reverend Williams's pleas to the Massachusetts government to strengthen Deerfield, it remained largely undefended, and in late February 1704 it fell to an enemy force almost as large as the town's meager population. Many of the inhabitants were killed outright, including two of Williams's sons; the survivors were force-marched to Canada, an ordeal that proved fatal to Mrs. Williams.

In captivity, Williams shouldered a double burden: he sought, like any parent, to comfort his surviving children and to secure their freedom along with his own. At the same time, Williams tried to satisfy the spiritual needs of his congregation, most of it scattered among eastern Canada's Indian and French settlements. Williams especially feared that some of his flock would succumb to Catholic pressures and desert their Puritan heritage. Accordingly, his narrative abounds with theological debate. More than any surviving captivity account, *The Redeemed Captive* reveals the battle for the mind and heart that so often followed close upon the military conflict. Williams also reflects the gulf between New England and New France: as Europeans, the colonists of both areas had much in common, especially an abhorrence of falling completely under Indian control, but as wartime enemies and religious rivals—in an age of intense loyalties and pervasive intolerance—Puritan and Canadian were worlds apart.

In November 1706, Cotton Mather recorded in his diary that "it pleased the Lord, to grant a safe and quick Return, (an Harvest of many Prayers,) unto near threescore more of our Captives, and among the rest, unto the pious and worthy Minister, Mr. *Williams*, after he had spent almost three Years in a sad Captivity." On December 5, Williams preached from Mather's pulpit "unto a great Auditory"; the sermon was subsequently published as an addendum to Williams's story of his captivity. Although Mather hints that he may have had a hand in both literary endeavors, Williams is justifiably credited with sole authorship. But that the two clergymen discussed the captivity-redemption experience and how best to turn it to God's glory is also certain, and Mather may have prompted the Deerfield minister to write about his ordeal. Mather undoubtedly concurred in the last line of Williams's sermon: "God accounts forgetting of *Mercies,* a forgetting of *Himself.*"

Encouraged by a compensation of forty pounds from the Massachusetts General Court, Williams soon returned to Deerfield, where his grateful parishioners built him a new house. He subsequently married his first wife's cousin, Abigail Allen Bissell (who bore him five more children), much to the dismay of Judge Samuel Sewall who interpreted the Bible as forbidding such unions. Williams continued his involvement in the Anglo-French struggle. In 1711 he served as chaplain of a New England expedition against Port Royal and later joined a delegation to Canada for the release of English prisoners. To his profound regret he was unable to redeem his daughter Eunice.

The Redeemed Captive, Returning to Zion. A Faithful History of Remarkable Occurences in the Captivity and the Deliverance of Mr. John Williams, Minister of the Gospel first appeared in 1707, printed in Boston by Bartholemew Green. The text used here is a slightly modified version of Edward W. Clark's edition of Williams's *Redeemed Captive,* published in 1976 by the University of Massachusetts Press and reprinted here with its permission. Readers who seek more information about Williams and his narrative than is available in this anthology should consult the University of Massachusetts Press edition, which has an introductory essay and extensive annotations.

The Dedication
TO HIS EXCELLENCY,
JOSEPH DUDLEY, ESQ.
Captain-General and Governor-in-Chief,
in and over her Majesty's Province of the
Massachusetts Bay in New England, etc.[1]

SIR,

It was a satirical answer, and deeply reproachful to mankind, which the Philosopher gave to that question, "What soonest grows old?" [He] replied, "Thanks." The reproach of it would not be so sensible, were there not sensible demonstrations of the truth of it in those that wear the character of the ingenuous. Such as are at first surprised at and seem to have no common relish of divine goodness, yet too soon lose the impression: "they sang God's praise, but soon forgot His works." That it should be thus with respect to our benefactors on earth is contrary to the ingenuity of human nature; but, that our grateful resentments of the signal favors of heaven should soon be worn off by time is to the last degree criminal and unpardonable.

It would be unaccountable stupidity in me not to maintain the most lively and awful sense of divine rebukes which the most holy God has seen meet in spotless sovereignty to dispense to me, my family and people in delivering us into the hands of those that hated us, who led us into a strange land: "my soul has these still in remembrance and is humbled in me;" however, God has given us plentiful occasion to sing of mercy as well as judgment. The wonders of divine mercy, which we have seen in the land of our captivity and deliverance therefrom, cannot be forgotten without incurring the guilt of the blackest ingratitude.

To preserve the memory of these, it has been thought advisable to publish a short account of some of those signal appearances of divine power and goodness for hoping it may serve to excite the praise, faith, and

---

1. Joseph Dudley (1647–1720) was a son of Thomas Dudley, second governor of the Massachusetts Bay Colony. Joseph graduated from Harvard in 1665 and served in both the lower and upper houses of the colonial legislature; in the mid-1680s he was acting governor. His cooperation with royal authorities during the Andros regime (1686–1689) put him at odds with many of his contemporaries, and during his own governorship (1702–1715) Dudley was increasingly unpopular. Williams, of course, was grateful for Dudley's help in redeeming New England captives.

hope of all that love God, and may peculiarly serve to cherish a grateful spirit, and to render the impressions of God's mighty works indelible on my heart, and on those that with me have seen the wonders of the Lord and tasted of His salvation, that we may not fall under that heavy charge made against Israel of old, Psalms 78:11, 42: "They forgot His works and the wonders He showed them. They remembered not His hand, nor the day that He delivered them from the enemy."

And I cannot, Sir, but think it most agreeable to my duty to God our supreme redeemer, to mention your Excellency's name with honor since heaven has honored you as the prime instrument in returning our captivity. Sure I am [that] the laws of justice and gratitude, which are the laws of God, do challenge from us the most public acknowledgments of your uncommon sympathy with us, your children, in our bonds expressed in all endearing methods of parental care and tenderness. All your people are cherished under your wings, happy in your government, and are obliged to bless God for you. And among your people those that are immediately exposed to the outrages of the enemy have peculiarly felt refreshment from the benign influences of your wise and tender conduct and are under the most sensible engagements to acknowledge your Excellency, under God, as the breath of their nostrils.

Your uncommon sagacity and prudence in contriving to loose the bonds of your captived children, your unwearied vigor and application in pursuing them to work our deliverance, can never be enough praised. It is most notorious that nothing was thought too difficult by you to effect this design in that you readily sent your own son, Mr. William Dudley, to undergo the hazards and hardships of a tedious voyage that this affair might be transacted with success, which must not be forgotten, as an expression of your great solicitude and zeal to recover us from the tyranny and oppression of our captivity.[2]

I doubt not but that the God, whom herein you have served, will remember and gloriously reward you, and may heaven long preserve you at our helm, a blessing so necessary for the tranquility of this province in this dark and tempestuous season; may the best of blessings from the Father of

2. In 1705 the governor's son William led a Massachusetts delegation to Quebec to arrange the return of English captives. It was generally successful, although a substantial number of children and a few adults remained in Canada. Dudley's achievement was the culmination of negotiations launched in December 1704 by Ensign John Sheldon of Deerfield. On Sheldon's persistent efforts to redeem the captives, including some of his own kin, see George Sheldon, *A History of Deerfield, Massachusetts . . . with a Special Study of the Indian Wars in the Connecticut Valley*, 2 vols. (Deerfield, 1895), I, 324–342.

Lights be showered down upon your person, family, and government, which shall be the prayer of,

Your Excellency's
most humble, obedient,
and dutiful servant,
John Williams

The Redeemed Captive Returning to Zion

The history I am going to write proves that days of fasting and prayer, without reformation, will not avail to turn away the anger of God from a professing people. And yet witnesseth how very advantageous gracious supplications are to prepare particular Christians patiently to suffer the will of God in very trying public calamities! For some of us, moved with fear, set apart a day of prayer to ask of God, either to spare and save us from the hands of our enemies or to prepare us to sanctify and honor Him in what way soever He should come forth towards us. The places of Scripture from whence we were entertained were Gen. 32:10-11: "I am not worthy of least of all the mercies and of all the truth which thou hast showed unto thy servant. Deliver me, I pray thee, from the hand of my brother, from the hand of Esau, for I fear him, lest he will come and smite me and the mother with the children" (in the forenoon). And Gen. 32:26: "And he said, 'Let me go, for the day breaketh'; and he said, 'I will not let thee go, except thou bless me' " (in the afternoon). From which we were called upon to spread the causes of fear relating to our own selves or families before God; as also how it becomes us with an undeniable importunity to be following God with earnest prayers for His blessing in every condition. And it is very observable how God ordered our prayers in a peculiar manner to be going up to Him to prepare us with a right Christian spirit to undergo and endure suffering trials.

Not long after, the holy and righteous God brought us under great trials as to our persons and families which put us under a necessity of spreading before Him in a wilderness the distressing dangers and calamities of our relations; yea, that called on us notwithstanding seeming present frowns, to resolve by His grace not to be sent away without a blessing. Jacob in wrestling has the hollow of his thigh put out of joint, and it is said to him, "Let me go"; yet he is rather animated to an heroical Christian resolution to continue earnest for the blessing than discouraged from asking.[3]

3. Genesis 32:24-28.

On the twenty-ninth of February, 1703/4, not long before break of day, the enemy came in like a flood upon us, our watch being unfaithful: an evil, whose awful effects in a surprisal of our fort, should bespeak all watchmen to avoid, as they would not bring the charge of blood upon themselves. They came to my house in the beginning of the onset and, by their violent endeavors to break open doors and windows with axes and hatchets, awakened me out of sleep; on which I leaped out of bed, and running toward the door, perceived the enemy making their entrance into the house. I called to awaken two soldiers in the chamber and returned towards my bedside for my arms. The enemy immediately brake into the room, I judge to the number of twenty, with painted faces and hideous acclamations. I reached up my hands to the bed tester for my pistol, uttering a short petition to God for everlasting mercies for me and mine on the account of the merits of our Glorified Redeemer, expecting a present passage through the Valley of the Shadow of Death, saying in myself as Isaiah 38:10–11: "I said in the cutting off my days, 'I shall go to the gates of the grave. I am deprived of the residue of my years.' I said, 'I shall not see the Lord, even the Lord, in the land of the living. I shall behold man no more with the inhabitants of the world.'" Taking down my pistol, I cocked it and put it to the breast of the first Indian who came up, but my pistol missing fire, I was seized by three Indians who disarmed me and bound me naked, as I was in my shirt, and so I stood for near the space of an hour. Binding me, they told me they would carry me to Quebeck. My pistol missing fire was an occasion of my life's being preserved, since which I have also found it profitable to be crossed in my own will. The judgment of God did not long slumber against one of the three which took me, who was a captain, for by sunrising he received a mortal shot from my next neighbor's house, who opposed so great a number of French and Indians as three hundred and yet were no more than seven men in an ungarrisoned house.[4]

I cannot relate the distressing care I had for my dear wife, who had lain-in but a few weeks before, and for my poor children, family, and Christian neighbors. The enemy fell to rifling the house and entered in great numbers into every room of the house. I begged of God to remember mercy in the midst of judgment, that He would so far restrain their

4. Williams may have exaggerated the number of assailants against the nearby home of Benoni Stebbins, but surely the settlers' plight was precarious. For details of the attack see Francis Parkman, *A Half-Century of Conflict*, New Library Edition, 2 vols. (Boston, 1903), I, 62–64.

wrath as to prevent their murdering of us, that we might have grace to glorify His name, whether in life or death, and, as I was able, committed our state to God. The enemies who entered the house were all of them Indians and Macquas,[5] insulted over me awhile, holding up hatchets over my head threatening to burn all I had. But yet God beyond expectation made us in a great measure to be pitied, for though some were so cruel and barbarous as to take and carry to the door two of my children and murder them, as also a Negro woman,[6] yet they gave me liberty to put on my clothes, keeping me bound with a cord on one arm, till I put on my clothes to the other, and then changing my cord, they let me dress myself and then pinioned me again. [They] gave liberty to my dear wife to dress herself and our children.

About sun an hour high we were all carried out of the house for a march and saw many of the houses of my neighbors in flames, perceiving the whole fort, one house excepted, to be taken. Who can tell what sorrows pierced our souls when we saw ourselves carried away from God's sanctuary to go into a strange land exposed to so many trials, the journey being at least three hundred miles we were to travel, the snow up to the knees, and we never inured to such hardships and fatigues, the place we were to be carried to a popish country.

Upon my parting from the town, they fired my house and barn. We were carried over the [Deerfield] River to the foot of the mountain, about a mile from my house, where we found a great number of our Christian neighbors, men, women, and children, to the number of an hundred, nineteen of which were afterward murdered by the way and two starved to death near Cowass[7] in a time of great scarcity or famine the savages underwent there. When we came to the foot of our mountain, they took away our shoes and gave us, in the room of them, Indian shoes[8] to prepare us for our travel. Whilst we were there, the English beat out a company that remained in the town and pursued them to the river, killing and wounding many of them, but the body of the army, being alarmed, they repulsed those few English that pursued them.

I am not able to give you an account of the number of the enemy slain,

5. Caughnawaga (Christian Mohawk) Indians from the Montreal area. Williams called the Mohawks "Macquas," as did many of his contemporaries.

6. The murdered members of Williams's household were six-year-old John Williams, Jr., six-week-old Jerusha Williams, and Parthena, a slave woman.

7. Near present-day Newbury, Vermont.

8. Moccasins.

but I observed after this fight no great insulting mirth as I expected and saw many wounded persons, and for several days together they buried [several] of their party and one of chief note among the Macquas. The governor of Canada[9] told me his army had that success with the loss but of eleven men, three Frenchmen, one of which was the lieutenant of the army, five Macquas, and three Indians; but after my arrival at Quebeck I spake with an Englishman who was taken the last war and married there and of their religion, who told me they lost above forty and that many were wounded. I replied the governor of Canada said they lost but eleven men. He answered, " 'Tis true that there were but eleven killed outright at the taking of the fort, but that many others were wounded, among who was the ensign of the French." But, said he, "They had a fight in the meadow, and that in both engagements they lost more than forty. Some of the soldiers, both French and Indians then present, told me so," said he, adding that, "The French always endeavor to conceal the number of their slain."

AFTER THIS we went up the mountain and saw the smoke of the fires in the town and beheld the awful desolations of our town, and, before we marched any farther, they killed a sucking child of the English. There were slain by the enemy of the inhabitants of our town to the number of thirty-eight besides nine of the neighboring towns. We traveled not far the first day; God made the heathen so to pity our children that, though they had several wounded persons of their own to carry upon their shoulders for thirty miles before they came to the river, yet they carried our children, incapable of traveling, upon their shoulders and in their arms.

When we came to our lodging-place the first night,[10] they dug away the snow and made some wigwams, cut down some of the small branches of spruce trees to lie down on, and gave the prisoners somewhat to eat, but we had but little appetite. I was pinioned and bound down that night, and so I was every night whilst I was with the army. Some of the enemy who brought drink with them from the town fell to drinking, and in their drunken fit they killed my Negro man,[11] the only dead person I either saw at the town or on the way. In the night an Englishman made his escape; in the morning I was called for and ordered by the general to tell the English

9. For a sketch of Phillippe de Rigaud de Vaudreuil (c. 1643–1725)—musketeer, "mayor" of Montreal, and later, governor of New France—see *Dictionary of Canadian Biography,* ed. George W. Brown et al., II (Toronto, 1969), 565–574.

10. Probably near present-day Greenfield, Massachusetts.

11. Frank, husband of Parthena. The surviving records give no last name.

that, if any more made their escape, they would burn the rest of the prisoners.[12]

He that took me was unwilling to let me speak with any of the prisoners as we marched; but on the morning of the second day, he being appointed to guard the rear, I was put into the hands of my other master who permitted me to speak to my wife when I overtook her and to walk with her to help her in her journey. On the way we discoursed of the happiness of them who had a right to an house not made with hands, eternal in the heavens and God for a father and a friend; as also that it was our reasonable duty quietly to submit to the will of God and to say the will of the Lord be done. My wife told me her strength of body began to fail and that I must expect to part with her, saying she hoped God would preserve my life and the lives of some, if not all of our children with us, and commended to me, under God, the care of them.[13] She never spake any discontented word as to what had befallen us, but with suitable expressions justified God in what had befallen us.

We soon made an halt in which time my chief surviving master[14] came up, upon which I was put upon marching with the foremost, and so made to take my last farewell of my dear wife, the desire of my eyes and companion in many mercies and afflictions. Upon our separation from each other we asked, for each other, grace sufficient for what God should call us to. After our being parted from one another, she spent the few remaining minutes of her stay in reading the holy Scriptures, which she was wont personally every day to delight her soul in reading, praying, meditating of and over, by herself in her closet, over and above what she heard out of them in our family worship.

I was made to wade over a small river and so were all the English, the water above knee-deep, the stream very swift; and after that to travel up a small montain; my strength was almost spent before I came to the top of it. No sooner had I overcome the difficulty of that ascent, but I was per-

12. Twenty-three-year-old John Alexander escaped. The "general" of the French and Indian expedition was Jean Baptiste Hertel de Rouville, who had earlier led raids along the New Hampshire and Maine frontiers. See *Dictionary of Canadian Biography*, II, 284–286 (which errs concerning several details of the raid on Deerfield).

13. Eleazar, the eldest of the Williamses' eight children was not in Deerfield when the Indians attacked. As John Williams states, two of his children were killed during the assault; captured along with their parents were Samuel (fifteen), Esther (thirteen), Stephen (ten), Eunice (seven), and Warham (four).

14. The three Indians whom Williams described as having disarmed and bound him all claimed him as their prize. One of them, as Williams relates, was killed before the retreat began.

mitted to sit down and be unburdened of my pack. I sat pitying those who were behind and entreated my master to let me go down and help up my wife, but he refused and would not let me stir from him. I asked each of the prisoners as they passed by me after her, and heard that in passing through the abovesaid river, she fell down and was plunged over head and ears in the water; after which she traveled not far, for at the foot of this mountain the cruel and bloodthirsty savage who took her, slew her with his hatchet at one stroke, the tidings of which were very awful; and yet such was the hardheartedness of the adversary that my tears were reckoned to me as a reproach.

My loss and the loss of my children was great; our hearts were so filled with sorrow that nothing but the comfortable hopes of her being taken away in mercy, to herself, from the evils we were to see, feel, and suffer under (and joined to the assembly of the spirits of just men made perfect, to rest in peace and joy unspeakable, and full of glory, and the good pleasure of God thus to exercise us) could have kept us from sinking under at that time. That Scripture, Job 1:21, "Naked came I out of my mother's womb, and naked shall I return thither. The Lord gave and the Lord hath taken away, blessed be the name of the Lord," was brought to my mind and from it that an afflicting God was to be glorified, with some other places of Scripture to persuade to a patient bearing [of] my afflictions.

We were again called upon to march with a far heavier burden on my spirits than on my back; I begged of God to overrule in His providence that the corpse of one so dear to me, and of one whose spirit He had taken to dwell with Him in glory, might meet with a Christian burial and not be left for meat to the fowls of the air and beasts of the earth, a mercy that God graciously vouchsafed to grant. For God put it into the hearts of my neighbors to come out as far as she lay to take up her corpse, recarry it to the town, and decently to bury it soon after. In our march they killed another sucking infant of one of my neighbors and before night a girl of about eleven years of age. I was made to mourn at the consideration of my flock's being so far a flock of slaughter, many being slain in town and so many murdered in so few miles from the town, and from fears what we must yet expect from such who delightfully imbrued their hands in the blood of so many of His people.

When we came to our lodging-place,[15] an Indian captain from the Eastward spake to my master about killing of me and taking off my scalp. I lifted up my heart to God to implore His grace and mercy in such a time

15. Probably at present-day Brattleboro, Vermont.

of need. And afterwards I told my master if he intended to kill me I desired he would let me know of it, assuring him that my death after a promise of quarter would bring the guilt of blood upon him. He told me he would not kill me. We lay down and slept, for God sustained and kept us.

In the morning we were all called before the chief sachems of the Macquas and Indians that a more equal distribution might be made of the prisoners among them; at my going from the wigwam, my best clothing was taken from me. As I came nigh the place appointed, some of the captives met me and told me they thought the enemies were going to burn some of us for they had peeled off the bark from several trees and acted very strangely. To whom I replied they could act nothing against us but as they were permitted of God, and I was persuaded He would prevent such severities. When we came to the wigwam appointed, several of the captives were taken from their former masters and put into the hands of others, but I was sent again to my two masters who brought me from my house.

In our fourth day's march the enemy killed another of my neighbors, who being nigh the time of travail, was wearied with her journey. When we came to the great river,[16] the enemy took sleighs to draw their wounded, several of our children, and their packs, and marched a great pace. I traveled many hours in water up to the ankles. Near night I was very lame, having before my travel wronged my ankle bone and sinews; I thought, so did others, that I should not be able to hold out to travel far. I lifted up my heart to God (my only refuge) to remove my lameness and carry me through with my children and neighbors if He judged it best; however, I desired God would be with me in my great change if He called me by such a death to glorify Him, and that He would take care of my children and neighbors and bless them. And within a little space of time I was well of my lameness, to the joy of my children and neighbors who saw so great an alteration in my traveling.

On the Saturday the journey was long and tedious; we traveled with such speed that four women were tired and then slain by them who led them captive. On the Sabbath day[17] we rested, and I was permitted to pray and preach to the captives. The place of Scripture spoken from was Lam. 1:18: "The Lord is righteous, for I have rebelled against his commandment. Hear, I pray you, all people, and behold my sorrow. My virgins and my young men are gone into captivity." The enemy, who said to

16. Connecticut River.
17. Sunday, March 5, 1704/5 (O.S.). The captives were then at a tributary of the Connecticut River about twenty-five miles north of Brattleboro. The tributary was was subsequently named the Williams River.

us, "Sing us one of Zion's songs," were ready some of them to upbraid us because our singing was not so loud as theirs. When the Macquas and Indians were chief in power, we had this revival in our bondage to join together in the worship of God and encourage one another to a patient bearing of the indignation of the Lord till He should plead our cause. When we arrived to New France, we were forbidden praying one with another or joining together in the service of God.

The next day, soon after we marched, we had an alarm on which many of the English were bound; I was then near the front and my masters not with me so I was not bound. This alarm was occasioned by some Indians shooting at geese that flew over them that put them into a considerable consternation and fright, but, after they came to understand they were not pursued by the English, they boasted that the English would not come out after them as they had boasted before we began our journey in the morning. They killed this day two women who were so faint they could not travel.

The next day in the morning before we traveled, one Mary Brooks, a pious young woman, came to the wigwam where I was and told me she desired to bless God who had inclined the heart of her master to let her come to take her farewell of me. Said she, "By my falls on the ice yesterday I wronged myself, causing an abortion this night so that I am not able to travel far. I know they will kill me today, but," says she, "God has (praised be His name) by His spirit with His word strengthened me to my last encounter with death." And [she] mentioned to me some places of Scripture so seasonably sent in for her support. "And," says she, "I am not afraid of death; I can, through the grace of God, cheerfully submit to the will of God. Pray for me," said she at parting, "that God would take me to Himself." Accordingly she was killed that day. I mentioned it to the end I may stir up all in their young days to improve the death of Christ by faith to a giving them a holy boldness in the day of death.

The next day we were made to scatter one from another into smaller companies, and one of my children [was] carried away with Indians belonging to the Eastern parts.[18] At night my master came to me with my pistol in his hand, and put it to my breast, and said, "Now I will kill you, for," said he, "at your house you would have killed me with it if you could." But by the grace of God I was not much daunted, and whatever his intention might be, God prevented my death.

18. The Abenaki Indians. The parties separated at present-day White River Junction, Vermont.

The next day I was again permitted to pray with that company of captives with me, and we allowed to sing a Psalm together. After which I was taken from all the company of the English, excepting two children of my neighbors, one of which, a girl of four years of age, was killed by her Macqua master the next morning, the snow being so deep when we left the river that he could not carry the child and his pack too.

When the Sabbath came, one Indian stayed with me and a little boy nine years old while the rest went a-hunting. And when I was here, I thought with myself that God had now separated me from the congregation of His people who were now in His sanctuary where He commandeth the blessing, even life forever, and made to bewail my unfruitfulness under and unthankfulness for such a mercy. When my spirit was almost overwhelmed within me at the consideration of what had passed over me and what was to be expected, I was ready almost to sink in my spirit. But God spoke those words with a greater efficacy than man could speak them for my strengthening and support: Psalms 118:17: "I shall not die but live and declare the works of the Lord"; Psalms 42:11: "Why art thou cast down, o my soul? and why art thou disquieted within me? Hope thou in God, for I shall yet praise Him who is the health of my countenance and my God"; Nehem. 1:8–9: "Remember I beseech thee, the word thou commandedest thy servant Moses, saying, 'If ye transgress, I will scatter you abroad among the nations; but, if ye turn unto me, and keep my commandments and do them, though there were of you cast out unto the uttermost part of the heavens, yet will I gather them from thence and will bring them unto the place that I have chosen to set my name there.' " Those three places of Scripture, one after another by the grace of God, strengthened my hopes that God would so far restrain the wrath of the adversary that the greatest number of us left alive should be carried through so tedious a journey. That though my children had no father to take care of them, that word quieted me to a patient waiting to see the end the Lord would make, Jer. 49:11: "Leave thy fatherless children, I will preserve them alive and let thy widows trust in me." Accordingly God carried them wonderfully through great difficulties and dangers.

My youngest daughter, aged seven years, was carried all the journey and looked after with a great deal of tenderness. My youngest son, aged four years, was wonderfully preserved from death; for, though they that carried him or drawed him on sleighs were tired with their journeys, yet their savage cruel tempers were so overruled by God that they did not kill him, but in their pity he was spared and others would take care of him; so that four times on the journey he was spared and others would take care of him, till at last he arrived at Mont-Royal [Montreal] where a French gentlewoman, pitying the child, redeemed it out of the hands of the heathen. My son Samuel and my eldest daughter were pitied so as to be drawn on sleighs when unable to travel. And though they suffered very much through scarcity of food and tedious journeys, they were carried through to Mont-Royal. And my son Stephen, about eleven years of age, [was] wonderfully preserved from death in the famine whereof three English persons died and after eight months brought into Shamblee [Chambly].

My master returned on the evening of the Sabbath and told me he had killed five moose. The next day we removed to the place where he killed them. We tarried there three days till we had roasted and dried the meat. My master made me a pair of snowshoes, "For," said he, "you cannot possibly travel without, the snow being knee-deep." We parted from thence heavy laden; I traveled with a burden on my back, with snowshoes, twenty-five miles the first day of wearing them and again the next day till afternoon, and then we came to the French River.[19] My master at this place took away my pack and drew the whole load on the ice, but my bones seemed to be misplaced and I unable to travel with any speed. My feet were very sore, and each night I wrung blood out of my stockings when I pulled them off. My shins also were very sore, being cut with crusty snow in the time of my traveling without snowshoes. But finding some dry oak leaves by the river banks, I put them to my shins and in once applying of them they were healed. And here my master was very kind to me, would always give me the best he had to eat, and by the goodness of God, I never wanted a meal's meat during my captivity though some of my children and neighbors were greatly wounded (as I may say) with the arrows of famine and pinching want, having for many days nothing but roots to live upon and not much of them either. My master gave me a piece of a Bible, never disturbed me in reading the Scriptures, or in praying to God. Many of my neighbors also found that mercy in their journey to have Bibles, psalm books, catechisms, and good books put into their hands with liberty to use them; and yet after their arrival at Canada all possible endeavors were used to deprive them of them. Some of them say their Bibles were demanded by the French priests and never re-delivered to them, to their great grief and sorrow.

MY MARCH on the French River was very sore, for, fearing a thaw, we traveled a very great pace; my feet were so bruised and my joints so dis-

19. Now called the Winooski River.

torted by my traveling in snowshoes that I thought it unpossible to hold out. One morning a little before break of day my master came and awakened me out of my sleep, saying, "Arise, pray to God, and eat your breakfast, for we must go a great way today." After prayer I arose from my knees, but my feet were so tender, swollen, bruised, and full of pain that I could scarce stand upon them without holding on the wigwam. And then the Indians said, "You must run today."

I answered, "I could not run."

My master, pointing out to his hatchet, said to me, "Then I must dash out your brains and take off your scalp."

I said, "I suppose then you will do so, for I am not able to travel with speed." He sent me away alone on the ice.

About sun half an hour high he overtook me for I had gone very slowly, not thinking it possible to travel five miles. When he came up, he called me to run; I told him I could go no faster; he passed by without saying one word more so that sometimes I scarce saw anything of him for an hour together. I traveled from about break of day till dark, never so much as set down at noon to eat warm victuals, eating frozen meat which I had in my coat pocket as I traveled. We went that day two of their day's journey as they came down. I judge we went forty or forty-five miles that day. God wonderfully supported me and so far renewed my strength that in the afternoon I was stronger to travel than in the forenoon. My strength was restored and renewed to admiration. We should never distrust the care and compassion of God who can give strength to them who have no might and power to them who are ready to faint.

When we entered on the lake [Champlain], the ice was very rough and uneven, which was very grievous to my feet that could scarce endure to be set down on the smooth ice on the river: I lifted up my cry to God in ejaculatory requests that He would take notice of my state and some way or other relieve me. I had not marched above half a mile before there fell a moist snow about an inch and a half deep that made it very soft for my feet to pass over the lake to the place where my master's family was—wonderful favors in the midst of trying afflictions!

We went a day's journey from the lake to a small company of Indians who were a-hunting; they were after their manner kind to me and gave me the best they had, which was mooseflesh, groundnuts, and cranberries but not bread; for three weeks together I eat no bread. After our stay there and undergoing difficulties in cutting of wood, [I] suffered from lousiness having lousy old clothes of soldiers put upon me when they stripped me of mine to sell to the French soldiers of the army. We again began a march for Shamblee; we stayed at a branch of the lake and feasted two or three days on geese we killed there.

AFTER ANOTHER day's travel we came to a river where the ice was thawed;[20] we made a canoe of elm bark in one day and arrived on a Saturday near noon at Shamblee, a small village where is a garrison and a fort of French soldiers. This village is about fifteen miles from Mont-Royal. The French were very kind to me; a gentleman of the place took me into his house and to his table and lodged me at night on a good feather bed. The inhabitants and officers were very obliging to me the little time I stayed with them and promised to write a letter to the governor-in-chief[21] to inform him of my passing down the river. Here I saw a girl taken from our town, and a young man who informed me that the greatest part of the captives were come in and that two of my children were at Mont-Royal, and that many of the captives had been in three weeks before my arrival—mercy in the midst of judgment!

As we passed along the river towards [Fort] Sorel, we went into an house where was an Englishwoman of our town who had been left among the French in order to her conveyance to the Indian fort. The French were very kind to her and to myself and gave us the best provision they had, and she embarked with us to go down to St. Francois Fort.[22] When we came down to the first inhabited house at Sorel, a Frenchwoman came to the riverside and desired us to go into her house, and, when we were entered, she compassioned our state and told us she had in the last war[23] been a captive among the Indians and therefore was not a little sensible of our difficulties. She gave the Indians something to eat in the chimney-corner and spread a cloth on the table for us with napkins, which gave such offense to the Indians that they hasted away and would not call in at the fort. But wherever we entered into houses, the French were very courteous.

When we came to St. Francois River, we found some difficulty by rea-

20. Probably the Richelieu River.

21. Vaudreuil. See *Dictionary of Canadian Biography*, II, 565–574.

22. An Abenaki stronghold.

23. King William's War, the American phase of Europe's War of the League of Augsburg, 1689–1697. For a modern account see Douglas Edward Leach, *Arms for Empire: A Military History of the British Colonies in North America, 1607–1763* (New York, 1973), and for a more detailed classic account see Francis Parkman, *Count Frontenac and New France under Louis XIV*, New Library Edition (Boston, 1903). Important correctives to Parkman's view are William J. Eccles, *Frontenac the Courtier Governor* (Toronto, 1959); and Eccles, *Canada under Louis XIV, 1663–1701* (Toronto, 1964).

son of the ice, and, entering into a Frenchman's house, he gave us a loaf of
bread and some fish to carry away with us; but we passed down the river
till night, and there seven of us supped on the fish, called bullhead or pout,
and did not eat it up, the fish was so very large. The next morning we met
with such a great quantity of ice that we were forced to leave our canoe
and travel on land. We went to a French officer's house, who took us into
a private room out of the sight of the Indians, and treated us very courteously.

THAT NIGHT we arrived at the fort called St. Francois, where we found
several poor children who had been taken from the Eastward the summer
before, a sight very affecting, they being in habit very much like Indians
and in manner very much symbolizing with them. At this fort lived two
Jesuits, one of which was made superior of the Jesuits at Quebeck. One of
these Jesuits met me at the fort gate and asked me to go into the church
and give God thanks for preserving my life; I told him I would do that in
some other place. When the bell rang for evening prayers, he that took
me bid me go, but I refused.

The Jesuits came to our wigwam and prayed a short prayer and invited
me to sup with them and justified the Indians in what they did against us,
rehearsing some things done by Major Walden above thirty years ago,[24]
and how justly God retaliated them in the last war, and inveighed against
us for beginning this war with the Indians. And [then they] said we had
before the last winter, and in the winter, been very barbarous and cruel in
burning and killing Indians. I told them that the Indians in a very perfidi-
ous manner had committed murders on many of our inhabitants after the
signing articles of peace, and, as to what they spake of cruelties, they were
undoubtedly falsehoods, for I well knew the English were not approvers of
inhumanity or barbarity towards enemies.

They said that an Englishman had killed one of St. Casteen's relations,[25] which occasioned this war; for, say they, the nations in a general
counsel had concluded not to engage in the war, on any side, till they
themselves were first molested, and then all of them as one would engage

24. For the eventful career of Richard Waldron, or Walderne, who in 1676 treacherously captured about two hundred Indians and in 1689 was tortured to death in apparent retaliation, see George M. Bodge, *Soldiers in King Philip's War*, 3rd ed. (Boston,
1906), 293–317; and note 18 to Gyles's narrative, above.

25. Jean-Vincent d'Abbadie de Saint-Castin (1652–1707) played an important role in
the imperial border wars, as did his son Bernard Anselme d'Abbadie de Saint-Castin
(1689–1720). The elder St. Castin married an Abenaki woman; their son was simultaneously a French officer and an Indian chief. See *Dictionary of Canadian Biography*, II, 3–7.

against them that began a war with them; and that upon the killing of Casteen's kinsman, a post was dispatched to Canada to advertise the Macquas and Indians that the English had begun a war. On which they gathered up their forces, and the French joined with them to come down on the Eastern parts; and, when they came near New England, several of the Eastern Indians told them of the peace made with the English and the satisfaction given them from the English for that murder. But the Macquas told them it was now too late, for they were sent for and were now come and would fall on them if without their consent they made a peace with the English. [They] said also that a letter was shown them sent from the governor of Port Royal, which he said was taken in an English ship, being a letter from the queen of England to our governor writing how she approved his designs to ensnare and deceitfully to seize on the Indians; so that being enraged from that letter and being forced as it were, they began the present war. I told them the letter was a lie forged by the French.

The next morning the bell rang for Mass. My master bid me to go to church. I refused. He threatened me and went away in a rage. At noon the Jesuits sent for me to dine with them, for I eat at their table all the time I was at the fort. And after dinner they told me the Indians would not allow of any of their captives staying in their wigwams whilst they were at church and were resolved by force and violence to bring us all to church if we would not go without. I told them it was highly unreasonable so to impose upon those who were of a contrary religion, and to force us to be present at such service as we abhorred was nothing becoming Christianity. They replied they were savages and would not hearken to reason but would have their wills; [they] said also [that] if they were in New England themselves, they would go into the churches to see their ways of worship.

I answered the case was far different, for there was nothing (themselves being the judges) as to matter or manner of worship but what was according to the word of God in our churches; and therefore it could not be an offense to any man's conscience. But among them there were idolatrous superstitions in worship; they said, "Come and see and offer us conviction of what is superstitious in [our] worship." To which I answered that I was not to do evil that good might come on it, and that forcing in matters of religion was hateful. They answered the Indians were resolved to have it so, and they could not pacify them without my coming; and they would engage they should offer no force or violence to cause any compliance with their ceremonies.

The next Mass my master bid me go to church. I objected; he arose and forcibly pulled me out by head and shoulders out of the wigwam to the

184

church that was nigh the door. So I went in and sat down behind the door, and there saw a great confusion instead of gospel order. For one of the Jesuits was at the altar saying Mass in a tongue unknown to the savages, and the other between the altar and the door saying and singing prayers among the Indians at the same time saying over their Pater Nosters and Ave Mary [Marias] by tale from their chaplets, or beads on a string. At our going out, we smiled at their devotion so managed, which was offensive to them, for they said we made a derision of their worship. When I was here, a certain savagess died; one of the Jesuits told me she was a very holy woman who had not committed one sin in twelve years.

After a day or two the Jesuits asked me what I thought of their way now [that] I saw it? I told them I thought Christ said of it as Mark 7:7–9: "Howbeit in vain do they worship me, teaching for doctrines the commandments of man. For laying aside the commandment of God, ye hold the tradition of men as the washing of pots and cups and many such like things ye do. And He said unto them, 'Full well ye reject the commandment of God that ye may keep your own tradition.' " They told me they were not the commandments of men but apostolical traditions of equal authority with the holy Scriptures. And that after my death I would bewail my not praying to the Virgin Mary, and that I should find the want of intercession for me with her Son, judging me to hell for asserting the Scriptures to be perfect rule of faith, and said I abounded in my own sense, entertaining explications contrary to the sense of the pope regularly sitting with a general council explaining Scripture and making articles of faith. I told them it was my comfort that Christ was to be my judge and not they at the Great Day, and, as for their censuring and judging of me, I was not moved with it.

One day a certain savagess taken prisoner in King Philip's War, who had lived at Mr. Buckley's at Wethersfield,[26] called Ruth, who could speak English very well, who had been often at my house but was now proselyted to the Romish faith, came into the wigwam. And with her [came] an English maid who was taken the last war,[27] who was dressed up in Indian apparel, could not speak one word of English, who said she could neither tell her own name or the name of the place from whence she was taken. These two talked in the Indian dialect with my master a long time after which my master bade me to cross myself. I told him I would not; he commanded me several times, and I as often refused.

26. Perhaps Rev. Gershom Bulkeley (1636–1712), pastor at Wethersfield, Connecticut, and surgeon to his colony's troops in King Philip's War.
27. King William's War. This English maid has not been further identified.

Ruth said, "Mr. Williams, you know the Scripture and therefore act against your own light, for you know the Scripture saith, 'Servants, obey your masters.' He is your master and you his servant."

I told her she was ignorant and knew not the meaning of the Scripture, telling her [that] I was not to disobey the great God to obey any master, and that I was ready to suffer for God if called thereto.[28] On which she talked to my master; I suppose she interpreted what I said.

My master took hold of my hand to force me to cross myself, but I struggled with him and would not suffer him to guide my hand; upon this he pulled off a crucifix from his own neck and bade me kiss it, but I refused once again. He told me he would dash out my brains with his hatchet if I refused. I told him I should sooner choose death than to sin against God; then he ran and caught up his hatchet and acted as though he would have dashed out my brains. Seeing I was not moved, he threw down his hatchet, saying he would first bite off all my nails if I still refused; I gave him my hand and told him I was ready to suffer. He set his teeth in my thumbnails and gave a grip with his teeth, and then said, "No good minister, no love God, as bad as the devil," and so left off.

I have reason to bless God who strengthened me to withstand; by this he was so discouraged as nevermore to meddle with me about my religion. I asked leave of the Jesuits to pray with those English of our town that were with me, but they absolutely refused to give us any permission to pray one with another and did what they could to prevent our having any discourse together.

After a few days the Governor de Vaudreuil, governor-in-chief, sent down two men with letters to the Jesuits desiring them to order my being sent up to him to Mont-Royal, upon which one of the Jesuits went with my two masters and took me along with them, as also two more of Deerfield, a man and his daughter about seven years of age.[29] When we came to the lake,[30] the wind was tempestuous and contrary to us so that they

28. Williams was adhering to a standard Puritan position. William Perkins, a major English Puritan spokesman, asserted that a Protestant servant should not obey a master who ordered him to attend Mass (*The Workes of That Famous and Worthy Minister of Christ . . . Mr. William Perkins,* 3 vols., [London, 1612–1637], I, 758). Similarly, Williams's contemporary, Benjamin Wadsworth of Massachusetts, argued in *The Well-Ordered Family* (Boston, 1712) that children and servants should obey their parents and masters only in "lawful things." Ordering a servant to blaspheme God by attending Mass did not fit the Puritans' notion of lawful.

29. Not further identified. Several father-daughter pairs had been taken at Deerfield. See Emma Lewis Coleman, *New England Captives Carried to Canada between 1677 and 1760 . . .* , 2 vols. (Portland, Me., 1925), II, 34–35.

30. Lake St. Pierre on the St. Lawrence River.

were afraid to go over; they landed and kindled a fire and said they would wait awhile to see whether the wind would fall or change.

I went aside from the company among the trees and spread our case with the temptations of it before God and pleaded that He would order the season so that we might not go back again but be furthered on our voyage that I might have opportunity to see my children and neighbors and converse with them and know their state. When I returned, the wind was more boisterous, and then a second time, and the wind was more fierce; I reflected upon myself for my unquietness and the want of a resigned will to the will of God. And a third time [I] went and bewailed before God my anxious cares and the tumultuous working of my own heart, begged a will fully resigned to the will of God, and thought that by the grace of God I was brought to say amen to whatever God should determine.

Upon my return to the company the wind was yet high; the Jesuit and my master said, "Come, we will go back again to the fort, for there is no likelihood of proceeding in our voyage, for very frequently such a wind continues three days, sometimes six."

After it continued so many hours, I said to them, "The will of the Lord be done," and the canoe was put again into the river and we embarked.

No sooner had my master put me into the canoe and put off from the shore, but the wind fell, and coming into the middle of the river they said, "We may go over the lake well enough." And so we did.

I promised if God gave me opportunity I would stir up others to glorify God in a continued persevering, committing their straits of heart to Him: He is a prayer-hearing God and the stormy winds obey Him. After we passed over the lake, the French wherever we came were very compassionate to us.

WHEN I CAME to Mont-Royal, which was eight weeks after my captivity, the Governor de Vaudrel [Vaudreuil] redeemed me out of the hands of the Indians, gave me good clothing, took me to his table, gave me the use of a very good chamber, and was in all respects relating to my outward man courteous and charitable to admiration. At my first entering into his house, he sent for my two children who were in the city[31] that I might see them and promised to do what he could to get all my children and neighbors out of the hands of the savages. My change of diet after the difficulties of my journeys caused an alteration in my body; I was physicked, blooded, and very tenderly taken care of in my sickness.[32]

31. Probably Esther and Warham.

32. Bloodletting and purgatives were standard seventeenth- and eighteenth-century remedies for almost any ailment. Williams was properly grateful for such medical assistance, although in fact it undoubtedly prolonged his recuperation.

The governor redeemed my eldest daughter[33] out of the hands of the Indians, and she was carefully tended in the hospital until she was well of her lameness and by the governor provided for with respect during her stay in the country. My youngest child was redeemed by a gentlewoman in the city as the Indians passed by.[34] After the Indians had been at their fort and discoursed with the priests, they came back and offered to the gentlewoman a man for the child, alleging that the child could not be profitable to her, but the man would, for he was a weaver and his service would much advance the design she had of making cloth. But God overruled so far that this temptation to the woman prevailed not for an exchange, for had the child gone to the Indian fort in an ordinary way, it had abode there still, as the rest of the children carried there do.

The governor gave orders to certain officers to get the rest of my children out of the hands of the Indians and as many of my neighbors as they could. After six weeks a merchant of the city obtained my eldest son[35] that was taken to live with him; he took a great deal of pains to persuade the savages to part with him. An Indian came to the city (Sagamore George of Pennacook) from Cowass and brought word of my son Stephen's being near Cowass, and some money was put into his hand for his redemption and a promise of full satisfaction if he brought him; but the Indian proved unfaithful, and I never saw my child till a year after.[36]

The governor ordered a priest to go along with me to see my youngest daughter among the Macquas and endeavor her ransom.[37] I went with him; he was very courteous to me, and, from his parish which was near the Macqua fort, he wrote a letter to the Jesuit to desire him to send my child to see me and to speak with them that took her to come along with it [her].[38] But the Jesuit wrote back a letter that I should not be permitted to

33. Thirteen-year-old Esther.
34. Four-year-old Warham.
35. Fifteen-year-old Samuel, the eldest *captive* son.
36. For Stephen's account of this episode, see George Sheldon, ed., *What Befell Stephen Williams in His Captivity* (Deerfield, Mass., 1889), 9.
37. Eunice, who was never redeemed. She married a Caughnawaga Indian and converted to Catholicism. For more on Eunice see Coleman, *New England Captives*, II, 54–64; and Alexander Medlicott, Jr., "Return to the Land of Light: a Plea to an Unredeemed Captive," *New England Quarterly*, 38 (1965), 202–216.
38. Eunice was held captive at the Caughnawaga village of St. Louis. In this passage and elsewhere in his narrative, Williams often used "it" to mean Eunice or Warham. The neuter pronoun was quite commonly applied before the nineteenth century to infants and young children.

speak with or see my child; if I came, that my labor would be lost, and that the Macquas would as soon part with their hearts as my child. At my return to the city I with a heavy heart carried the Jesuit's letter to the governor who, when he read it, was very angry and endeavored to comfort me, assuring me I should see it and speak with it, and he would to his utmost endeavor its ransom. Accordingly he sent to the Jesuits who were in the city and bade them improve their interest for the obtaining the child.

After some days he went with me in his own person to the fort. When we came thither, he discoursed with the Jesuits after which my child was brought into the chamber where I was. I was told I might speak with her but should be permitted to speak to no other English person there. My child was about seven years old; I discoursed with her near an hour; she could read very well and had not forgotten her catechism. And [she] was very desirous to be redeemed out of the hands of the Macquas and bemoaned her state among them, telling me how they profaned God's Sabbaths and said she thought that a few days before they had been mocking the devil, and that one of the Jesuits stood and looked on them.

I told her she must pray to God for His grace every day. She said she did as she was able and God helped her. But, says she, "They force me to say some prayers in Latin, but I don't understand one word of them; I hope it won't do me any harm." I told her she must be careful she did not forget her catechism and the Scriptures she had learned by heart. She told the captives after I was gone, as some of them have informed me, almost everything I spake to her and said she was much afraid she should forget her catechism, having none to instruct her. I saw her once a few days after in the city but had not many minutes of time with her, but what time I had I improved to give her the best advice I could.

The governor labored much for her redemption; at last he had a promise of it in case he would procure for them an Indian girl in her stead. Accordingly he sent up the river some hundreds of leagues for one,[39] but it was refused when offered by the governor: he offered them a hundred pieces of eight for her redemption, but it was refused. His lady went over to have begged her from them, but all in vain; it's there still and has forgotten to speak English. Oh! That all who peruse this history would join in their fervent requests to God, with whom all things are possible, that this poor child, and so many others of our children who have been cast upon God from the womb and are now outcast ready to perish, might be gathered from their dispersions and receive sanctifying grace from God!

39. That is, up the St. Lawrence River to the Great Lakes.

When I had discoursed with the child and was coming out of the fort, one of the Jesuits went out of the chamber with me and some soldiers to convey me to the canoe. I saw some of my poor neighbors who stood with longing expectations to see me and speak with me and had leave from their savage masters so to do. I was by the Jesuit himself thrust along by force and permitted only to tell them some of their relations they asked after were well in the city, and that with a very audible voice, being not permitted to come near to them.

After my return to the city I was very melancholy, for I could not be permitted so much as to pray with the English who dwelled in the same house. And the English who came to see me were most of them put back by the guard at the door and not suffered to come and speak with me. Sometimes the guard was so strict that I could scarce go aside on necessary occasions without a repulse; and whenever I went out into the city (a favor the governor himself never refused when I asked it of him) there were spies to watch me and to observe whether I spake to the English. Upon which I told some of the English they must be careful to call to mind and improve former instructions and endeavor to stand at a further distance for awhile, hoping that after a short time I should have more liberty of conversing with them. But some spies sent out found on a Sabbath day more than three (the number we by their order published were not to exceed together) of us in company, who informed the priest; the next day one of the priests told me I had a greater number of the English with me and that I had spoken something reflecting on their religion. I spake to the governor that no forcible means might be used with any of the captives respecting their religion; he told me he allowed no such thing. I am persuaded that the governor, if he might act as himself, would not have suffered such things to be done as have been done and that he never did know of several things acted against the English.

At my first coming to Mont-Royal, the governor told me I should be sent home as soon as Captain Baptiste was returned and not before,[40] and that I was taken in order to his redemption. The governor sought by all means to divert me from my melancholy sorrows and always showed a willingness for seeing my children. And one day I told him of my design of walking into the city; he pleasantly answered, "Go, with all my heart." His eldest son went with me as far as the door and saw the guard stop me; he

40. Pierre Maisonnat, alias Baptiste (1663–1714), was a notorious privateer along the Canadian and New England coasts. He was captured by the English in 1697 and again in 1702; in 1706 he was exchanged for Mr. Williams. See *Dictionary of Canadian Biography*, II, 449–450.

went in and informed his father, who came to the door and asked why they affronted the gentleman going out. They said it was their order. But with an angry countenance he said his orders were that I should not be stopped, but within a little time I had my orders to go down to Quebeck.

Another thing showing that many things are done without the governor's consent though his name be used to justify them: *viz.,* I asked the priest after I had been at Mont-Royal two days leave to go and see my youngest child; he said, "Whenever you would see it, tell me and I will bring it to you, for," says he, "the governor is not willing you should go thither." And yet not many days after when we were at dinner, the governor's lady (seeing me sad) spoke to an officer at the table who could speak Latin to tell me that after dinner I should go along with them and see my two children. And accordingly after dinner I was carried to see them, and, when I came to the house, I found three or four English captives who lived there, and I had leave to discourse with them. And not long after the governor's lady asked me to go along with her to the hospital to see one of my neighbors sick there.

One day one of the Jesuits came to the governor and told the company there that he never saw such persons as were taken from Deerfield. Said he, "The Macquas will not suffer any of their prisoners to abide in their wigwams whilst they themselves are at Mass but carry them with them to the church, and they can't be prevailed with to fall down on their knees to pray there, but no sooner are they returned to their wigwams, but they fall down on their knees to prayer." He said they could do nothing with the grown persons there, and they hindered the children's complying. Whereupon the Jesuits counseled the Macquas to sell all the grown persons from the fort—a stratgem to seduce poor children. Oh Lord! Turn the counsels of these Ahit[h]ophels[41] into foolishness, and make the counsels of the heathen of none effect!

Here I observed they were wonderfully lifted up with pride after the return of Captain Montinug from Northampton with news of success;[42] they boasted of their success against New England. And they sent out an army as they said of seven hundred men, if I mistake not, two hundred of which were French, in company of which army went several Jesuits, and said they would lay desolate all the places on Connecticut River. The superior of the priests told me their general was a very prudent and brave commander of undaunted courage, and he doubted not but they should have

41. That is, false advisers. 2 Samuel 15-17.
42. Probably Jacques Testard de Montigny (1663-1737).

great success. This army went away in such a boasting, triumphant manner that I had great hopes God would discover and disappoint their designs; our prayers were not wanting for the blasting such a bloody design.

The superior of the priests said to me, "Don't flatter yourselves in hopes of a short captivity, for," said he, "there are two young princes contending for the kingdom of Spain, and a third that care is to be taken for his establishment on the English throne." And [he] boasted what they would do to Europe, and that we must expect not only [in] Europe but in New England the establishment of popery.[43]

I said, "Glory not, God can make great changes in a little time and revive His own interest and yet save His poor afflicted people."

Said he, "The time for miracles is past, and in the time of the last war the King of France was, as it were, against all the world and yet did very great things, but now the kingdom of Spain is for him, and the Duke of Bavaria, and the Duke of Savoy, etc." And spake in a lofty manner of great things to be done by them and having the world, as I may say, in subjection to them.

I was sent down to Quebeck in company of Governor de Ramesey, governor of Mont-Royal,[44] and the superior of the Jesuits, and ordered to live with one of the council, from whom I received many favors for seven weeks. He told me it was the priest's doing to send me down before the governor came down, and that, if I went much to see the English, or they came much to visit me, I should yet certainly be sent away where I should have no converse with the English.

After my coming down to Quebeck, I was invited to dine with the Jesuits, and to my face they were civil enough. But after a few days a young gentleman came to my chamber and told me that one of the Jesuits (after we had done dinner) made a few distichs of verse and gave them to his scholars to translate into French. He showed them to me. The import of them was that the King of France's grandson had sent out his huntsmen, and that they had taken a wolf, who was shut up, and now he hopes the

43. On Spain's chaotic political situation in the early eighteenth century see Henry A. F. Kamen, *The War of Succession in Spain, 1700-15* (Bloomington, Ind., 1969). A good account of the impact of the War of the Spanish Succession on New France is Gustave Lanctot, *A History of Canada,* trans. Margaret M. Cameron, 3 vols. (Cambridge, Mass., 1963-1965), II, especially chaps. 15, 18-19.

44. "Governor de Ramesey"—Claude de Ramezay (1659-1724)—was, in effect, mayor of Montreal; he was later acting governor of New France. See *Dictionary of Canadian Biography,* II, 545-548.

sheep would be in safety. I knew at the reading of them what he aimed at but held my peace as though I had been ignorant of the Jesuit's intention. Observing this reproaching spirit, I said in my heart [that] if God will bless, let men curse if they please, and I looked to God in Christ the great shepherd to keep his scattered sheep among so many Romish ravenous wolves and to remember the reproaches wherewith His holy name, ordinances, and servants were daily reproached. And upon an observation of the time of these verses being composed, I find that near the same time the bishop of Canada with twenty ecclesiastics were taken by the English as they were coming from France and carried into England as prisoners of war.[45]

One Sabbath day morning I observed many signs of approaching rain, a great moisture on the stones of the hearth and chimney jams. I was that day invited to dine with the Jesuits, and when I went up to dinner, it began to rain a small drizzling rain. The superior told me they had been praying for rain that morning, "And lo," says he, "it begins to rain." I told him I could tell him of many instances of God's hearing our prayers for rain. However, in the afternoon there was a general procession of all orders, priests, Jesuits, and friars, and the citizens in great pomp, carrying (as they said) as an holy relic one of the bones of St. Paul.

The next day I was invited to the priest's Seminary to dinner; "Oh," said they, "we went in procession yesterday for rain, and see what a plentiful rain followed." I answered we had been answered when praying for rain when no such signs of rain, and the beginnings of rain preceded, as now with them, before they appointed or began their procession, etc. However, they upbraided me that God did not approve of our religion in that He disregarded our prayers and accepted theirs. For, said they, "We hear you had days of fasting and prayer before the fleet came to Quebeck; God would not regard your prayers but heard ours, and almost in a miraculous way preserved us when assaulted and refused to hear your fastday prayers for your preservation but heard ours for your desolation and our success."[46]

They boasted also of their king and his greatness and spake of him as

45. On July 26, 1704 (New Style), English warships captured the French royal merchant ship *Seine*, which was returning the bishop of Quebec, Mgr. Jeanne-Baptiste de La Crois de Saint-Vallier, and several priests to Canada. The bishop remained in England until his exchange in 1709.

46. The Jesuits apparently refer to Sir William Phips's abortive attack on Quebec in 1690. For details on the campaign see Francis Parkman, *Frontenac and New France under Louis XIV*, new Library Edition (Boston, 1903), chaps. 12–13.

though there could be no settlement of the world but as he pleased, reviling us as in a low and languishing case, having no king but being under the government of a queen.[47] And [they] spake as though the Duke of Bavaria would in a short time be emperor.[48]

From this day forward God gave them to hear sorrowful tidings from Europe, that a war was commenced against the Duke of Savoy and so their enemies increased, their bishop taken and two millions of wealth with him. News every year more distressing and impoverishing of them; and the Duke of Bavaria so far from being emperor that he is dispossessed of his dukedom; and France so far from being strengthened by Spain that the kingdom of Spain [is] like to be an occasion of the weakening and impoverishing their own kingdom—they themselves reporting so. And their great army going against New England turned back ashamed, and they discouraged and disheartened and every year very exercising fears and cares as to the savages who live up the river. Before the return of that army they told me we were led up and down and sold by the heathen as sheep for the slaughter, and they could not devise what they should do with us, we should be so many prisoners when the army returned.

The Jesuits told me it was a great mercy that so many of our children were brought to them, and that, now especially since they were not like speedily to be returned, there was hope of their being brought over to the Romish faith. They would take the English children born among them and, against the consent of their parents, baptize them. One Jesuit came to me and asked whether all the English at Lorette, a place not far from Quebeck where the savages lived, were baptized. I told him they were. He said, "If they be not, let me know of it that I may baptize them for fear they should die and be damned if they died without baptism." Says he, "When the savages went against you, I charged them to baptize all children before they killed them, such was my desire of your eternal salvation though you were our enemies."[49]

There was a gentleman called Monsieur de Beauville, a captain, the brother of the lord intendant, who was a good friend to me and very cour-

47. Queen Anne, daughter of James II and sister of Queen Mary (d. 1694), held the English throne from 1702 to 1714.

48. For the complicated history of the War of the Spanish Succession (Queen Anne's War in North America), see John R. Wolfe, *The Emergence of the Great Powers, 1685–1715* (New York, 1951); and Douglas E. Leach, *Arms for Empire: A Military History of the British Colonies in North America, 1607–1763* (New York, 1973), chap. 4.

49. Williams records this conversation sarcastically. According to Puritan theology, baptism would not save the children's souls.

teous to all the captives; he lent me an English Bible and, when he went to France, gave it me.

All means were used to seduce poor souls. I was invited one day to dine with one of chief note. As I was going, [I] met with the superior of the Jesuits coming out of the house, and he came in after dinner; and presently it was propounded to me, if I would stay among them and be of their religion, I should have a great and honorable pension from the king every year. The superior of the Jesuits turned to me and said, "Sir, you have manifested much grief and sorrow for your separation from so many of your neighbors and children; if you will now comply with this offer and proposal, you may have all your children with you, and here will be enough for an honorable maintenance for you and them."

I answered, "Sir, if I thought your religion to be true, I would embrace it freely without any such offer, but so long as I believe it to be what it is, the offer of the whole world is of no more value to me than a blackberry." And [I] manifested such an abhorrence of this proposal that I speedily went to take my leave and be gone.

"Oh! Sir," said he, "set down, why [are you] in such a hurry, you are alone in your chamber, divert yourself a little longer," and fell to other discourse. And within half an hour says again, "Sir, I have one thing earnestly to request of you. I pray pleasure me!"

I said, "Let your Lordship speak."

Said he, "I pray come down to the palace tomorrow morning and honor me with your company in my coach to the great church, it being then a saint's day."

I answered, "Ask me anything wherein I can serve you with a good conscience, and I am ready to gratify you, but I must ask your excuse here," and immediately went away from him. Returning unto my chamber, I gave God thanks for His upholding of me and also made an inquiry with myself whether I had by any action given encouragement for such a temptation.

NOT MANY DAYS after and a few days before Governor de Vaudrel coming down, I was sent away fifteen miles down the river that I might not have opportunity of converse with the English. I was courteously treated by the French and the priest of that parish; they told me he was one of the most learned men in the country; he was a very ingenious man, zealous in their way but yet very familiar. I had many disputes with the priests who came thither, and, when I used their own authors to confute some of their positions, my books borrowed of them were taken away from me, for they said I made an ill use of them. They, many of them having boasted of their unity in doctrine and profession, were loath I should show them from their own best approved authors as many different opinions as they could charge against us.

Here again a gentleman in the presence of the old bishop and a priest offered me his house and whole living with assurance of honor, wealth, and employment if I would embrace their ways. I told them I had an indignation of soul against such offers on such terms as parting with what was more valuable than all the world, alleging, "What is a man profited if he gain the whole world and lose his own soul? Or what shall a man give in exchange for his soul?"

I was sometimes told I might have all my children if I would comply and must never expect to have them on any other terms; I told them my children were dearer to me than all the world, but I would not deny Christ and His truths for the having of them with me; I would still put my trust in God who could perform all things for me.

I am persuaded that the priest of that parish where I [was] kept abhorred their sending down the heathen to commit outrages against the English, saying it was more like committing murders than managing a war. In my confinement in this parish I had my undisturbed opportunities to be humbly imploring grace for ourselves, for soul and body, for His protecting presence with New England, and His disappointing the bloody designs of enemies, that God would be a little sanctuary to us in a land of captivity, and that our friends in New England might have grace to make a more thankful and fruitful improvement of means of grace than we had done, who by our neglects found ourselves out of God's sanctuary.

ON THE TWENTY-FIRST of October 1704, I received some letters from New England with an account that many of our neighbors escaped out of the desolations in the fort, and that my dear wife was recarried and decently buried. and that my eldest son who was absent in our desolation was sent to college[50] and provided for, which occasioned thanksgiving to God in the midst of afflictions and caused prayers even in Canada to be going daily up to heaven for a blessing upon benefactors showing such kindness to the desolate and afflicted.

The consideration of such crafty designs to ensnare young ones and to turn them from the simplicity of the gospel to Romish superstition was

---

50. Eleazar Williams (1668–1742) attended Harvard (B.A. 1708) while his family was in Canada. He later became the Congregational minister at Mansfield, Connecticut.

very exercising; sometimes they would tell me my children, sometimes my neighbors, were turned to be of their religion. Some made it their work to allure poor souls by flatteries and great promises, some threatened, some offered abusive carriages to such as refused to go to church and be present at Mass; for some they industriously contrived to get them married among them. A priest drew up a compendium of the Romish Catholic faith and pretended to prove it by the Scriptures, telling the English that all they required was contained in the Scriptures, which they acknowledged to be the rule of faith and manners, but it was by Scriptures horribly perverted and abused. I could never come to the sight of it, though I often earnestly entreated a copy of it, until I was ashipboard for our voyage for New England, but hearing of it I endeavored to possess the English with their danger of being cheated with such a pretense. I understood they would tell the English that I was turned that they might gain them to change their religion; these their endeavors to seduce to popery were very exercising to me.[51]

And in my solitariness I drew up these following sorrowful, mournful considerations (though unused to and unskillful in poetry) yet in a plain style for the use of some of the captives who would sometimes make their secret visits to me, which at the desire of some of them are here made public.

Some Contemplations of the Poor and Desolate State of the Church at Deerfield

The sorrows of my heart enlarged are,
Whilst I my present state with past compare,
I frequently unto God's house did go,
With Christian friends, His praises forth to show,
But now I solitary sit, both sigh and cry,
Whilst my flock's misery think on do I.
     Many, both old and young, were slain outright,
Some in a bitter season take their flight.
Some burned to death, and others stifled were,
The enemy no sex or age would spare.
The tender children with their parents sad
Are carried forth as captives, some unclad.

51. John Williams's son Stephen, then with the Indians, reported hearing a rumor that his father had defected to the Catholics for £200 per year; Stephen thought some of the captives believed it. Sheldon, ed., *What Befell Stephen Williams*, 10.

Some murdered in the way unburied left,
And some through famine were of life bereft.
After a tedious journey some are sold,
Some kept in heathen hands; all from Christ['s] fold
By popish rage and heathenish cruelty
Are banished. Yea, some compelled to be
Present at Mass. Young children parted are
From parents and such as instructors were.
Crafty designs are used by papists all
In ignorance of truth them to enthrall.
Some threatened are unless they comply
In heathen hands again be made to lie.
To some large promises are made if they
Will truths renounce and choose their popish way.
   Oh Lord! mine eyes on Thee shall waiting be
Till Thou again turn our captivity.
Their Romish plots Thou canst confound, and save
This little flock, this mercy I do crave.
Save us from all our sins and yet again
Deliver us from them who truth disdain.
   Lord! for Thy mercy sake Thy covenant mind,
And in Thy house again rest let us find.
   So we Thy praises forth will show and speak
Of all Thy wondrous works, yea we will seek
The advancement of Thy great and glorious name,
Thy rich and sovereign grace we will proclaim.

The hearts of some were ready to be discouraged and sink, saying they were "out of sight and so out of mind." I endeavored to persuade them we were not forgotten, that undoubtedly many prayers were continually going up to heaven for us. Not long after came Capt. Livingston and Mr. Sheldon with letters from his excellency our governor to the governor of Canada about the exchange of prisoners, which gave a revival to many and raised expectations of a return. These visits from New England to Canada so often greatly strengthened many who were ready to faint and gave some check to the designs of the papists to gain proselytes.[52]

But God's time of deliverance was not yet come; as to some particular

52. Various New England agents visited Canada between 1705 and 1707 to negotiate the captives' release.

persons their temptations and trials were increased, and some abused because they refused a compliance with their superstitions. A young woman of our town met with a new trial. For on a day a Frenchman came into the room where she was and showed her his beads and boasted of them, putting them near to her; she knocked them out of his hands on the floor, for which she was beaten and threatened with death and for some days imprisoned. I pleaded with God His overruling this first essay for the deliverance of some as a pledge of the rest being delivered in due time.

I improved Capt. de Beauville, who had always been very friendly, to intercede with the governor for the return of my eldest daughter, and for his purchasing my son Stephen from the Indians at St. Francois Fort, and for liberty to go up and see my children and neighbors at Mont-Royal.[53] Divine Providence appeared to a moderating [of] my affliction in that five English persons of our town were permitted to return with Capt. Livingston, among whom went my eldest daughter.[54] And my son Stephen was redeemed and sent to live with me. He was almost quite naked and very poor; he had suffered much among the Indians. One of the Jesuits took upon him to come to the wigwam and whip him on some complaint that the squaws had made that he did not work enough for them.[55]

As to my petition for going up to Mont-Royal to see my children and neighbors, it was denied, as my former desire of coming up to the city before Capt. Livingston's coming was. God granted me favor as to two of my petitions, but yet brought me by His grace to be willing that He should glorify Himself in disposing of me and mine as He pleased and knew to be most for His glory. And almost always before any remarkable favor I was brought to lie down at the foot of God and made to be willing that God should govern the world so as might be most for His own honor and brought to resign all to His holy sovereignty. A frame of spirit when wrought in me by the grace of God giving the greatest content and satisfaction, and very often a forerunner of the mercy asked of God or a plain demonstration that the not obtaining my request was best for me. I had no small refreshing in having one of my children with me for four months.

53. Capt. de Beauville, brother of the intendant, helped to redeem English captives from the Indians and to return them to New England in exchange for French prisoners held there. He arranged the release of Esther and Stephen Williams, among others.

54. In December 1704–May 1705, Capt. John Livingston of Albany, a son-in-law of Governor Fitz-John Winthrop of Connecticut, and John Wells of Deerfield accompanied Ensign Sheldon to Canada.

55. For Stephen's account of this episode see Sheldon, ed., *What Befell Stephen Williams*, 10–11.

And the English were many of them strengthened with hopes that the treaty between the governments would issue in opening a door of escape for all.

In August Mr. Dudley and Capt. Vetch arrived, and great encouragements were given as to an exchange of all in the spring of the year; and some few again were sent home, among whom I obtained leave to send my son Stephen.[56] Upon Mr. Dudley's and Capt. Vetch's petitioning, I was again permitted to go up to Quebeck. But disputing with a mendicant friar who said he was an Englishman sent from France to endeavor the conversion of the English at Quebeck, who arrived at Canada while our gentlemen were there, I was by the priests' means ordered again to return to Chateauriche [Chateau Richer], and no other reason given but because I discoursed with that priest and their fear I should prevent his success among the captives.

But God showed His dislike of such a persecuting spirit: for the very next day, which was September 20, Old Style, October 1, New Style,[57] the Seminary, a very famous building, was most of it burned down, occasioned by a joiner's letting a coal of fire drop down among the shavings. The chapel in the priests' garden and the great cross were burned down, the library of the priests burned up. This Seminary and another library had been burned but about three years before. The day after my being sent away by the priests's means from Quebeck, there was a thunderstorm and the lightning struck the Seminary in the very place where the fire now began.

A little before Mr. Dudley's arrival came a soldier into my landlord's house barefoot and barelegged, going on a pilgrimage to Saint Anne.[58] For, said he, "My captain, who died some years ago, appeared to me and told me he was in purgatory, and told me I must go a pilgrimage to Saint Anne doing penance, and get a Mass said for him, and then he should be delivered." And many believed him and were much affected with it, came and told me of it to gain my credit of their devised purgatory. The soldier told me the priests had counseled him to undertake this pilgimage. And I am apt to think [they] ordered his calling in at my lordlord's [landlord's] that I might see and speak with him. I laughed at the conceit that a soldier

56. William Dudley sailed from Boston to Quebec in the summer of 1705 in Capt. Samuel Vetch's brigantine. They brought proposals for an exchange of prisoners which led to the release of several Deerfield captives, including Stephen and Samuel Williams. In November, Dudley and Vetch brought them to Boston.

57. See note 1 to Mary Rowlandson's narrative.

58. Probably the mission of St. Anne on the Ile de Montréal.

must be pitched upon to be sent on this errand, but they were much displeased and lamented my obstinacy in that I would not be reclaimed from a denial of purgatory by such a "miraculous Providence."

As I was able, I spread the case before God, beseeching of Him to disappoint them of their expectations to proselyte any of the captives by this stratagem, and by the goodness of God it was not very serviceable, for the soldier's conversation was such that several among the French themselves judged it to be a forgery. And though the captain spoken of was the governor's lady's brother, I never more heard any concernment or care to get him out of purgatory.

One of the parish where I lived told me that on the twenty-second of July 1705, he was at Quebeck at the mendicant friars' church on one of their feast days in honor of a great saint of their order and that at five o'clock Mass in the morning, near two hundred persons present, a great grey cat broke or pushed aside some glass, and entered into the church, and passed along it near the altar, and put out five or six candles that were burning, and that no one could tell which way the cat went out; and he thought it was the devil.

When I was in the city in September, I saw two English maids who had lived with the Indians a long time. They told me that an Indian had died at the place where they were; and that when sundry of his relations were together in order to his burial, the dead arose and informed them that at his death he went to hell, and there he saw all the Indians that had been dead since their embracing the popish religion, and warned them to leave it off, or they would be damned too, and lay down dead again. They said the Indians were frightened and very melancholy, but the Jesuit to whom they told this told them it was only a delusion of the devil to draw them away from the true religion, adding that he knew for certain that all those Indians who had been dead, spoken of by that Indian, were in heaven, only one squaw was gone to hell who died without baptism. These maids said also that many of the Indians much lamented their making a war against the English at the instigation of the French.

THE PRIESTS, after Mr. Dudley's going from Canada, were ready to think their time was short for gaining English proselytes and doubled their diligence and wiles to gain over persons to their persuasion. I improved all opportunities I could to write to the English that in that way I might be serviceable to them, but many or most of my letters treating about religion were intercepted and burned. I had a letter sent down to me by order of the governor that I had a liberty of writing to my children and friends which should be continued, provided I wrote about indifferent things and said nothing in them about the points in controversy between them and us. And if I were so hardy as to write letters otherwise, they should endeavor to prevent their being delivered. Accordingly I found many of them were burned. But sometimes notice would be given to the English that there were letters written, but they were burned, so that their writing was somewhat useful though never perused by the English because they judged those letters condemned popery. Many of our letters written from New England were never delivered because of some expressions about religion in them.

And, as I said before, after Mr. Dudley's departure from Quebeck endeavors were very vigorous to seduce [us]. Some were flattered with large promises, others threatened and beaten because they would not turn. And when two English women who had always opposed their religion were sick in the hospital, they kept with them night and day till they died, and their friends kept from coming to visit them. After their death they gave out that they died in the Romish faith and were received into their communion. Before their death Masses were said for them, and they [were] buried in the churchyard with all their ceremonies. And after this letters [were] sent into all parts to inform the English that these two women turned to their religion before their death, and that it concerned them to follow their example, for they could not be more obstinate than those women were in their health against the Romish faith and yet on a deathbed embraced it. They told the English who lived near that our religion was a dangerous religion to die in. But I shall hereafter relate the just grounds we have to think these things were falsehoods.

I was informed there was an English girl bid to take and wear the cross and cross herself. She refused; they threatened her and showed her the cross. At length she had her choice, either to cross herself and take the cross, or be whipped—she chose to be whipped. And they took up her clothes and made as though they would correct her, her, but seeing her choosing indeed to suffer rather than comply, they desisted and tied the cross about her neck. Some were taken and shut up among their religious, and all sorts of means used to gain them.

I received a letter from one of my neighbors wherein he thus bewails:

I obtained leave of my master to go to the Macqua fort to see my children that I had not seen for a long time. I carried a letter from my master to show that I had leave to come. When I came to the fort, I heard one of my children was in the woods. I went to see a boy

202

I had there who lived with one of the Jesuits; I had just asked him of his welfare, he said his master would come presently; he durst not stay to speak with me now being in such awe of his master. On which I withdrew, and when his master came in, I went and asked leave of him to speak with my child and showed him my letter. But he absolutely refused to let me see or speak with him; and said I had brought no letter from the governor and would not permit me to stay in the fort, though I had traveled on foot near fifty miles for no other errand than to see and speak with my children.

The same person with another Englishman last spring obtained leave of the governor-general to go to the same fort on the same errand and carried letters from the governor to the Jesuits that he might be permitted to speak with his children. The letter was delivered to the Jesuits, who told him his son was not at home but gone a-hunting. Whenas he was hid from them, as he heard afterward, so the poor man lost his labor a second time. These men say that when they returned to Mont-Royal, one Laland,[59] who was appointed as a spy always to observe the motions of the English, told them that one of the Jesuits had come in before them and had told the governor that the lad was gone out a-hunting. And that the Englishman who accompanied this poor man went out into the woods in hopes of finding the lad and saw him, but the lad run away, and that he followed him and called after him, but he would not stop but holding but a gun threatened to shoot him down if he followed him, and so he was discouraged and turned back. And says Laland, "You will never leave going to see your children and neighbors till some of you are killed." But the men told him it was an absolute lie, let who would report it, for they had neither seen the lad nor did they go into the woods to search after him. They judge this was told to the governor to prevent any English for the future going to see their children and neighbors.

Some of ours say they have been little better than absolutely promised to have their children who are among the savages in case they themselves would embrace popery. And that the priests had said they had rather the children should be among the Indians as they were than be brought out by the French and so be in readiness to return to New England.

A maid of our town was put into a religious house among the nuns for more than two years, and all sorts of means, by flatteries, threatenings, and abusive carriages, used to bring her to turn. They offered her money

59. Jean LaLande, a French interpreter.

which when refused, especially the latter part of the time, they threatened her very much, sent for her before them, and commanded her to cross herself. She refused. They hit her a box on the ear, bid her again; still she refused. They ordered a rod with six branches full of knots to be brought, and, when she refused, they struck her on the hands with their renewing their commands, and she stood to her refusals till her hands were filled with wales with the blows. But one said, "Beat her no more; we will give her to the Indians if she won't turn." They pinched her arms till they were black and blue, and made her go into their church, and, because she would not cross herself, struck her several blows with their hands on her face.

A squaw was brought in and said she was sent to fetch her to the Indians, but she refused. The squaw went away and said she would bring her husband with her tomorrow, and she should be carried away by force. She told me she remembered what I told her one day after the nuns had threatened to give her away to the Indians, that they only said so to affright her, that they never would give her away. The nuns told her she should not be permitted anymore to speak to the English and that they would afflict her without giving her any rest if she refused. But God preserved her from falling. This poor girl had many prayers going up to heaven for her daily and by name because her trials were more known to some of the English than the trials of others who lived more remote from them.

Here might be a history by itself of the trials and sufferings of many of our children and young ones who have been abused and after separation from grown persons made to do as they would have them.

I SHALL HERE give an account of what was done to one of my children, a boy between fifteen and sixteen years of age, two hundred miles distance from me, which occasioned grief and sorrow that I want words to utter, and yet kept under such awe that he never durst write anything to me for fear of being discovered in writing about religion. They threatened to put him to the Indians again if he would not turn, telling him he was never bought out of their hands but only sojourned with them, but, if he would turn, he should never be put into their hands anymore. The priests would spend whole days in urging of him.

He was sent to school to learn to read and write French; the schoolmaster sometimes flattered him with promises if he would cross himself, then threatened him if he would not. But when he saw flattering promises of rewards and threatenings were ineffectual, he struck him with a stick he had in his hand; and when he saw that would not do, he made him get down on his knees about an hour and then came and bid him make the sign of the cross, and that without any delay; he still refused. Then he gave him a couple of strokes with a whip he had in his hand, which whip had three branches and about twelve great knots tied in it. And again bid him make the sign of the cross, and if it was any sin he would bear it himself. And said also, "You are afraid you shall be changed if you do it, but," said he, "you will be the same, your fingers won't be changed." And after he had made him shed many tears under his abuses and threatenings, he told him he would have it done; and so through cowardice and fear of the whip, he made the sign.

[He] did so for several days together; with much ado he was brought to cross himself. And then the master told him he would have it done without his particular bidding him. And when he came to say his lesson and crossed not himself, the master said, "Have you forgot what I bid you do?"

"No sir," said he.

Then the schoolmaster said, "Down on your knees." And so kept him for an hour and a half till school was done, and so did for about a week. When he saw this would not do, he took the whip, "What, won't you do it?" said he, "I will make you." And so again frightened him to a compliance.

After this [he] commanded him to go to the church; when he refused, he told him he would make him. And one morning [he] sent four of the biggest boys of the school to draw him by force to Mass. These with other severities and witty stratagems were used, and I utterly ignorant of any attempt made upon him to bring him to change his religion. His fear was such that he never durst write any of these things lest his letters should fall into their hands, and he should again be delivered to the Indians. Hearing of an opportunity of writing to him by one of the parish where I was, going up to Mont-Royal, I wrote a letter to him and had by him a letter from my son which I shall here insert.

Honored Father,

I have received your letter bearing date January 11th, 1705/6, for which I give you many thanks with my duty and my brother's. I am sorry you have not received all the letters I have writ to you, as I have not received all yours. According to your good counsel I do almost every day read something of the Bible and so strengthen my faith.

As to the captives newly brought, Lancaster is the place of two of them and Marlborough that of the third: the governor of Mont-Royal has them all three. There is other news that will seem more strange to you: that two English women who in their lifetime were dreadfully set against the Catholic religion did on their deathbed embrace it. The one Abigail Turbet,[60] the other of them Esther Jones,[61] both of them known to you.

Abigail Turbet sent for Mr. Meriel[62] the Sabbath before she died. [She] said (many a time upon several following days) that she committed her soul into his hands and was ready to do whatever he pleased. She desired him to go to the Chapel St. Anne and there to say a holy Mass for her that she might have her sins pardoned and the will of the Lord accomplished upon her. Her cousin Mrs. Badston, now Stilson, asked her whether she should be willing to do as she said; she answered, yes. And upon the Tuesday she was taken into the Catholic Church in the presence of John Laland, and Madam Grizalem, an Englishwoman, and Mrs. Stilson, also with many French people besides.

She was anointed with oil on the same day; according to her will then upon the Wednesday an image of Christ crucified was brought to her, she caused it to be set up over against her at the curtains of her bed and looked continually upon the same; and also a little crucifix brought unto her, she took it, and kissed it, and laid it upon her stomach. She did also make the sign of the cross upon herself when she took any meat or drink. She promised to God that if she should recover she would go to the Mass every day. She, having on her hand a crucifix, saying, "Oh my Lord that I should have known thee so late!"

She did also make a prayer to the Virgin Mary the two last days of the week. She could utter no word, but by kissing the crucifix, endeavoring the crossing herself, she gave every evidence of her faith; she died Saturday the 24th of November [1705] at three a clock in the afternoon. The next day the priest did commend that woman's soul to the prayers of the congregation in the Mass; in the afternoon she was honorably buried in the churchyard next to the church close

60. Abigail Cass Turbet (1674–1705) was captured at Cape Porpoise (now Kennebunkport, Maine), probably in 1703.

61. Esther Ingersoll Jones (1665–1705) of Northampton, Massachusetts, was captured at Pascomuck (now in Easthampton) in 1704. See Coleman, *New England Captives*, I, 320–321.

62. Father Henri-Antoine de Meriel, a Sulpican priest. (See Coleman, *New England Captives*, I, 40; and *Dictionary of Canadian Biography*, II, 467–468.) The Order of St. Sulpice had virtual control of Montreal during this period.

to the body of the Justice Pese's[63] wife, all the people being present at her funeral.

The same day in the evening Mr. Meriel with an Englishwoman went to Esther Jones; she did at first disdain, but a little after she confessed there were seven sacraments;[64] Christ's body present, the sacrament of the Mass, the inequality of power among the pastors of the church; and, being returned to wait by her all night long, he read and expounded to her some part of the Catholic Confession of Faith to her satisfaction. About midnight he asked her whether she might not confess her sins. "I doubt not but I may," said she. And two hours after she made unto him a fervent confession of all the sins of her whole life. When he said he was to offer Christ to His Father for her, she liked it very well.

The superior of the nuns being come in to see her, she now desired that she might receive Christ's body before she died. She did also show Mrs. Stilson a great mind to receive the sacrament of extreme unction and said that if ever she should recover and get home she would have reproached the ministers for their neglecting that sacrament so plainly commanded by St. James. In the afternoon after she had begged pardon for her wavering and the Catholic Confession of Faith was read aloud to her in the hearing of Mr. Craston, Mrs. Stilson, and another Englishwoman, and she owned the same;[65] about seven a clock the same day she said to Mr. Dubison, "Shall not they give me the holy communion?" But her tongue was then so thick that she could hardly swallow anything. She was then anointed with holy oil, but before she said to Mr. Meriel, "Why have you not yet, sir, forgiven my sins?"

In the following night that priest and Mr. Dubison were continually by her and sometimes praying to God in her name and praying to the Virgin Mary and other saints. She said also, "I believe all. I am

63. Perhaps Justice of the Peace.

64. Puritan doctrine recognized only two sacraments—baptism and communion. This description and the subsequent Catholic beliefs set forth in Samuel's description of Esther Jones's conversion emphasize the differences between Calvinist and Catholic doctrines.

65. That is, Esther Jones acknowledged her belief in the Catholic confession. Mr. Craston is not identified; the name may be a badly garbled phonetic spelling of a French name. Mrs. Stilson (Anne Odiorne Batson, 1673–?) was captured in 1703 and baptized as a Catholic in 1705. The next year she married another captive, John Stilson of Pemaquid, Maine. Mr. Dubison may be Jacques-Charles Renaud Dubuisson (1666–1739), a Canadian officer who was stationed in Quebec during the years of Williams's captivity and in 1704 was assistant town major of Quebec.

very glad Christ was offered to His Father for me." Six or seven hours before she died, a crucifix was showed to her by Mr. Dubison, she took it and laid it upon her heart and kissed it, and the nuns hung it with a pair of beads upon her neck. A little before she died Mr. Dubison asked her to pray for him in heaven; she promised him.

So she gave up the ghost at ten of the clock the 27th of November [1705] whilst the high Mass was saying; she was soon commended to the prayers. On the fourth day of the week following [she] was buried after the Mass had been said for her. She was laid by Abigail Turbet.

Jan. 23rd, 1705/6

I have here transcribed the letter in the very words of it without the least alteration: the same for substance was sent to several other captives. When I had this letter, I presently knew it to be of Mr. Meriel's composing, but the messenger who brought the letter brought word that my son had embraced their religion. Afterwards when some blamed him for letting me know of it because they said they feared my sorrow would shorten my days, he told me he thought with himself that if he was in my case he should be willing to know the worst and, therefore, told me as he would have desired to have known if in my place. I thanked him, acknowledging it a favor to let me know of it, but the news was ready to overwhelm me with grief and sorrow.

I made my complaint to God and mourned before Him; sorrow and anguish took hold upon me. I asked of God to direct me what to do and how to write and find out an opportunity of conveying a letter to him and committed this difficulty to His providence. I now found a greater opposition to a patient, quiet, humble resignation to the will of God than I should otherwise have known if not so tried. Here I thought of my afflictions and trials; my wife and two children killed and many of my neighbors; and myself and so many of my children and friends in a popish captivity separated from our children, not capable to come to instruct them in the way they ought to go, and cunning crafty enemies using all their subtlety to insinuate into young ones such principles as would be pernicious. I thought with myself how happy many others were, in that they had their children with them under all advantages to bring them up in the nurture and admonition of the Lord, while we were separated one from another and our children in great peril of embracing damnable doctrines.

Oh! That all parents who read this history would bless God for the advantages they have of educating their children and faithfully improve it! I mourned when I thought with myself that I had one child with the Mac-quas,[66] a second turned to popery,[67] and a little child of six years of age in danger from a child to be instructed in popery,[68] and knew full well that all endeavors would be used to prevent my seeing or speaking with them. But in the midst of all these God gave me a secret hope that He would magnify His power and free grace and disappoint all their crafty designs. When I looked on the right hand and on the left, all refuge failed, and none showed any care for my soul. But God brought that word to uphold me who is able to do exceeding abundantly above what we can ask or think. As also that—is anything too hard for God? I prayed to God to direct me and wrote very short the first time and in general terms, fearing lest if I should write about things in controversy, my letters would not come to him. I therefore addressed him with the following letter:

Son Samuel,

Yours of January 23rd I received and with it had the tidings that you had made an abjuration of the Protestant faith for the Romish— news that I heard with the most distressing, afflicting, sorrowful spirit that ever I heard any news. Oh! I pity you; I mourn over you day and night! Oh, I pity your weakness that through the craftiness of man you are turned from the simplicity of the gospel! I persuade myself you have done it through ignorance. Oh! Why have you ne-glected to ask your father's advice in an affair of so great importance as the change of religion! God knows that the catechism in which I instructed you is according to the word of God and so will be found in the Day of Judgment. Oh! Consider and bethink yourself what you have done! And whether you ask me or not, my poor child, I cannot but pray for you that you may be recovered out of the snare you are taken in. Read the Bible, pray in secret, make Christ's righ-teousness your only plea before God for justification. Beware of all immorality and of prophaning God's Sabbaths.

Let a father's advice be asked for the future in all things of weight and moment. What is a man profited if he gain the whole world and lose his own soul? Or what shall a man give in exchange for his soul? I desire to be humbled under the mighty hand of God thus afflicting of me. I would not do as you have done for ten thousand worlds. My

66. Eunice, then at the Caughnawaga mission near Montreal.
67. Samuel, then at Montreal.
68. Warham, also at Montreal.

heart aches within me, but I will yet wait upon the Lord, to Him will I commit your case day and night. He can perform all things for me and mine and can yet again recover you from your fall. He is a God forgiving iniquity, transgression, and sin; to the Lord our God belong forgivenesses though we have rebelled. I charge you not to be instrumental to ensnare your poor brother Warham, or any other, and to add sin to sin. Accept of my love and don't forsake a father's advice, who, above all things, desires that your soul may be saved in the day of the Lord.

What I mournfully wrote, I followed with my poor cries to God in heaven to make effectual, to cause in him a consideration of what he had done. God saw what a proud heart I had and what need I had to be so answered out of the whirlwind that I might be humbled before Him. Not having any answer to my letter for some weeks, I wrote the following letter as I was enabled of God and sent to him by a faithful hand, which by the blessing of God was made effectual for his good and the good of others who had fallen to popery, and for the establishing and strengthening of others to resist the essays of the adversary to truth. God brought good out of this evil and made what was designed to promote their interest an occasion of shame to them.

Son Samuel,

I have waited till now for an answer from you hoping to hear from you why you made an abjuration of the Protestant faith for Romish. But since you continue to neglect to write to me about it as you neglected to take any advice or counsel from a father when you did it, I cannot forbear writing again and making some reflections on the letter you wrote me last, about the two women. It seems to me from those words of Abigail Turbet's in your letter, or rather of Mr. Meriel which you transcribed for him—"Abigail Turbet sent for Mr. Meriel, she committed her soul into his hand, and was ready to do whatsoever he pleased"—I say it seems rational to believe that she had not the use of her reason; it's an expression to be abhorred by all who have any true sense of religion. Was Mr. Meriel a God, a Christ? Could he bear to hear such words and not reject them, replying, "Don't commit your soul into my hands, but see that you commit your soul into the hands of God through Christ Jesus and do whatever God commands you in His holy word."

As for me I am a creature and can't save your soul but will tell you of Acts 4:12: "Neither is there salvation in any other, for there is no other name under heaven given among men whereby we must be saved." Had he been a faithful minister of Jesus Christ, he would have said, " 'Tis an honor due to Christ alone." The holy apostle says: "Now unto Him that is able to keep you and present you faultless before the presence of His glory with exceeding joy to the only wise God our Saviour be glory, and majesty, dominion and power, both now and ever, amen" (Jude 24 and 25 verses).

As to what you write about praying to the Virgin Mary and other saints, I make this reply: had Mr. Meriel done his duty, he should have said to them as 1 John 2:1–2: "If any man sin, we have an advocate with the Father, Jesus Christ the righteous, and He is the propitiation for our sins." The Scriptures say, "There is one God and one mediator between God and man, the man Christ Jesus." Yea, Christ said, "Go and preach, he that believeth and is baptized shall be saved." The apostle in Gal. 1:8 saith: "But though we or an angel from heaven preach any other gospel unto you than that we have preached to you, let him be accursed." They never preached [or] prayed to the Virgin Mary or other saints.

As you would be saved, hear what the apostle saith, Heb. 4:13, etc.: "Neither is there any creature that is not manifest in His sight, but all things are naked and opened unto the eyes of Him with whom we have to do. Seeing then that we have a great high priest that is entered into the heavens, Jesus the Son of God, let us hold fast our profession, for we have not an high priest that cannot be touched with the feeling of our infirmities but was in all points tempted like as we are, yet without sin; let us therefore come boldly unto the throne of grace that we may obtain mercy and find grace to help in time of need." Which words do hold forth how that Christ Jesus is in every respect qualified to be a mediator and intercessor, and I am sure they can't be applied to any mere creature to make them capable of our religious trust.

When Roman Catholics have said all they can, they are not able to prove that the saints in heaven have a knowledge of what prayers are directed to them. Some say they know them one way, others say they have the knowledge of them another way, and that which they have fixed upon as most probable to them is that they know of them from their beholding the face of God, seeing God they know these prayers, but this is a great mistake. Though the saints see and know God in a glorious manner, yet they have not an infinite knowledge, and it does no ways follow that, because they see God, they know all prayers that are directed to them upon the earth. And God has nowhere in His world told us that the saints have such a knowledge.

Besides, were it a thing possible for them to have a knowledge of what prayers are directed to them, it does not follow that they are to be prayed to or have religious honor conferred upon them. The Romanists can neither give one Scripture precept or example for praying to them, but God has provided a mediator who knows all our petitions and is faithful and merciful enough, and we have both Scripture and precept and example to look to Him as our mediator and advocate with the Father. Further it can't be proved that it's consistent with the saints being creatures as well as with their happiness to have a knowledge of prayers from all parts of the world at the same time from many millions together about things so vastly differing one from another. And then to present those supplications for all that look to them; it's not humility but will worship. Col. 2:18: "Let no man beguile you of your reward in a voluntary humility, worshiping of angels." Verse 23: "Which things indeed have a show of wisdom, will worship and humility."

For what humility can it be to distrust the way that God has provided and encouraged us to come to Him in and impose upon God a way of our own devising? Was not God angry with Jeroboam for imposing upon Him after such a sort? 1 Kings 12:33: "So he offered upon the altar which he had made in Bethel the fifth day of the eighth month which he devised of his own heart." Therefore Christ saith, Mark 7:7: "Howbeit in vain do they worship me, teaching for doctrines the commandments of men." Before the coming of Christ and His entering into heaven as an intercessor, Heb. 7:25: "Wherefore He is able to save them to the uttermost that come to God by Him, seeing He ever liveth to make intercession for them." I say before Christ's entering into heaven as an intercessor [there is] not one word of any prayer to saints. What reason can be given that now there is of so many saints to make intercession when Christ as a priest is entered into heaven to make intercession for us?

The answer that the Romanists give is a very fable and falsehood, namely that there were no saints in heaven till after the Resurrection and Ascension of Christ but were reserved in a place called *Limbus Patrum* and so had not the beatifical vision. See Gen. 5:24: "Enoch walked with God and was not, for God took him." If he was not taken into heaven, what can be the sense of those words "for God took him?" Again, 2 Kings 2:1, when the Lord would take up Elijah into heaven by a whirlwind, verse 11: "There appeared a chariot of fire and horses of fire and parted them both asunder, and Elijah went up by a whirlwind into heaven." Must the truth of the Scripture be called in question to uphold their notions? Besides, 'tis not consistent with reason to suppose that Enoch and Elijah, instead of having a peculiar privilege vouchsafed to them for their eminency in holiness, should be less happy for so long a time than the rest of the saints deceased who are glorified in heaven, which must be if they are yet kept, and must be till the Day of Judgment, out of heaven and the beatifical vision in an earthly paradise, according to some of the Romanists, or in some other place they know not where, according to others.

Religious worship is not to be given to the creature, Matt. 4:9-10, and saith, "All these things will I give thee if thou will fall down and worship me. Then saith Jesus to him, 'Get thee hence Satan, for it is written thou shalt worship the Lord thy God, and Him only shalt thou serve.' " That phrase, "and Him only shalt thou serve," excludes all creatures. Rev. 22:8-9: "I fell down to worship before the feet of the angel which showed me these things. Then saith he to me, 'see thou do it not, for I am thy fellow servant, and of thy fellow servant, and of thy breathren the Prophets, and of them which keep the sayings of this book—worship God.' " Which plainly shows that God only is to be worshiped with a religious worship. None can think that Saint John intended to give the highest divine worship to the angel, "Don't fall down and worship me; it's God's due, worship God." So Acts 10:25-26: "As Peter was coming in, Cornelius met him and fell down at his feet and worshiped him, but Peter took him up, saying, 'Stand up, I myself also am a man.' "

See also Lev. 19:10, the words of the Second Commandment (which the Romanists either leave out or add to their First Commandment saying, "Thou shalt have no other gods before me," adding etc.); I say the words of the Second Commandment are, "Thou shalt not make to thyself any graven image, or any likeness of anything that is in heaven above, or that is in the earth beneath, or that is in the waters under the earth; thou shalt not bow down thyself to them nor serve them, for I the Lord thy God am a jealous God, etc." These words being inserted in the letter that came from your brother Eleazar in New England the last summer was the cause of the letter's being sent down from Mont-Royal and not given to you when so near you, as I suppose there being no other clause of the letter that could be objected against and the reason why found at Quebeck, when I sent it to you a second time and enclosed in a letter written by myself.

The brazen serpent made by divine appointment as a type of Christ, when abused to superstition, was by reforming Hezekiah broken in pieces. As to what the Romanists plead about the lawfulness of image and saint worship from those likenesses of things made in Solomon's Temple, it's nothing to the purpose. We don't say it is not lawful to make or have a picture, but those carved images were not in the Temple to be adored, bowed down to, or worshiped. There is no manner of consequence that because there were images in Solomon's Temple that were not adored and worshiped that therefore it's now lawful to make and fall down before images and pray to them and so worship them. Religous worshiping of saints can't be defended from but is forbidden in the Scriptures, and, for fear of losing their disciples, the Romanists keep away from them the Bible and oblige them to believe as they say they must believe. As though there was no use to be made of our reason about our souls, and yet the Beroeans were counted noble for searching the Scriptures to see whether the things preached by Saint Paul were so or no. They dare not allow you liberty to speak with your father or others for fear their errors should be discovered to you.

Again you write that "Esther Jones confessed that there was an inequality of power among the pastors of the church." An argument to convince the world that because the priests in fallacious ways caused a woman distempered with a very high fever, if not distracted, to say she confessed there was an inequality of power among the pastors of the church; therefore, all the world are obliged to believe that there is a pope. An argument to be sent from Dan to Beersheba everywhere, where any English captives are, to gain their belief of a pope.

Can any rational man think that Christ in the sixteenth chapter of Matthew gave Saint Peter such a power as the papists speak of? Or that the Disciples so understood Christ? When immediately there arose a dispute among them who should be the greatest in the Kingdom of Heaven? Matt. 18:1: "At the same time came the Disciples of Jesus, saying, 'Who is the greatest in the Kingdom of Heaven?' " The rock spoken of in sixteenth of Matthew [is] not the person of Peter but the confession made by him, and the same power is given to all the Disciples if you compare one Scripture with another, not one word in any place of Scripture of such a vicarship power as of a pope, nor any solid foundation of proof that Peter had a greater authority than the rest of the Apostles. 1 Cor. 4:6. "That you might learn in us not to think of men above that which is written." Yea, the Apostle condemns them, 1 Cor. 1:12, for their contentions, "one saying I am of Paul, I of Apollos, and I of Caephas"; no more of Peter's being a foundation than any of the rest. "For we are built upon the foundation of the Apostles and Prophets, Jesus Christ Himself being the chief cornerstone," not one word in any of Peter's epistles showing that he had greater power than the other Apostles.

Nay, if the Scriptures give any preference, it is to Saint Paul rather than Saint Peter. 1 Cor. 3:10: "According to the grace of God which is given to me as a wise master builder, I have laid the foundation." 1 Cor. 5:3–4: "For I verily as absent in body but present in spirit, have judged already as though I were present concerning him that hath so done this deed. In the name of our Lord Jesus Christ when ye are gathered together, and my spirit, with the power of our Lord Jesus Christ," etc. 1 Cor. 7:1: "Now concerning the things whereof ye wrote to me"; application made not to Saint Peter but Paul for the decision of a controversy or scruple. 1 Cor. 11:2: "Now I praise you brethren that you remember me in all things and keep the ordinances as I delivered them to you." Either those spoken of, Acts 15, or in his ministry and epistles, 2 Cor. 2:10, "For your sake forgave I it in the person of Christ." 2 Cor. 11:28: "That which cometh upon me daily, the care of all the churches." 2 Cor. 12:11–12: "For in nothing am I behind the very chiefest of the Apostles, though I be nothing. Truly the signs of an Apostle were wrought among you in all patience, in signs and wonders, and mighty deeds," and in other places.

Again if you consult Acts 15 where you have an account of the first synod or council, you will find that the counsel or sentence of the Apostle James is followed, verse 19, "Wherefore my sentence is," etc., not a word that St. Peter was chief. Again, you find Peter himself sent forth by the other Apostles, Acts 8:14, "The Apostles sent unto them Peter and John." When the church of the Jews found fault with Peter for going to the gentiles when he went to Cornelius, he does not say, "Why do you question me or call me to an account? I am Christ's vicar on earth." When Paul reproved Peter, Gal. 2, he does not defend himself by mentioning an infallibility in himself as Christ's vicar or reprove Paul for his boldness.

The Roman Catholic Church can't be a true church of Christ in that it makes laws directly contrary to the laws and commands of Christ. As for example, in withholding the wine or the cup from the laity in the Lord's Supper; whenas Christ commands the same to drink who were to eat. Their evasion that the blood is in the body , and so they partake of both in eating, is a great fallacy built on a false foundation of transubstantiation. For when men eat, they can't be said to drink, which Christ commands, for Christ commands that we take the cup and drink, which is not done in eating; besides, the priests themselves won't be so put off. The words "this is my body" do only intend this doth signify or represent my body, which will appear if you compare Scripture with Scripture, for after the consecration the Holy Ghost calls it bread and the fruit of the vine. Exod. 12:11, "It is the Lord's Passover," that is, it represents it. In all the Evangelists you read of killing and eating the Passover a few lines or verses before these words, "this is my body," which plainly show that our Savior in the same way of figurative expression speaks of the Gospel Sacrament.

If these words were taken as the Romanists expound them, he must eat his own body himself, whole and entire in his own hands; and after that each one of the Disciples eat him entire, and yet he set at the table whole, untouched at the same time; contradictions impossible to be defended by any rational arguments. Yea, his whole body must be now in Heaven and in a thousand other places and in the mouth of every communicant at the same time, and that both as a broken and unbroken sacrifice and be subject to putrefaction. Christ is said to be a door, a true vine, a way, a rock. What work shall we make if we expound these in a literal manner as the Romanists do when they say "this is my body" is meant of the real body of Christ in the Eucharist? It's said, 1 Cor. 10:4: "And did all drink the same spiritual drink. For they drank of that spiritual rock that followed them—and that rock was Christ." Was Christ literally a rock, think you? Yea, it is absurd to believe that a priest uttering a few words over a wafer not above an inch square can make it a God or the body of Christ entire as it was offered on the cross. [It is] a blasphemy to pretend to a power of making God at their pleasure, and then eat Him and give Him to others to be eaten or shut Him up in their altars, that they can utter the same words and make a God or not make a God according to their intention, and that the people are obliged to believe that it is God and so adore it when they never hear any word of consecration nor know the priest's intention.

As to what you write about the holy Mass, I reply it's wholly an human invention; not a word of such a sacrifice in the whole Bible, its being a sacrifice propitiatory daily to be offered is contrary to the holy Scriptures, Heb. 7:27: "Who needeth not daily, as those high priests, to offer up sacrifice first for his own sins and then for the peoples', for this He did once when He offered up Himself." And yet the Romanists say there is need that He be offered up as a sacrifice to God every day. Heb. 9:12: "By His own blood He entered in once into the holy place, having obtained eternal redemption for us." And 25–28: "Nor yet that He should offer Himself often, as the high priest entereth into the holy place, every year with the blood of others. For then must He often have suffered since the foundation of the world. But now once in the end of the world, hath He appeared to put away sin by the sacrifice of Himself. As it is appointed unto men once to die, but after this the judgment: so Christ was once offered to bear the sins of many." Heb. 10:10: "By which will we are sanctified through the offering of the body of Jesus Christ once for all." Verse 12: "But this man, after He had offered one sacrifice for sins, forever sat down on the right hand of God." Verse 14: "For by one offering He hath perfected forever them that are sanctified." By which Scriptures you may see that the Mass is not of divine appointment but an human invention. Their evasion of a bloody and an unbloody sacrifice is a sham; the holy Scriptures speak not one word of Christ being offered as a sacrifice propitiatory after such a sort as they call an unbloody sacrifice. All the ceremonies of the Mass are human inventions that God never commanded.

As to what in the letter about praying for the women after their death is very ridiculous. For as the tree falls, so it lies, as death leaves, judgment will find; no change after death from an afflicted to an happy place and state. Purgatory is a fancy for the enriching the clergy and impoverishing the laity. The notion of it [is] a fatal snare to many souls who sin with hopes of easy getting priestly absolutions at death and buyinig off torments with their money. The soul at death goes immediately to judgment and so to heaven or hell. No authentic place of Scripture mentions so much as one word of any such place or state. Mr. Meriel told me if I found one error in our religion it was enough to cause me to disown our whole religion. By his argument you may see what reason you have to avoid that religion that is so full of errors.

Bethink yourself and consult the Scriptures, if you can get them (I mean the Bible). Can you think their religion is right when they are afraid to let you have an English Bible? Or to speak with your father, or other of your Christian neighbors, for fear they should give you such convictions of truth that they can't remove? Can that religion be true that can't bear an examination from the Scriptures that are a perfect rule in matters of faith? Or that must be upheld by ignorance, especially ignorance of the holy Scriptures? These things have I written as in my heart I believe.

I long for your recovery and will not cease to pray for it. I am now a man of sorrowful spirit, and look upon your fall as the most aggravating circumstance of my afflictions, and am persuaded that no pains will be wanting to prevent me from seeing or speaking with you; but I know that God's grace is all-sufficient; He is able to do exceeding abundantly above what I can ask or think. Don't give way to discouragement as to a return to New England; read over what I have written and keep it with you if you can; you have no friend on earth that wisheth your eternal salvation more heartily than your father. I long to see and speak with you, but I never forget you; my love to you and to your brother and sister, and to all our fellow prisoners. Let me hear from you as often as you can. I hope God will appear for us before it be long.

There are a great many other things in the letter that deserve to be refuted, but I shall be too tedious in remarking of them all at once, yet [I] would not pass over that passage in the letter that Esther Jones confessed that there were seven sacraments. To which I answer that some of the most learned of the Romish religion confessed (without the distracting pains of violent fever) and left it upon record in print that it can't be convincingly made out from the Scripture that there are seven sacraments, and that their most incontestable proof is from tradition, and by their traditions they might have found seventeen as well as seven, considering that four popes successively spent their lives purging and correcting old authors. But no man can out of the holy Scriptures prove more than two sacraments of divine institution under the New Testament, namely baptism and the Lord's Supper.

If you make the Scriptures a perfect rule of faith, as you ought to do, you can't believe as the Romish Church believes. Oh! See that you sanctify the Lord Himself in your heart and make Him your fear and dread. "Fear not them that can kill the body, and after that have no more that they can do, but rather fear Him that has power to destroy soul and body in hell-fire." The Lord have mercy upon you and show you mercy for the worthiness and righteousness' sake of Jesus Christ, our great and glorious redeemer and advocate who makes intercession for transgressors. My prayers are daily to God for you, for your brother and sister, yea for all my children and fellow prisoners. I am your afflicted and sorrowful father.

John Williams

Chateauriche, March 22, 1706

God, who is gloriously free and rich in His grace to vile sinners, was pleased to bless poor and weak means for the recovery of my child so taken and gave me to see that He did not say to the House of Jacob, "Seek you me in vain." Oh! That every reader would in every difficulty make Him their refuge; He is a hopeful stay. To alleviate my sorrow, I received the following letter in answer to mine.

Mont-Royal, May 12, 1706

Honored Father,

I received your letter which you sent by   , which good letter I thank you for and for the good counsel which you gave me; I desire to be thankful for it and hope it will be for the good of my soul. I may say as in the Psalms: "The sorrows of death compassed me, and the pains of hell got hold on me. I found trouble and sorrow, then called I upon the name of the Lord. O Lord, I beseech Thee deliver my soul! Gracious is the Lord and righteous, yea our God is merciful."

As for what you ask me about my making an abjuration of the Protestant faith for the Romish, I durst not write so plain to you as I would but hope to see and discourse with you. I am sorry for the sin I have committed in changing of religion, for which I am greatly to blame. You may know that Mr. Meriel, the schoolmaster, and others were continually at me about it; at last I gave over to it, for which I am very sorry.

As for that letter you had from me, it was a letter I transcribed for Mr. Meriel. And for what he said about Abigail Turbet and Esther Jones, nobody heard them but he as I understand. I desire your

219

prayers to God for me to deliver me from my sins. Oh, remember me in your prayers! I am your dutiful son, ready to take your counsel.

Samuel Williams

This priest, Mr. Meriel, has brought many letters to him and bid him write them over and send them, and so he has done for many others. By this as also by Mrs. Stilson's saying she does not think that either of these women did change their religion before their death (she affirms also that oftentimes during their sickness, whilst they had the use of their reason, they protested against the Romish religion and faith), it's evident that these women never died papists, but that it was a wily stratagem of the priests to advance their religion, for letters were sent immediately after their death to use this as a persuasive argument to gain others. But God in His providence gave in farther conviction of their fallaciousness in this matter.

For the last summer one Biggilow of Marlborough,[69] a captive at Mont-Royal, was very sick in the hospital and in the judgment of all with a sickness to death. Then the priests and others gave out that he was turned to be of their religion and taken into their communion. But contrary to their expectation he was brought back from the gates of death and would comply with none of their rites, saying that whilst he had the use of his reason he never spake anything in favor of their religion. And that he never disowned the Protestant faith, nor would he now. So that they were silenced and put to shame. There is no reason to think that these two women were any more papists than he, but they are dead and cannot speak. One of the witnesses spoken of in the forementioned letter told me she knew of no such thing and said Mr. Meriel told her that he never heard a more fervent and affectionate prayer than one which Esther Jones made a little before her death. I am verily persuaded that he calls that [fervent] prayer [directed] to God [just before her death] so full of affection and confession, the confession made by her of the sins of her whole life. These two women always in their health, and so in their sickness, opposed all popish principles as all that knew them can testify so long as they could be permitted to go and speak with them. One of these women was taken from the Eastward, and the other, namely Esther Jones, from Northampton.

69. John Bigelow, a carpenter. See Coleman, *New England Captives*, I, 310–313.

IN THE BEGINNING of March 1706, Mr. Sheldon came again to Canada with letters from his Excellency our governor at which time I was a few days at Quebeck.[70] And when I was there, one night about ten a clock there was an earthquake that made a report like a cannon and made the houses to tremble. It was heard and felt many leagues all along the Island of St. Lawrence and other places. When Mr. Sheldon came the second time, the adversaries did what they could to retard the time of our return to gain time to seduce our young ones to popery. Such were sent away who were judged ungainable, and most of the younger sort still kept, some still flattered with promises of reward and great essays to get others married among them. One [was] debauched and then in twenty-four hours of time published, [she was] taken into their communion and married, but the poor soul has had time since to lament her sin and folly with a bitter cry and asks your prayers that God of His sovereign grace would yet bring [her] out of the horrible pit she has thrown herself into. Her name was Rachael Storer of Wells.[71]

In April one Zebediah Williams of our town died.[72] He was a very hopeful and pious young man who carried himself so in his captivity as to edify several of the English and recover one fallen to popery taken the last war; though some were enraged against him on these accounts, yet even the French where he sojourned and with whom he conversed would say he was a good man, one that was very prayerful to God and studious and painful in reading the holy Scriptures, a man of a good understanding, a desirable conversation. In the beginning of his last sickness he made a visit (before he went to the hospital, at Quebeck) to my great satisfaction and our mutual consolation and comfort in our captivity, as he had several times before, living not above two miles from me over the river at the Island of St. Lawrence about six weeks or two months.

After his death the French told me Zebediah was gone to hell and damned. For, said they, he has appeared since his death (to one Joseph Egerly [Edgerly], an Englishman who was taken the last war) in flaming

70. On his second expedition to Canada, Ensign Sheldon was accompanied by John Wells of Deerfield and Joseph Bradley of Haverhill. In May 1706 they embarked for Boston with fifty-four redeemed captives.

71. Rachael Storer was captured in 1703. She soon converted to Catholicism and was baptized as Marie Françoise; in 1706 she married a Canadian soldier, Jean Berger. See Coleman, *New England Captives*, I, 398, 423–425.

72. Zebediah Williams, no relation to John, had been captured near Deerfield several months before the surprise assault in which the bulk of the town's captives were taken. He died in Quebec. Coleman, *New England Captives*, II, 33, 38–39.

fire, telling him he was damned for refusing to embrace the Romish religion when such pains were used to bring him to the true faith and for being instrumental to draw him away from the Romish Communion forsaking the Mass, and was therefore now come to advertise him of his danger. I told them I judged it to be a popish lie, saying I bless God our religion needs no lies to uphold, maintain, and establish it as theirs did. But they affirmed it to be true, telling me how God approved of their religion and witnessed miraculously against ours. But I still told them I was persuaded his soul was in heaven and that these reports were only devised fables to seduce souls.

For several weeks they affirmed it, telling me that all who came over the river from the island affirmed it to be a truth. I begged of God to blast this hellish design of theirs so that in the issue it might be to render their religion more abominable and that they might not gain one soul by such a stratagem. After some weeks had passed in such assertions, there came one into my landlord's house affirming it to be a truth reported of Zebediah, saying Joseph Egerly had been over the river and told one of our neighbors this story.

After a few hours I saw that neighbor and asked him whether he had seen Edgerly lately; he said, "Yes."

"What news told he to you?"

"None," said he.

Then I told him what was affirmed as a truth; he answered [that] Egerly said nothing like this to him, and he was persuaded he would have told him if there had been any truth in it.

About a week after this came one John Boult from the Island of St. Lawrence, a lad taken from Newfoundland, a very serious sober lad of about seventeen years of age; he had often before come over with Zebediah to visit me. At his coming in, he much lamented the loss of Zebediah and told me that for several weeks they had told him the same story, affirming it to be a truth, and that Egerly was so awakened by it as to go again to Mass every day, urging him since God in such a miraculous way offered such conviction of the truth of their religion and the falsehood and danger of ours, to come over to their religion or else his damnation would be dreadfully aggravated.

He, said he, could have no rest from them day and night, but, said he, "I told them their religion was contrary to the word of God, and therefore I would not embrace it, and that I did not believe what they said. And," says he to me, "One day I was sitting in the house and Egerly came in, and I spake to him before the whole family in the French tongue, for he could not speak much English, and asked him of this story. He answered, 'It's a great falsehood,' saying, 'He never appeared to me, nor have I ever reported any such thing to anybody.' And that he had never been at the Mass since Zebediah's death." At the hearing of which they were silenced and put to shame; we blessed God together for discovering their wickedness, and disappointing them in what they aimed at, and prayed to God to deliver us and all the captives from delusions, and recover them who had fallen, and so parted.

After which I took my pen and wrote a letter to one Mr. Samuel Hill, an English captive taken from Wells who lived at Quebeck, and his brother Ebenezar Hill[73] to make a discovery of this lying plot to warn them of their danger and assure them of the falsehood of this report, but the letter fell into the hands of the priests and was never delivered. This Egerly came home with us so that they gained nothing but shame by this stratagem. God often disappoints the crafty devices of wicked men.

IN THE LATTER END of summer they told me they had news from New England by one who had been a captive at Boston who said that the ministers at Boston had told the French captives that the Protestant religion was the only true religion, and that as a confirmation of it they would raise a dead person to life before their eyes for their conviction, and that, having persuaded one to feign himself dead, they came and prayed over him and then commanded him in the name of Christ (whose religion they kept pure) to arise; they called and commanded, but he never arose, so that instead of raising the dead they killed the living, which the bereaved relations discovered. I told them it was an old lie and calumny against Luther and Calvin new vamped and that they only changed the persons and place, but they affirmed it to be a truth; I told them I wondered they were so fond of a faith propagated and then maintained by lying words.

We were always out of hopes of being returned before winter, the season proving so cold in the latter end of September, and were praying to God to prepare our hearts with all holy submission to His holy will to glorify His holy name in a way of passive obedience in the winter. For my own part I was informed by several who came from the city that the lord intendant[74] said if more returned and brought word that Battis [Baptiste]

73. Samuel and Ebenezar Hill had been captured in Maine at Wells and Saco, respectively, in August 1703. See Coleman, *New England Captives,* I, 401–403; II, 17–19.

74. Probably Antoine-Denis Raudot (1679–1737), intendant of New France from 1705 to 1710. See *Dictionary of Canadian Biography,* II, 549–554.

was in prison, he would put me into prison and lay me in irons.[75] They would not permit me to go into the city, saying I always did harm when I came to the city, and if at any time I was in the city, they would persuade the governor to send me back again.

In the beginning of last June the superior of the priests came to the parish where I was and told me he saw I wanted my friend Captain de Beauville and that I was ragged. "But" says he, "your obstinacy against our religion discourages [us] from providing better clothes." I told him it was better going in a ragged coat than with a ragged conscience.

In the beginning of last June went out an army of five hundred Macquas and Indians with an intention to have fallen on some English towns down Connecticut River, but lighting on a Scalacook Indian, who ran away in the night, they were discouraged, saying he would alarm the whole country.[76] About fifty as some say, or eighty as others, returned; thus, God restrained their wrath.

When they were promising themselves another winter to draw away the English to popery, came news of an English brigantine a-coming and that the honorable Captain Samuel Appleton, Esq., was coming ambassador to fetch off the captives, and Captain John Bonner with him.[77] I cannot tell you how the clergy and others labored to stop many of the prisoners; to some liberty, to some money and yearly pensions were offered if they would stay. Some they urged to tarry at least till the spring of the year, telling them it was so late in the year they would be lost by shipwreck if they went now; some younger ones they told if they were home they would be damned and burn in hell forever, to affright them; day and night they were urging of them to stay. And I was threatened to be sent abroad without a permission to come ashore again if I should again discourse with any of the English who were turned to their religion.

At Mont-Royal especially, all crafty endeavors were used to stay the English. They told my child[78] if he would stay he should have an honorable pension from the king every year and that his master, who was an old man and the richest in Canada, would give him a great deal, telling him if he returned he would be poor, for, said they, your father is poor, [he] has

75. Baptiste was being held in Boston, where authorities threatened to hang him as a privateer.

76. Probably a Scatacook (Schaghticoke) Indian from western Connecticut. If so, the Connecticut colonists were saved by a friendly Indian's discovery of invading forces.

77. In early October 1706, Capt. Samuel Appleton arrived at Quebec with French prisoners to exchange for New Englanders and cash for the purchase of others, which presumably would repay Canadians who had ransomed English captives from the Indians. Capt. John Bonner was a prominent Boston mariner and cartographer.

78. Probably Samuel.

lost all his estate; it was all burned. But he would not be prevailed with to stay; and others were also in like manner urged to stay, but God graciously brake the snare and brought them out. They endeavored in the fall of the year to have prevailed with my son to have gone to France when they saw he would not come to their communion anymore.

One woman belonging to the Eastern parts, who had by their persuasions married an English captive taken the last war, came away with her husband, which made them say they were sorry they ever persuaded her to turn to their religion and then to marry. For, instead of advancing their cause by it, they had weakened it, for now they had not only lost her, but another they thought they had made sure of. Another woman belonging to the Eastward, who had been flattered to their religion, to whom a Bible was denied till she promised to embrace their religion and then had the promise of it for a little time, opening her Bible while in the church and present at Mass, she read the fourth chapter of Deuteronomy and received such conviction while reading that before her first communion she fell off from them and could never be prevailed with anymore to be of their religion.

We have reason to bless God who has wrought deliverance for so many, and yet to pray to God for a door of escape to be opened for the great number yet behind, not much short of an hundred, many of which are children, and of these not a few among the savages and having lost the English tongue, will be lost and turn savages in a little time unless something extraordinary prevent.

The vessel that came for us in its voyage to Canada struck on a bar of sands and there lay in very great hazard for four tides, and yet they saw reason to bless God for striking there, for had they got over the bar, they should at midnight in a storm of snow have run upon a terrible ledge of rocks.

We came away from Quebeck October twenty-five [1706] and by contrary winds and a great storm we were retarded, and then driven back nigh the city, and had a great deliverance from shipwreck, the vessel striking twice on a rock in that storm. But through God's goodness we all arrived in safety at Boston November twenty-one, the number of captives fifty-seven, two of which were my children. I have yet a daughter of ten years of age and many neighbors whose case bespeaks your compassion and prayers to God to gather them, being outcasts ready to perish.

At our arrival at Boston we found the kindnesses of the Lord in a wonderful manner in God's opening the hearts of many to bless God with us and for us wonderfully to give for our supplies in our needy state. We are under obligation to praise God for disposing the hearts of so many to so

225

great charity and under great bonds to pray for blessing on the heads, hearts, and families of them who so liberally and plentifully gave for our relief. It's certain that the charity of the whole country of Canada, though moved with the doctrine of merit, does not come up to the charity of Boston alone, where notions of merit are rejected, but acts of charity [are] performed out of a right Christian spirit from a spirit of thankfulness to God out of obedience to God's command and unfeigned love and charity to them that are of the same family and household of faith.[79] The Lord grant that all who devise such liberal things may find accomplishment of the promises made by God in their own person and theirs after them from generation to generation.

I SHALL ANNEX a short account of the troubles beginning to arise at Canada. On May sixteen [1706] arrived a canoe at Quebeck that brought letters from Mississippi written the May preceding giving an account that the plague was there, and that one hundred and fifty French in a very little time had died of it, and that the savages called the Lezilouways[80] were very turbulent, and had with their arrows wounded a Jesuit in five places, and killed a Frenchman that waited on him. In July news came that the nations up the river were engaged in a war, one against the other, and that the French living so among them and trading with them were in great danger, that the Mitchel-macquinas [Michilimackinacs] had made war with the Mizianmies [Miamis?] and had killed a mendicant friar and three other Frenchmen and eleven savages at a place called the Straits [Detroit?] where they are settling a garrison and place for traffic; the Mitchell-macquinas had taken sixteen Frenchmen prisoners and burned their trading houses. These tidings made the French very full of perplexing troubles, but the Jesuits are endeavoring to pacify them, but the troubles when we came away were rather increasing than lessening, for the last letters from the French prisoners at Mitchel-macquina report that the savages sent out two companies, one of a hundred and fifty and another of a hundred sixty, against the savages at the Straits, and they feared they would engage as well against the French as the Indians.[81]

79. Williams here objects to Catholic belief in the redemptive value of "works"—that meritorious acts can influence God's selection of the saved and the damned. The Puritans contended that only divinely inspired faith led to salvation.

80. Not identified. Presumably a subtribe in the vicinity of Wisconsin.

81. For a modern account of an episode at Detroit that was probably the basis for part of Williams's confusing paragraph, see Lanctot, *History of Canada,* II, 157–158.

A nineteenth-century depiction of Elizabeth Hanson and her daughter in captivity. From John Frost's *Pictorial History of Indian Wars and Captivities* (New York, 1873). Courtesy of Columbia University Libraries.

1728 published

· ELIZABETH HANSON ·
"GOD'S MERCY SURMOUNTING
MAN'S CRUELTY"

Queen Anne's War ended in 1713 with the Peace of Utrecht. That event should have brought relief to New England's war-weary frontier, but the ancient rivalry between French Canada and the British colonies scarcely abated. French soldiers and missionaries continued to seek Indian allies in Maine and New Hampshire, and the Puritan colonies clung to their imperial designs on both Indian and French territory. Scattered raids and counter-raids persisted for more than a decade. In the summer of 1724 a French and Indian war party hit Dover Township, New Hampshire. Among the captives was Elizabeth Meader Hanson (1684–1737).

Mrs. Hanson was not, strictly speaking, a Puritan. Her husband John was described by a contemporary, Samuel Penhallow, as "a stiff Quaker, full of enthusiasm." Presumably his wife had the same religious convictions; her narrative hints strongly at contempt for the Puritan clergy. In any event, John Hanson took Quaker pacifism seriously, for he lived on an isolated and undefended farm, and (according to the same commentator) "ridiculing the military power [he] would on no account be influenced to come into the garrison, by which means the whole family (then at home) being eight in number were all killed or taken." John Hanson knew the danger well enough: his paternal grandmother had been killed by Indians in 1689, an aunt was captured the same year and never heard of again, and an uncle was killed in 1693.

Puritans and Quakers differed bitterly on many issues, yet both sects drew heavily on England's protestant heritage, and accordingly they had much more in common than they recognized at the time. In New England, moreover, most Quakers grew up in a predominantly Puritan environment—both theologically and socially. Thus Elizabeth Hanson's narrative, while characteristically Puritan in its pietistic rhetoric and general theme, reflects also the Quaker emphasis on God's communication with mankind through an "inner light"; Quakers were therefore somewhat more individualistic than Puritans, at least in New England. Mary Rowlandson and most of the orthodox Puritan captives sought to awaken the whole community, even all New England, with their messages of God's redeeming mercy; Elizabeth Hanson, however, aimed her lessons more directly at the individual reader. Moreover, by Hanson's day the social and religious ethic that had dominated the founding and early growth of New England had lost much of its communitarian character and intensity, even among staunch Congregationalists. There is, of course, no precise chronological end to American Puritanism, but scholars of the subject generally agree that by the second quarter of the eighteenth century it had ceased to be the overriding theme of New England's history. Hanson's narrative thus chronologically and symbolically marks the end of Puritan captivity narratives.

God's Mercy Surmounting Man's Cruelty, Exemplified in the Captivity and Redemption of Elizabeth Hanson has an intriguing and complex publication history. Two versions of the Hanson text, one American and one English, appeared during the eighteenth century. All American editions contain the intials E.H. at the end of the text, while the English editions are attributed to Samuel Bownas, a noted English Quaker preacher. The successive English editions illustrate an attempt to "refine" the narrative's style according to eighteenth-century literary taste. The following modernized version is based on the first American edition, published by Thomas Keimer at Philadelphia in 1728. It has a direct and simple style that later editions lack.

Remarkable and many have been the providences of God towards His people for their deliverance in a time of trouble by which we may behold as in lively characters the truth of that saying that "He is a God nigh at hand and always ready to help assist those that fear Him and put their confidence in Him."

The sacred writings give us instances of the truth hereof in days of old as in the case of the Israelites, Job, David, Daniel, Paul, Silas, and many others. Besides which our modern histories have plentifully abounded with instances of God's fatherly care over His people in their sharpest trials, deepest distresses, and sorest exercises by which we may know He is a God that changeth not but is the same yesterday, today, and forever.

Among the many modern instances I think I have not met with a more singular one of the mercy and preserving hand of God than in the case of

ELIZABETH HANSON

Elizabeth Hanson,[1] wife of John Hanson of Knoxmarsh in Kecheachey [Cocheco], in Dover Township in New England, who was taken into captivity the 27th day of the 6th month called August, 1724, and carried away with four children[2] and a servant by the Indians, which relation as it was taken from her own mouth by a friend differs very little from the original copy but is even almost in her own words (what small alteration is made being partly owing to the mistake of the transcriber) which take as follows:

As soon as they discovered themselves (having, as we understood by their discourse, been skulking in the fields some days watching their opportunity when my dear husband with the rest of our men were gone out of the way),[3] two of these barbarous savages came in upon us, next eleven more, all naked with their guns and tomahawks, came into the house in a great fury upon us and killed one child immediately as soon as they entered the door, thinking thereby to strike in us the greater terror and to make us more fearful of them.

Then in as great fury the captain came up to me, but at my request he gave me quarter. There being with me our servant and six of our children, two of the little ones being at play about the orchard and my youngest child but fourteen days old, whether in cradle or arms I now mind not, being in that condition, I was very unfit for the hardships I after met with, which are briefly contained in the following pages.

They next go to rifling the house in a great hurry (fearing, as I suppose, a surprise from our people, it being late in the afternoon) and packed up some linen, woolen, and what other things pleased them best. And when they had done what they would, they turned out of the house immediately and being at the door, two of my younger children, one six and the other four years old, came in sight and, being under a great surprise, cried aloud,

1. The identity of the narrator of the opening paragraphs—and recorder of the remainder of the story in which Elizabeth Hanson appears in the first person—is uncertain, though presumably it was Samuel Bownas who claimed to have transcribed the narrative directly from her. But Bownas's edition did not appear until 1760, and the 1728 edition, from which this text is taken, makes no mention of Bownas. For further discussion of this matter see Richard VanDerBeets, ed., *Held Captive by Indians: Selected Narratives, 1642–1836* (Knoxville, Tenn., 1973), 130–132.

2. The children were Sarah (sixteen), Elizabeth (fourteen), Ebenezer or David (six), and an infant whose only recorded name is "Mary Ann Frossway" (Marie Anne Françoise), given by a Canadian priest who baptized her.

3. The broader setting of the raid, as well as some important details, are in *History of the Wars of New England, with the Eastern Indians* [1703–1725] (Boston, 1726).

231

upon which one of the Indians, running to them, takes one under each arm and brings them to us. My maid prevailed with the biggest to be quiet and still, but the other could by no means be prevailed with but continued screeching and crying very much in the fright, and the Indians, to ease themselves of the noise and to prevent the danger of a discovery that might arise from it, immediately before my face knocked its brains out. I bore this as well as I could, not daring to appear disturbed or show much uneasiness lest they should do the same to the other but should have been exceeding glad they had kept out of sight till we had been gone from our house.

Now having killed two of my children, they scalped them (a practice common with these people, which is whenever they kill any English people they cut the skin off from the crown of their heads and carry it with them for a testimony and evidence that they have killed so many, receiving sometimes a reward of a sum of money for every scalp)[4] and then put forward to leave the house in great haste without doing any other spoil than taking what they had packed together with myself and little babe fourteen days old, the boy six, and two daughters, the one about fourteen and the other about sixteen years, [and] with my servant girl.

It must be considered that, I having lain-in but fourteen days and being but very tender and weakly, being removed now out of a good room well accommodated with fire, bedding, and other things suiting a person in my condition, it made these hardships to me greater than if I had been in a strong and healthy frame, yet for all this I must go or die. There was no resistance.

In the condition aforesaid we left the house, each Indian having something, and I with my babe and three children that could go of themselves. The captain, though he had as great a load as he could well carry and was helped up with it, did for all that carry my babe for me in his arms, which I took to be a favor from him. Thus we went through several swamps and some brooks, they carefully avoiding all paths of any track like a road lest by our footsteps we should be followed.

We got that night, I suppose, not quite ten miles from our house on a direct line; then, taking up their quarters, [they] lighted a fire, some of them lying down while others kept watch. I, being both wet and weary and lying on the cold ground in the open woods, took but little rest.

However, early in the morning we must go just as day appeared, traveling very hard all that day through sundry rivers, brooks, and swamps,

4. See note 13 to Rowlandson's narrative.

they, as before, carefully avoiding all paths for the reason already assigned. At night I was both wet and tired exceedingly, having the same lodging on the cold ground in the open woods. Thus for twenty-six days, day by day, we traveled very hard sometimes a little by water over lakes and ponds. And in this journey we went up some very high mountains so steep that I was forced to creep up on my hands and knees, under which difficulty the Indian, my master, would mostly carry my babe for me which I took as a great favor of God that his heart was so tenderly inclined to assist me though he had, as is said, a very heavy burden of his own. Nay, he would sometimes take my very blanket so that I had nothing to do but take my little boy by the hand for his help and assist him as well as I could, taking him up in my arms a little at times because [he was] so small, and when we came at very bad places, he would lend me his hand or coming behind would push me up before him. In all which he showed some humanity and civility more than I could have expected, for which privilege I was secretly thankful to God as the moving cause thereof.

Next to this we had some very great runs of water and brooks to wade through in which, at times, we met with much difficulty, wading often to our middle and sometimes our girls were up to their shoulders and chins, the Indians carrying my boy on their shoulders. At the side of one of these runs or rivers the Indians would have my eldest daughter Sarah to sing them a song. Then was brought into her remembrance that passage in the 137th Psalm, "By the rivers of Babylon there we sat down, yea we wept when we remembered Zion; we hanged our harps on the willows in the midst thereof, for there they that carried us away captives required of us a song, and they that watched us required of us mirth." When my poor child had given me this account, it was very affecting, and my heart was very full of trouble, yet on my child's account I was glad that she had so good an inclination which she yet further manifested in longing for a Bible that we might have the comfort in reading the Holy Text at vacant times for our spiritual comfort under our present affliction.

Next to the difficulties of the rivers were the prodigious swamps and thickets very difficult to pass through, in which places my master would sometimes lead me by the hand a great way together and give me what help he was capable of under the straits we went through, and, we passing one after another, the first made it pretty passable for the hindmost.

By the greatest difficulty that deserves the first to be named was want of food, having at times nothing to eat but pieces of old beaverskin matchcoats which the Indians having hid (for they came naked as is said before) which in their going back again they took with them, and they were used more for food than raiment.⁵ Being cut out in long, narrow straps, they gave us little pieces which, by the Indians' example, we laid on the fire till the hair was singed away, and then we eat them as a sweet morsel, experimentally knowing that "to the hungry soul every bitter thing is sweet."

It's to be considered further that of this poor diet we had but very scanty allowance so that we were in no danger of being overcharged. But that which added to my troubles was the complaints of my poor children, especially the little boy. Sometimes the Indians would catch a squirrel or a beaver and at other times we met with nuts, berries, and roots they digged out of the ground, with the bark of some trees. But we had no corn for a great while together, though some of the younger Indians went back and brought some corn from the English inhabitants, the harvest not being gathered, of which we had a little allowed us. But when they caught a beaver, we lived high while it lasted, they allowing me the guts and garbage for myself and children. But not allowing us to clean and wash them as they ought made the food very irksome to us, in the conceit of our minds, to feed upon; and nothing besides pinching hunger could have made it anyway tolerable to be borne. But "that makes every bitter thing sweet."

The next difficulty was no less hard to me, for my daily travel and hard living made my milk dry almost quite up, and how to preserve my poor babe's life was no small care on my mind, having no other sustenance for it many times but cold water, which I took in my mouth and let it fall on my breast (when I gave it the teat) to suck in with what it could get from the breast. And when I had any of the broth of the beaver or other guts, I fed my babe with it as well as I could. By which means through care to keep it as warm as I could, I preserved its life till I got to Canada, and then I had some other food, of which more in its place.

Having by this time got considerably on the way, the Indians part, and we must be divided amongst them. This was a sore grief to us all. But we must submit, and no way to help ourselves. My eldest daughter was first taken away and carried to another part of the country far distant from us where for the present we must take leave of her though with a heavy heart.

5. Indian "match-coats" were fur capes. According to William Wood, "Many of [the Indians] wear skins about them, in form of an Irish mantle, and of these some be bear's skins, moose's skins, and beaver skins sewed together, otter skins, and raccoon skins, most of them in winter having his deep-furred cat skin, like a long large muff, which he shifts to that arm which lieth most exposed to the wind. Thus clad, he bustles better through a world of cold in a frost-paved wilderness than the furred citizen in his warmer stove." *New England's Prospect*, ed. Alden T. Vaughan (Amherst, Mass., 1977), 84.

We did not travel far after this before they divided again, taking my second daughter and servant maid from me into another part of the country. So, I having now only my babe at my breast and little boy six years old, we remained with the captain still. But my daughter and servant underwent great hardships after they were parted from me, traveling three days without any food, taking nothing for support but cold water, and the third day what with the cold, the wet, and hunger the servant fell down as dead in a swoon, being both very cold and wet. At which the Indians with whom they were, were surprised, showing some kind of tenderness, being unwilling then to lose them by death, having got them so near home, hoping if they lived by their ransom to make considerable profit by them.

In a few days after this they got near their journey's end where they had more plenty of corn and other food. But flesh often fell very short, having no other way to depend on for it but hunting, and when that failed, they had very short commons. It was not long ere my daughter and servant were likewise parted; and my daughter's master being sick was not able to hunt for flesh. Neither had they any corn in that place but were forced to eat bark of trees for a whole week.

Being almost famished in this distress, Providence so ordered that some other Indians, hearing of their misery and want, came to visit them (these people being very kind and helpful to one another which is very commendable)[6] and brought unto them the guts and liver of a beaver which afforded them a good repast, being but four in number, the Indian, his wife and daughter, and my daughter.

By this time my master and our company got to our journey's end where we were better fed at times, having some corn and venison and wild fowl or what they could catch by hunting in the woods. And my master, having a large family (being fifteen in number), we had at times very short commons, more especially when game was scarce.

But here our lodging was still on the cold ground in a poor wigwam (which is a kind of little shelter made with the rinds of trees and mats for a covering something like a tent).[7] These are so easily set up and taken down that they oft remove them from one place to another. Our shoes and stockings being done and our other clothes worn out in that long journey through the bushes and swamps and the weather coming in very hard, we were poorly defended from the cold for want of necessaries, which caused

---

6. The Indians' willingness to share food and to help the needy was widely recognized and applauded by the settlers. See, for example, Wood, *New England's Prospect,* 87–91.

7. On wigwams see note 11 to Rowlandson's narrative.

one of my feet, one of the little babe's, and both the little boy's to freeze. And this was no small exercise, yet through mercy we all did well.

Now though we got to our journey's end, we were never long in one place but very often moved from one place to another, carrying their wigwams with them, which they could do without much difficulty. This, being for the conveniency of hunting, made our accommodations much more unpleasant than if we had continued in one place, by reason the coldness and dampness of the ground where our wigwams were pitched made it very unwholesome and unpleasant lodging.

Being now got to the Indian fort, many of the Indians came to visit us and, in their way, welcomed my master home and held a great rejoicing with dancing, firing guns, beating on hollow trees instead of drums, shouting, drinking, and feasting after their manner in much excess for several days together which, I suppose, in their thoughts was a kind of thanks to God put up for their safe return and good success. But while they were in their jollitry and mirth, my mind was greatly exercised towards the Lord that I, with my dear children separated from me, might be preserved from repining against God under our affliction on the one hand and on the other we might have our dependence on Him who rules the hearts of men and can do what pleases in the kingdoms of the earth, knowing that His care is over them who put their trust in Him. But I found it very hard to keep my mind as I ought under the resignation which is proper to be in under such afflictions and sore trials as at that time I suffered, in being under various fears and doubts concerning my children that were separated from me, which helped to add to and greatly increase my troubles. And herein I may truly say my afflictions are not to be set forth in words to the extent of them.

We had not been long at home ere my master went a-hunting and was absent about a week, he ordering me in his absence to get in wood, gather nuts, etc. I was very diligent, cutting the wood, and putting it in order, not having very far to carry it. But when he returned having got no prey, he was very much out of humor, and the disappointment was so great that he could not forbear revenging it on us poor captives. However he allowed me a little boiled corn for self and child, but with a very angry look threw a stick or corn cob at me with such violence as did bespeak he grudged our eating. At this his squaw and daughter broke out in a great crying. This made me fear mischief was hatching against us. And on it, I immediately went out of his presence into another wigwam; upon which, he comes after me and in great fury tore my blanket off my back and took my little boy from me and struck him down as he went along before him. But the poor child, not being hurted (only frightened) in the fall, he started up and ran away without crying; then the Indian, my master, left me, but his wife's mother came and sat down by me and told me I must sleep there that night. She, then going from me a little time, came back with a small skin to cover my feet withal, informing that my master intended now to kill us, and I, being desirous to know the reason, expostulated that in his absence I had been diligent to do as I was ordered by him. Thus, as well as I could, I made her sensible how unreasonable he was. Now, though she could not understand me nor I her, but by signs, we reasoned as well as we could. She therefore makes signs that I must die, advising me by pointing up with her fingers in her way, to pray to God, endeavoring by her signs and tears to instruct me in that which was most needful, *viz.* to prepare for death which now threatened me. The poor old squaw was so very kind and tender that she would not leave me all that night but laid herself down at my feet, designing what she could to assuage her son-in-law's wrath, who had conceived evil against me chiefly, as I understood, because the want of victuals urged him to it. My rest was little this night, my poor babe sleeping sweetly by me.

I dreaded the tragical design of my master, looking every hour for his coming to execute his bloody will upon us. But he, being weary with his hunting and travel in the woods (having toiled for nothing), went to rest and forgot it. Next morning he applied himself again to hunting in the woods, but I dreaded his returning empty and prayed secretly in my heart that he might catch some food to satisfy his hunger and cool his ill humor. He had been gone but a little time till returned with booty, having shot some wild duck, and now he appeared in a better temper, ordering the fowls to be dressed with speed, for these kind of people when they have plenty spend it as freely as they get it, spending in gluttony and drunkenness in two days' time as much as with prudent management might serve a week.[8] Thus do they live for the most part either in excess of gluttony and drunkenness or under great straits for want of necessaries. However, in this plentiful time I felt the comfort of it in part with the family, having a portion sent for me and my little ones which was very acceptable. Now, I thinking to myself the bitterness of death was over for this time, my spirits were a little easier.

Not long after this he got into the like ill humor again, threatening to take away my life. But I always observed whenever he was in such a temper he wanted food and was pinched with hunger. But when he had suc-

8. See note 18 to Stockwell's narrative.

cess in hunting to take either bears, beavers, bucks, or fowls on which he could fill his belly, he was better humored though he was naturally of a very hot and passionate temper, throwing sticks, stones, or whatever lay in his way on every slight occasion. This made me in continual danger of my life. But that God whose Providence is over all His works so preserved me that I never received any damage from him that was of any great consequence to me for which I ever desire to be thankful to my Maker.

When flesh was scarce, we had only the guts and garbage allowed to our part, and, not being permitted to cleanse the guts any otherwise than emptying the dung without so much as washing them as is before noted, in that filthy pickle we must boil them and eat them, which was very unpleasant. But hunger made up that difficulty so that this food which was very often our lot became pretty tolerable to a sharp appetite which otherwise by no means could have been dispensed with. Thus, I considered, none knows what they can undergo till they are tried, for what I had thought in my own family not fit for food would here have been a dainty dish and sweet morsel.

By this time, what with fatigue of spirits, hard labor, mean diet, and often want of natural rest, I was brought so low that my milk was dried up, my baby very poor and weak, just skin and bone for I could perceive all its joints from one end of the babe's back to the other. And how to get what would suit its weak appetite I was at a loss, on which one of the Indian squaws perceiving my uneasiness about my child began some discourse with me in which she advised me to take the kernels of walnuts and clean them and beat them with a little water, which I did, and when I had so done, the water looked like milk. Then she advised me to add to this water a little of the finest of the Indian corn meal and boil it a little together. I did so, and it became palatable and was very nourishing to the babe so that it began to thrive and look well, which was before more like to die than live. I found that with this kind of diet the Indians did often nurse their infants. This was no small comfort to me. But this comfort was soon mixed with bitterness and trouble which thus happened: my master, taking notice of my dear babe's thriving condition, would often look upon it and say when it was fat enough, it should be killed, and he would eat it. And pursuant to his pretense at a certain time he made me to fetch him a stick that he had prepared for a spit to roast the baby upon as he said which, when I had done, he made me sit down by him and undress the infant. When the child was naked, he felt its arms, legs, and thighs and told me it was not fat enough yet; I must dress it again until it was better in case.

Now though he thus acted, I could not persuade myself that he intended to do as he pretended but only to aggravate and afflict me.[9] Neither ever could I think but our lives would be preserved from his barbarous hands by the overruling power of Him in whose Providence I put my trust both day and night.

A little time after this my master fell sick, and in his sickness as he lay in his wigwam, he ordered his own son to beat my son. But the old squaw, the Indian boy's grandmother, would not suffer him to do it. Then his father, my master, being provoked, catches up a stick very sharp at one end and with great violence threw it from him at my son and hit him on the breast with which my child was much bruised, and the pain, with the surprise, made him turn as pale as death. I entreated him not to cry, and the boy, though but six years old, bore it with wonderful patience, not so much as in the least complaining, so that the child's patience assuaged the barbarity of his hard heart, who, no doubt, would have carried his passion and resentment higher had the child cried, as always complaining did aggravate his passion, and his anger grew hotter upon it. Some little time after on the same day he got upon his feet but far from being well. However, though he was sick, his wife and daughter let me know he intended to kill us, and I was under a fear, unless Providence now intercepted, how it would end. I therefore put down my child and, going out of his presence, went to cut wood for the fire as I used to do, hoping that would in part allay his passion. But withal ere I came to the wigwam again, I expected my children would be killed in this mad fit, having no other way but to cast my care upon God who had hitherto helped and cared for me and mine.

Under this great feud the old squaw, my master's mother-in-law, left him, but my mistress and her daughter abode in the wigwam with my master. And when I came with my wood, the daughter came to me, whom I asked if her father had killed my children, and she made me a sign, no, with a countenance that seemed pleased it was so, for instead of his further venting his passion on me and my children, the Lord in whom I trusted did seasonably interpose, and I took it as a merciful deliverance from him, and the Indian was under some sense of the same as himself did confess to them about him afterwards.

Thus it was a little after he got up on his feet [that] the Lord struck him with great sickness and a violent pain as appeared by the complaint he

9. Hanson's master was almost certainly throwing a scare into her. Cannibalism among the northeastern tribes was rare, and most recorded instances were ceremonial or symbolic, although the neighboring Mohawks had a reputation among both the Algonquians and the English of eating human flesh.

made in a doleful and hideous manner which, when I understood, not having yet seen him, I went to another squaw that was come to see my master which could both speak and understand English and inquired of her if my mistress (for so I always called her, and him master) thought that master would die. She answered, yes, it was very likely he would, being worse and worse. Then I told her he struck my boy a dreadful blow without any provocation at all and had threatened to kill us all in his fury and passion. Upon which the squaw told me my master had confessed the abuse he offered my child and that the mischief he had done was the cause why God afflicted him with that sickness and pain, and he had promised never to abuse us in such sort more. And after this he soon recovered but was not so passionate, nor do I remember he ever after struck either me or [my] children so as to hurt us or with that mischievous intent as before he used to do. This I took as the Lord's doing, and it was marvelous in my eyes.

Some few weeks after this my master made another remove, having as before made several. But this was the longest ever he made, it being two days' journey and mostly upon the ice. The first day's journey the ice was bare but the next day, some snow falling, made it troublesome, very tedious, and difficult traveling, and I took much damage in often falling, having the care of my babe that added not a little to my uneasiness. And the last night when we came to encamp, it being in the night, I was ordered to fetch water, but, having sat awhile on the cold ground, I could neither go nor stand but [by] crawling on my hands and knees. A young Indian squaw who came to see our people, being of another family, in compassion took the kettle and, knowing where to go, which I did not, fetched the water for me. This I took as a great kindness and favor that her heart was inclined to do me this service.

I now saw the design of this journey; my master, being, as I suppose, weary to keep us, was willing to make what he could of our ransom. Therefore, he went further towards the French and left his family in this place where they had a great dance, sundry other Indians coming to our people. This held some time, and while they were in it, I got out of their way in a corner of the wigwam as well as I could. But every time they came by me in their dancing, they would bow my head towards the ground and frequently kick me with as great fury as they could bear, being sundry of them barefoot and others having Indian moccasins. This dance held some time, and they made (in their manner) great rejoicings and noise.

It was not many days ere my master returned from the French, but he was in such a humor when he came back he would not suffer me in his presence. Therefore, I had a little shelter made with some boughs, they

240

having digged through the snow to the ground, the snow being pretty deep. In this hole I and my poor children were put to lodge, the weather being very sharp, and hard frost in the month called January made it more tedious to me and [my] poor babes. Our stay not being long in this place, he took me to the French in order for a chapman,[10] and when we came among them, I was exposed to sale, and he asked for me 800 livres. But the French, not complying with his demand, put him in a great rage, offering him but 600. He said in a great passion if he could not have his demand, he would make a great fire and burn me and the babe in the view of the city, which was named Port Royal.[11] The Frenchman bid the Indian make his fire. "And I will," says he, "help you if you think that will do you more good than 600 livres," calling my master "fool" and speaking roughly to him, bid him be gone. But at the same time the Frenchman was very civil to me and for my encouragement bid me be of good cheer for I should be redeemed and not go back with them again.

Retiring now with my master for this night, the next day I was redeemed for 600 livres, and in treating with my master the Frenchman queried why he asked so much for the babe's ransom, urging when it had its bellyful it would die. My master said, no, it would not die, having already lived twenty-six days on nothing but water, believing the babe to be a devil. The Frenchman told him, no, the child is ordered for longer life, and it has pleased God to preserve it to admiration. My master said, no, it was a devil, and he believed it would not die unless they took a hachet and beat its brains out. Thus ended their discourse, and I was, as aforesaid, with my babe ransomed for 600 livres; my little boy likewise at the same time for an additional sum of livres was redeemed also.

I now having changed my landlord, table, and diet, as well as my lodging, the French were civil beyond what I could either desire or expect. But the next day after I was redeemed, the Romish priests took my babe from me, and, according to their custom, they baptized it (urging if it died before that, it would be damned like some of our modern, pretended-reformed priests),[12] and they gave it a name as pleased them best which was Mary Ann Frossways, telling me my child, if it now died, would be saved, being baptized. And my landlord, speaking to the priest that bap-

10. That is, Hanson's master took her to a Frenchman who purchased captives.

11. This is Hanson's only indication of her location while in captivity.

12. "Modern, pretended-reformed priests" is the only clue in Hanson's narrative that she was a Quaker. Quakers rejected what they considered a "hireling clergy" in favor of individual laymen's recitations of God's effect on their spirit. Presumably Hanson here refers to Puritan clergymen.

tized it, said, "It would be well now Frossways was baptized for it to die, being now in a state to be saved." But the priest said, "No, the child, having been so miraculously preserved through so many hardships, it may be designed by God for some great work, and, by its life being still continued, may much more glorify God than if it should now die." A very sensible remark, and I wish it may prove true.

I having been about five months amongst the Indians, in about one month after I got amongst the French, my dear husband, to my unspeakable comfort and joy, came to me, who was now himself concerned to redeem his children, two of our daughters being still captives and only myself and two little ones redeemed; and through great difficulty and trouble he recovered the younger daughter. But the eldest we could by no means obtain from their hands, for the squaw to whom she was given had a son which she intended my daughter should in time be prevailed with to marry.[13] The Indians being very civil toward their captive women, not offering any incivility by any indecent carriage (unless they be much overgone in liquor) which is commendable in them so far.[14]

However, the affections they had for my daughter made them refuse all offers and terms of ransom so that after my poor husband had waited and made what attempts and endeavors he could to obtain his child, and all to no purpose, we were forced to make homeward, leaving our daughter to our great grief behind us amongst the Indians and set forwards over the lake with three of our children and servant maid in company with sundry others, and, by the kindness of Providence, we got well home on the first day of the seventh month 1725.[15] From which it appears I had been from home amongst the Indians and French about twelve months and six days. In the series of which time, the many deliverances and wonderful Providences of God unto us and over us have been, and I hope will so remain to be, as a continued obligation on my mind ever to live in that fear, love, and obedience to God, duly regarding by His grace with meekness and wisdom to approve myself by His spirit in all holiness of life and Godliness of con-

13. This episode suggests a greater acceptance of miscegenation by the Indians than by the English, who sanctioned intermarriage only if the Indian partner had become appreciably anglicized.

14. This is generally corroborated by other European captives.

15. The seventh month in the Julian (Old Style) calendar was September; it was July in the Gregorian (New Style) calendar. See not 1 to Rowlandson's narrative. Hanson apparently used the former because in late August a Newport, R.I., newspaper reported that the Hansons were there en route home from Canada via New York City.

versation to the praise of Him that hath called me, who is God blessed forever.

But my dear husband, poor man, could not enjoy himself in quiet with
us for want of his dear daughter Sarah that was left behind, and, not willing to omit anything for her redemption which lay in his power, he could
not be easy without making a second attempt. In order to which he took
his journey about the nineteenth day of the second month 1727, in company with a kinsman and his wife who went to redeem some of their children and were so happy as to obtain what they went about. But my dear
husband, being taken sick on the way, grew worse and worse, as we were
informed, and was sensible he should not get over it, telling my kinsman
that if it was the Lord's will he must die in the wilderness, he was freely
given up to it. He was under a good composure of mind and sensible to the
last moment and died as near as we can guess in about the halfway between Albany and Canada in my kinsman's arms and is at rest, I hope, in
the Lord. And though my own children's loss is very great, yet I doubt
not but his gain is much more. I, therefore, desire and pray that the Lord
will enable me patiently to submit to His will in all things He is pleased to
suffer to my lot while here, earnestly supplicating the God and Father of
all our mercies to be a father to my fatherless children and give unto them
that blessing which maketh truly rich and adds no sorrow to it, that as they
grow in years they may grow in grace and experience the joy of His salvation which is come by Jesus Christ our Lord and Savior, Amen.

Now though my husband died, by reason of which his labor was ended,
yet my kinsman prosecuted the thing and left no stone unturned that he
thought or could be advised was proper to the obtaining my daughter's
freedom but could by no means prevail, for, as is before said (she being in
another part of the country distant from where I was) and given to an old
squaw who intended to marry her in time to her son, using what persuad-
ing she could to effect her end, sometimes by fair means and sometimes by
severe. In the meantime a Frenchman interposed, and they by persuasion
enticed my child to marry in order to obtain her freedom by reason that
those captives married by the French are by that marriage made free
among them, the Indians having then no pretense longer to keep them as
captives. She therefore was prevailed upon, for the reasons afore assigned,
to marry, and she was accordingly married to the Frenchman.[16]

16. In 1727 Sarah married Jean Baptiste Sabourin, a Canadian militia captain from a
wealthy family. She remained permanently in Canada.

Thus, as well and as near as I can from my memory (not being capable of keeping a journal), I have given a short but a true account of some of the remarkable trials and wonderful deliverances which I never purposed to expose but that I hope thereby the merciful kindness and goodness of God may be magnified, and the reader hereof provoked with more care and fear to serve Him in righteousness and humility, and then my designed end and purpose will be answered.

E.H.

F I N I S

BIBLIOGRAPHY

INDEX

BIBLIOGRAPHY

I. Indian Captivity: Narratives and Analyses

The best place to launch a study of early American captivity narratives is with R. W. G. Vail's *The Voice of the Old Frontier* (Philadelphia, 1949), which contains an invaluable annotated bibliography of narratives published before 1800 and their various early editions. There is no thorough bibliography of all Indian captivities, but one should be forthcoming in the 111-volume *Narratives of North American Indian Captivities*, currently being published by Garland Publishing Company and the Newberry Library. In the meantime, a substantial list is the Newberry Library's *Narratives of Captivity Among the Indians of North America: A List of Books and Manuscripts on This Subject in the Edward E. Ayer Collection . . .* (Chicago, 1912); the same library's *Supplement to Narratives of Captivity . . .* (Chicago, 1928); and its "Deering Indian Captivities" (typescript, 1966).

Collections of narratives vary in scope and quality. Samuel G. Drake, *Indian Captivities* (Auburn, Mass., 1850), reprints nearly thirty major accounts; although Drake's transcriptions are not reliable, they have often been the source of subsequent editions. Charles H. Lincoln, ed., *Narratives of the Indian Wars, 1675–1699* (New York, 1913) contains reliable and extensively annotated versions of several New England narratives. Richard VanDerBeets, ed., *Held Captive by Indians: Selected Narratives, 1642–1836* (Knoxville, Tenn., 1973), covering almost two centuries and most of the continental United States, provides a valuable overview of some of the major narratives. Two anthologies written for a popular audience are Howard Peckham's *Captured by Indians* (New Brunswick, N.J., 1954), and Frederick Drimmer's *Scalps and Tomahawks* (New York, 1961). Valuable for its brief excerpts from the narratives and from American literary works reflecting the captivity narrative tradition is James Levernier and Hennig Cohen, *The Indians and Their Captives* (Westport, Conn., 1977) which emphasizes the narratives' influence on later generations of American writers. The huge Garland-Newberry collection, mentioned above, is being edited by Wilcomb E. Washburn, one of the foremost scholars on American Indian history; its 311 narratives will include virtually all of the nonfiction accounts. Microcard reproductions of most of the narratives written before 1800 are in Clifford K. Shipton, ed., *Early American Imprints*, issued by the American Antiquarian Society and Readex Microprint Corporation (Worcester, Mass., 1955–), which is available in most large libraries. A convenient guide to the microcard edition is Clifford K. Shipton and James E. Mooney, eds., *National Index of American Imprints through 1800; The Short-Title Evans,* 2 vols. (Barre, Mass., 1969).

1. *General Studies of North American Indian Captivity*

Scholarly writings on Indian captivity narratives are numerous and varied, largely because the narratives cross the traditional boundaries of several academic disciplines—especially anthropology, history, ethnography, and literature. Scholars are just now beginning to synthesize the methods of these disciplines, discovering in the process the narratives' multifaceted importance for the American past and their continuing influence in the present.

The following works are primarily concerned with the captivity experience in a broad context—literary, historical, psychological, or social. Not included here are books and articles that focus on New England; they are listed below in section 2. Many of the studies listed here, however, do give some attention to New England captivities.

Ackernecht, Erwin H. "White Indians: Psychological and Physiological Peculiarities of White Children Abducted and Reared by North American Indians." *Bulletin of the History of Medicine,* 15 (1944), 15–36.

Axtell, James. "The White Indians of Colonial America." *William and Mary Quarterly,* 3rd. ser., 32 (1975), 55–88; and "Letters to the Editor," ibid., 33 (1976), 143–153.

Barbeau, Marius. "Indian Captivities." *American Philosophical Society Proceedings,* 94 (1950), 522–548.

Barnett, Louise K. *The Ignoble Savage: American Literary Racism, 1790–1890.* Westport, Conn., 1975.

Behan, Dorothy Forbis. "The Captivity Story in American Literature, 1577–1826: An Examination of Written Reports in English, Authentic and Fictitious, of the Experiences of the White Men Captured by the Indians North of Mexico." Ph.D. dissertation, University of Chicago, 1952.

Carleton, Phillips D. "The Indian Captivity." *American Literature,* 15 (1943), 169–180.

Dondore, Dorothy A. "White Captives among the Indians." *New York History,* 13 (1932), 292–300.

Fiedler, Leslie. *The Return of the Vanishing American.* New York, 1968.

Green, Rayna D. "The Only Good Indian: The Image of the Indian in American Vernacular Tradition." Ph.D. dissertation, Indiana University, 1973.

Haberly, David T. "Women and Indians: *The Last of the Mohicans* and the Captivity Tradition." *American Quarterly,* 28 (1976), 431–441.

Hallowell, A. Irving. "American Indians, White and Black: The Phenomenon of Transculturalization." *Current Anthropology,* 4 (1963), 519–531.

Heard, J. Norman. *White into Red: A Study of the Assimilation of White Persons Captured by Indians.* Metuchen, N.J., 1973.

Keiser, Albert. *The Indian in American Literature.* New York, 1933.

CAPTIVITY NARRATIVES AND ANALYSES

Kolodny, Annette. "Review Essay" [of Wilcomb E. Washburn, ed., *Narratives of North American Indian Captivities*]. *Early American Literature*, 14 (1979), 228–235.

Levernier, James A. "Indian Captivity Narratives: Their Functions and Forms." Ph.D. dissertation, University of Pennsylvania, 1975.

Levernier, James A., and Hennig Cohen, eds. *The Indians and Their Captives.* Westport, Conn., 1977.

Meade, James. "The 'Westerns' of the East: Narratives of Indian Captivity from Jeremiad to Gothic Novel." Ph.D. dissertation, Northwestern University, 1971.

Pearce, Roy Harvey. "The Significances of the Captivity Narrative." *American Literature*, 19 (1947), 1–20.

Peckham, Howard H. *Captured by Indians: True Tales of Pioneer Survivors.* New Brunswick, N.J., 1954.

Swanton, John R. "Notes on the Mental Assimilation of Races." *Journal of the Washington Academy of Sciences*, 16 (1926), 493–502.

Vail, R. W. G. *The Voice of the Old Frontier.* Philadelphia, 1949. Chap. 2: "The Indians' Captives Relate Their Adventures."

VanDerBeets, Richard. *Held Captive by Indians: Selected Narratives, 1642–1836.* Knoxville, Tenn., 1973.

———— "The Indian Captivity Narrative: An American Genre." Ph.D. dissertation, University of the Pacific, 1973.

———— "The Indian Captivity Narrative as Ritual." *American Literature*, 43 (1972), 548–562.

———— "A Surfeit of Style: The Indian Captivity Narrative as Penny Dreadful." *Research Studies*, 39 (1971), 297–306.

———— " 'A Thirst for Empire': The Indian Captivity Narrative as Propaganda." *Research Studies*, 40 (1972), 207–215.

Washburn, Wilcomb E., ed. *Narratives of North American Indian Captivities.* 111 vols. New York, 1976– . Introductory essay.

2. New England Captivities

Because seventeenth- and eighteenth-century Puritans wrote many of the earliest and best captivity narratives, modern studies of the subgenre are fairly numerous. The following works discuss one of more Puritan narratives or captivity experiences.

Arner, Robert. "The Story of Hannah Duston: Cotton Mather to Thoreau." *American Transcendental Quarterly*, 18 (1973), 19–23.

Baker, Charlotte Alice. *True Stories of New England Captives Carried to Canada during the Old French and Indian Wars . . .* Greenfield, Mass., 1897.

Clark, Edward W. Introduction to John Williams, *The Redeemed Captive Returning to Zion.* Amherst, Mass., 1976.

249

BIBLIOGRAPHY

Coleman, Emma Lewis. *New England Captives Carried to Canada between 1677 and 1760 during the French and Indian Wars.* 2 vols. Portland, Me., 1925.

Diebold, Robert Kent. "A Critical Edition of Mrs. Mary Rowlandson's Captivity Narrative." Ph.D. dissertation, Yale University, 1972.

Gherman, Dawn L. "From Parlour to Tepee: The White Squaw on the American Frontier." Ph.D. dissertation, University of Massachusetts, 1975. A valuable discussion of Rowlandson's and Hanson's narratives and of Eunice Williams's captivity is on pp. 50–91.

Leach, Douglas Edward. "The 'Whens' of Mary Rowlandson's Captivity." *New England Quarterly,* 34 (1961), 352–363.

Lincoln, Charles H., ed. *Narratives of the Indian Wars, 1675–1699.* New York, 1913.

Medlicott, Alexander, Jr. "Return to the Land of Light: A Plea to an Unredeemed Captive." *New England Quarterly,* 38 (1965), 202–216.

Minter, David L. "By Dens of Lions: Notes on Stylization in Early Puritan Captivity Narratives." *American Literature,* 45 (1973), 335–347.

Morrison, Kenneth M. "The Wonders of Divine Mercy: A Review of John Williams' *The Redeemed Captive.*" *Canadian Review of American Studies,* 9 (1979), 56–62.

Richards, David A. "The Memorable Preservations: Narratives of Indian Captivity in the Literature and Politics of Colonial New England," 1675–1725. Honors thesis, Yale College, 1967.

Slotkin, Richard. *Regeneration through Violence: The Mythology of the American Frontier, 1600–1860.* Middletown, Conn., 1973. Especially pp. 94–145.

Trueman, Stuart. *The Ordeal of John Gyles.* Toronto, 1966. A "semi-fictional" reconstruction.

Vail, R. W. G. "Certain Indian Captivities of New England." *Massachusetts Historical Society Proceedings,* 68 (1944–1947), 113–131.

Whitford, Kathrun. "Hannah Dustin: The Judgment of History." *Essex Institute Historical Collections,* 108 (1972), 304–325.

II. New England and Canadian Contexts of Puritan Captivities

The authors of Puritan captivity narratives inevitably reflected the values and mores of their culture; a full appreciation of their trials and their writings therefore requires an understanding of early New England. Similarly, the experiences of the many New England captives who lived for a time in Canada can best be understood in the context of New France.

The literature on Puritan New England is vast. Unfortunately there is no thorough bibliography nor up-to-date guide to its bewildering shifts in interpretation. The most thorough guide to primary sources is George McCandlish's bibliography in the revised edition of Perry Miller and Thomas H. Johnson, eds., *The Puritans: A Sourcebook of their Writings,* 2 vols. (New York, 1963). McCandlish's lists of secondary works should be supplemented by Alden T. Vaughan, comp., *The American Colonies in the Seventeenth Century* (New York, 1971), and by standard guides to recent books and articles. The best general survey of early New England is Francis J. Bremer, *Puritan Experiment* (cited below). Thereafter the choices are limitless, but surely every reading list must include Perry Miller's magisterial study, *The New England Mind*, 2 vols. (Cambridge, Mass., 1939, 1953). The changing patterns of historical interpretation are best approached through Edmund S. Morgan, "The Historians of Early New England," in Ray Allen Billington, ed., *The Reinterpretation of Early American History* (San Marino, Calif., 1966); Michael McGiffert, "American Puritan Studies in the 1960s," *William and Mary Quarterly*, 3rd ser., 27 (1970); and Emil Oberholzer, "Puritanism Revisited," in Alden T. Vaughan and George Athan Billias, eds., *Perspectives on Early American History* (New York, 1973).

Readers who have time and the inclination should delve into the diverse body of Puritan writings—of which the captivity narratives are but one genre. There are several editions of most of the classic works such as William Bradford's *Of Plymouth Plantation* (the best modern version was edited by Samuel Eliot Morison [New York, 1952]; a more heavily annotated text that adheres to the original orthography was issued by the Massachusetts Historical Society, 2 vols. [Boston, 1912]); John Winthrop's *History of New England* (the best edition is James Savage's second version, Boston, 1853, but a meticulous new edition is being prepared by Richard S. Dunn and Letitia Yeandle); Samuel Sewall's *Diary* (the best version is edited by M. Halsey Thomas, 2 vols. [New York, 1973]); Cotton Mather's *Magnalia Christi Americana* (London, 1702; several subsequent editions are less satisfactory, but a definitive modern edition is in progress at Harvard University Press); and Michael McGiffert, ed., *God's Plot . . . Being the Autobiography and Journal of Thomas Shepard* (Amherst, Mass., 1972). Many other early Puritan sources—histories, sermons, and civil tracts—have been reissued in facsimile in three series by Arno Press: "Research Library of Colonial Americana," "A Library of American Puritan Writings," and "The Millennium in America." Still other works are available on Readex microcards in "Early American Imprints," cited in part I above. Convenient collections of Puritan documents are Miller and Johnson, eds., *The Puritans* (cited above), and Perry Miller, ed., *The American Puritans: Their Prose and Poetry* (Garden City, N.Y., 1956), which are literary in focus, and Alden T. Vaughan, ed., *The Puritan Tradition in America, 1620–1730* (New York, 1973), a historical collection. More specialized anthologies of source material are Edmund S. Morgan, ed., *Puritan Political Ideas, 1558–1794* (Indianapolis, 1965); A. W. Plumstead, ed., *The Wall and the Garden: Selected Massachusetts Election Sermons, 1670–1775* (Minneapolis, 1968), and Phyllis M. Jones and Nicholas R. Jones, eds., *Salvation in New England: Selections from the Sermons of the First Preachers* (Austin, Tex., 1977).

1. Puritan New England

This list of titles is necessarily highly selective and is limited almost exclusively to book-length monographs. Most biographies are omitted, as are almost all articles from scholarly journals. However, some of the best articles are reprinted in the anthologies (cited below) by Bercovitch, Hall, and Vaughan and Bremer.

Bailyn, Bernard. *The New England Merchants in the Seventeenth Century.* Cambridge, Mass., 1955.

Battis, Emory. *Saints and Sectaries: Anne Hutchinson and the Antinomian Controversy in the Massachusetts Bay Colony.* Chapel Hill, N.C., 1962.

Bercovitch, Sacvan. *The American Jeremiad.* Madison, Wis., 1978.

——— ed. *The Puritan Imagination: Essays in Revaluation.* Cambridge, Eng., 1975.

——— *The Puritan Origins of the American Self.* New Haven, 1975.

——— ed. *Typology and Early American Literature.* Amherst, Mass., 1972.

Boyer, Paul, and Stephen Nissenbaum. *Salem Possessed: The Social Origins of Witchcraft.* Cambridge, Mass., 1974.

Breen, T. H. *The Character of the Good Ruler: A Study of Puritan Political Ideas in New England, 1630–1730.* New Haven, 1970.

——— "Persistent Localism: English Social Change and the Shaping of New England Institutions." *William and Mary Quarterly,* 3rd ser., 32 (1975), 3–28.

——— "English Origins and New World Development: The Case of the Covenanted Militia in Seventeenth Century Massachusetts." *Past and Present,* 57 (1972), 74–96.

Bremer, Francis J. *The Puritan Experiment: New England Society from Bradford to Edwards.* New York, 1976.

Bushman, Richard L. *From Puritan to Yankee: Character and the Social Order in Connecticut, 1690–1765.* Cambridge, Mass., 1967.

Carroll, Peter N. *Puritanism and the Wilderness: The Intellectual Significance of the New England Frontier, 1629–1700.* New York, 1969.

Clark, Charles E. *The Eastern Frontier: The Settlement of Northern New England, 1610–1763.* New York, 1970.

Daniels, Bruce C. *The Connecticut Town: Growth and Development, 1635–1790.* Middletown, Conn., 1979.

Demos, John. *A Little Commonwealth: Family Life in Plymouth Colony.* New York, 1970.

Dunn, Richard S. *Puritans and Yankees: The Winthrop Dynasty of New England.* Princeton, N.J., 1962.

Elliott, Emory. *Power and the Pulpit in Puritan New England.* Princeton, N.J., 1975.

Emerson, Everett. *Puritanism in America, 1620–1750.* Boston, 1977.

Erikson, Kai. *Wayward Puritans: A Study in the Sociology of Deviance.* New York, 1966.

Foster, Stephen. *Their Solitary Way: The Puritan Social Ethic in the First Century of New England.* New Haven, 1971.

Gildrie, Richard P. *Salem, Massachusetts, 1626–1683: Covenant Community.* Charlottesville, Va., 1975.

NEW ENGLAND AND CANADIAN CONTEXTS

Greene, Lorenzo J. *The Negro in Colonial New England.* New York, 1942.

Greven, Philip J., Jr. *Four Generations: Population, Land, and Family in Colonial Andover, Massachusetts.* Ithaca, N.Y., 1970.

—— *The Protestant Temperament: Patterns of Child-Rearing, Religious Experience and the Self in Early America.* New York, 1977.

Hall, David D. *The Faithful Shepherd: A History of the New England Ministry in the Seventeenth Century.* Chapel Hill, N.C., 1972.

—— ed. *Puritanism in Seventeenth Century Massachusetts.* New York, 1968.

—— "Understanding the Puritans." In Herbert J. Bass, ed., *The State of American History.* Chicago, 1970.

Hanson, Chadwick. *Witchcraft at Salem.* New York, 1969.

Haskins, George L. *Law and Authority in Early Massachusetts.* New York, 1960.

Heimert, Alan. "Puritanism, the Wilderness, and the Frontier." *New England Quarterly,* 26 (1953), 361–382.

Holifield, E. Brooks. *The Covenant Sealed: The Development of Puritan Sacramental Theology in Old and New England, 1570–1720.* New Haven, 1974.

Jones, James W. *The Shattered Synthesis: New England Puritanism before the Great Awakening.* New Haven, 1973.

Jones, Mary Jeanne Anderson. *Congregational Commonwealth: Connecticut 1636–1662.* Middletown, Conn., 1968.

Konig, David Thomas. *Law and Society in Puritan Massachusetts: Essex County, 1629–1692.* Chapel Hill, N.C., 1979.

Langdon, George. *Pilgrim Colony: A History of New Plymouth, 1620–1691.* New Haven, 1966.

Levy, Babette. *Preaching in the First Half Century of New England History.* Hartford, Conn., 1945.

Lockridge, Kenneth A. *A New England Town; the First Hundred Years: Dedham, Massachusetts, 1636–1736.* New York, 1970.

—— "Land, Population and the Evolution of New England Society, 1630–1790." *Past and Present,* 39 (1969), 62–80.

Lowrie, Ernest Benson. *The Shape of the Puritan Mind: The Thought of Samuel Willard.* New Haven, 1974.

Lucas, Paul R. *Valley of Discord: Church and Society along the Connecticut River, 1636–1725.* New York, 1970.

McManis, Douglas R. *Colonial New England: A Historical Geography.* New York, 1975.

Middlekauff, Robert. *The Mathers: Three Generations of Puritan Intellectuals, 1596–1728.* New York, 1971.

Miller, Perry. *Errand into the Wilderness.* Cambridge, Mass., 1956.

—— *The New England Mind: From Colony to Province.* Cambridge, Mass., 1953.

—— *The New England Mind: The Seventeenth Century.* Cambridge, Mass., 1939.

—— *Orthodoxy in Massachusetts, 1630–1650.* Cambridge, Mass., 1933.

253

BIBLIOGRAPHY

Morgan, Edmund S. *The Puritan Dilemma: The Story of John Winthrop.* Boston, 1958.

———— *The Puritan Family: Religion and Domestic Relations in Seventeenth-Century New England.* Boston, 1944; rev. ed., New York, 1966.

———— *Roger Williams: The Church and the State.* New York, 1967.

———— *Visible Saints: The History of a Puritan Idea.* Ithaca, N.Y., 1963.

Morison, Samuel Eliot. *Builders of the Bay Colony.* Boston, 1930.

———— *The Founding of Harvard College.* Cambridge, Mass., 1935.

———— *Harvard College in the Seventeenth Century.* 2 vols. Cambridge, Mass., 1936.

———— *Intellectual Life of Colonial New England.* Ithaca, N.Y., 1956.

Murdock, Kenneth B. *Literature and Theology in Colonial New England.* Cambridge, Mass., 1949.

Oberholzer, Emil, Jr. *Delinquent Saints: Disciplinary Action in the Early Congregational Churches of Massachusetts.* New York, 1956.

Petit, Norman. *The Heart Prepared: Grace and Conversion in Puritan Spiritual Life.* New Haven, 1966.

Pope, Robert G. *The Half-way Covenant: Church Membership in Puritan New England.* Princeton, N.J., 1969.

Powell, Sumner Chilton. *Puritan Village: The Formation of a New England Town.* Middletown, Conn., 1963.

Rutman, Darrett B. *American Puritanism: Faith and Practice.* Philadelphia, 1970.

———— "God's Bridge Falling Down: 'Another Approach' to Puritanism Assayed." *William and Mary Quarterly,* 3rd ser., 19 (1962), 408–421.

———— *Husbandmen of Plymouth: Farms and Villages in the Old Colony, 1620–1692.* Boston, 1967.

———— *Winthrop's Boston: Portrait of a Puritan Town, 1630–1649.* Chapel Hill, N.C., 1965.

Shipton, Clifford. "The Locus of Authority in Colonial Massachusetts." In George Athan Billias, ed., *Law and Authority in Colonial America.* Barre, Mass., 1965.

Simpson, Alan. *Puritanism in Old and New England.* Chicago, 1955.

Solberg, Winton U. *Redeem the Time: The Puritan Sabbath in Early America.* Cambridge, Mass., 1977.

Stannard, David E. *The Puritan Way of Death: A Study in Religion, Culture, and Social Change.* New York, 1978.

Stoever, William K. B. *"A Faire and Easie Way to Heaven": Covenant Theology and Antinomianism in Early Massachusetts.* Middletown, Conn., 1978.

Towner, Lawrence W. " 'A Fondness for Freedom': Servant Protest in Puritan Society." *New England Quarterly,* 3rd ser., 19 (1962), 184–219.

Vaughan, Alden T., and Francis J. Bremer, eds. *Puritan New England: Essays on Religion, Society, and Culture.* New York, 1977.

Wall, Robert Emmet, Jr. *Massachusetts Bay: The Crucial Decade, 1640–1650.* New Haven, 1972.

NEW ENGLAND AND CANADIAN CONTEXTS

Ward, Harry M. *The United Colonies of New England, 1643–90.* New York, 1961.

Winslow, Ola Elizabeth. *Meetinghouse Hill, 1630–1783.* New York, 1952.

Young, J. William T., Jr. *God's Messengers: Religious Leadership in Colonial New England, 1700–1750.* Baltimore, 1976.

Ziff, Larzer. *Puritanism in America: New Culture in a New World.* New York, 1973.

Zuckerman, Michael. *Peaceable Kingdoms: New England Towns in the Eighteenth Century.* New York, 1970.

——— "The Social Context of Democracy in Massachusetts." *William and Mary Quarterly,* 3rd ser., 25 (1968), 523–544.

2. New France

The literature on early Canadian history is extremely rich, though less abundant than New England's. The best recent bibliographies are W. J. Eccles, *France in America* (cited below), 251–281; and Claude Thibault, comp., *Bibliographia Canadiana* (Don Mills, 1973). Still useful is Ernest Gagnon, *Essai du bibliographie canadienne,* 2 vols. (Québec, 1895–1913). Helpful historiographical essays include John Rule, "The Old Régime in America: A Review of Recent Interpretations of France in America," *William and Mary Quarterly,* 3rd ser., 19 (1962), 575–600; Robert Mandrou, "L'Histographie canadienne française: Bilan et perspectives," *Canadian Historical Review,* 51 (1970), 5–20; and Serge Gagnon, "The Historiography of New France, 1960–1974: Jean Hamelin to Louise Dechêne," *Journal of Canadian Studies,* 13, no. 1 (Spring 1978), 80–99.

Many of the important primary sources were published in the nineteenth century and a few have been issued in modern editions. Among the most relevant are *Collections des manuscrits contenant lettres, mémoires et autres documents historiques relatifs à la Nouvelle-France,* 4 vols. (Québec, 1883–1885); E. Z. Massicotte, ed., *Montréal sous le régime français... 1640–1760* (Montreal, 1919); Gabriel Sagard, *Histoire du Canada,* ed. Edwin Tross (Paris, 1866); H. Têtu and C. O. Gagnon, eds., *Mandements, lettres pastorales et circulaires des évêques de Québec,* 7 vols. (Québec, 1887); Reuben Gold Thwaites, ed., *The Jesuit Relations and Allied Documents* (73 vols., Cleveland, 1896–1901), supplemented by Joseph P. Donnelly, *Thwaites' Jesuit Relations: Errata and Addenda* (Chicago, 1967); Marc Lescarbot, *The History of New France* (Paris, 1609; modern ed. by W. L. Grant and H. P. Biggar, 3 vols. [Toronto, 1907–1914]); Pierre de Charlevoix, *History and General Description of New France,* ed. John Gilmary Shea, 6 vols. (New York, 1866–1872); Chrestien LeClercq, *The First Establishment of the Faith in New France,* ed. John Gilmary Shea, 2 vols. (New York, 1882); Dom Jamet, ed., *Histoire de l'Hôtel-Dieu de Québec* (Québec, 1939); Marie Morin, *Annales de l'Hôtel-Dieu de Montréal,* (Montréal, 1921); Joyce Marshall, trans. and ed., *Word from New France: The Selected Letters of Marie de l'Incarnation* (Toronto, 1967); Baron de Lahontan, *New Voyages to North-America,* ed. Reuben Gold Thwaites, 2 vols. (Chicago, 1905); and François Vachon de Belmont, *Histoire du Canada par*

BIBLIOGRAPHY

M. l'Abbe de Belmont, in Literary and Historical Society of Quebec, *Historical Documents,* 1st ser., 2 (Quebec, 1840). A convenient documentary history is Yves F. Zoltvany, ed., *The French Tradition in America* (New York, 1969). Two superb reference works are *Dictionary of Canadian Biography,* ed. George W. Brown et al., vols. I–III (Toronto, 1966–1974); and Marcel Trudel, *Initiation à la Nouvelle-France* (Montreal, 1968; English trans. [*Introduction to New France*], Toronto, 1978). Also important are Marcel Trudel, *Atlas de la Nouvelle France/An Atlas of New France* (Quebec, 1968); L. M. LeJeune, *Dictionnaire générale de biographie, histoire, littérature, etc. du Canada,* 2 vols. (Ottawa, 1931); and Jean Hamelin and André Beaulieu, *Guide de l'étudiant en histoire du Canada* (Quebec, 1965).

Listed below are some of the important modern monographs and a few older but still useful works. Most of them pertain to the period in which the captivities in this volume occurred, about 1675–1750.

Baillargeon, Georges E. *La Seminaire de Québec de 1685 à 1760.* Quebec, 1977.

Bédard, Marc-André. *Les Protestants en Nouvelle-France.* Quebec, 1978.

Brebner, J. B. *The Explorers of North America, 1492–1806.* London, 1933.

——— *New England's Outpost: Acadia Before the Conquest of Canada.* New York, 1927.

Cahall, Raymond Dubois. *The Sovereign Council of New France.* New York, 1915.

Clark, Andrew Hill. *Acadia: The Geography of Early Nova Scotia to 1760.* Madison, Wis., 1968.

Dechêne, Louise. *Habitants et marchands de Montréal au XVIIe siècle.* Paris, 1974.

Diamond, Sigmund. "An Experiment in Feudalism: French Canada in the Seventeenth Century." *William and Mary Quarterly,* 3rd ser., 17 (1961), 3–34.

Dubé, Jean-Claude. *Claude-Thomas Dupuy, Intendant de la Nouvelle-France, 1678–1738.* Montreal, 1969.

Eccles, W. J. *Canada Under Louis XIV, 1663–1701.* Toronto, 1964.

——— *The Canadian Frontier, 1543–1760.* New York, 1969.

——— *France in America.* New York, 1972.

——— *Frontenac: The Courtier Governor.* Toronto, 1959.

Frégault, Guy. *François Bigot: Administrateur français.* Montreal, 1968.

——— *Le XVIIIe Siècle canadien: Etudes.* Montreal, 1968.

Hamelin, Jean. *Economie et Société en Nouvelle-France.* Quebec, 1960.

Hammang, Francis H. *The Marquis de Vaudreuil: New France at the Beginning of the Eighteenth Century.* Louvian, 1938.

Harris, Richard Colebrook. *The Seigneurial System in Early Canada.* Madison, Wis., and Quebec, 1966.

Henripin, Jacques. *La population canadienne au début du XVIIIe siècle.* Paris, 1954.

Innis, Harold. *The Cod Fisheries. The History of an International Economy.* Toronto, 1940.

——— *The Fur Trade in Canada.* New Haven, 1930.
Jaenen, Cornelius J. *The Role of the Church in New France.* Toronto, 1976.
Lanctôt, Gustave. *Historie du Canada.* 3 vols. Montréal, 1960–1964. Also in English translation, Cambridge, Mass., 1963–1965.
Miquelon, Dale, ed. *Society and Conquest: The Debate on the Bourgeoisie and Social Change in French Canada, 1700–1850.* Toronto, 1977.
Morison, Samuel Eliot. *Samuel de Champlain, Father of New France.* Boston, 1972.
Munro, W. B. *The Seignorial System in Canada: A Study in French Colonial Policy.* New York, 1907.
Nish, Cameron, and Pierre Harvey. *The Social Structure of New France.* Toronto, 1968.
Parkman, Francis. *France and England in North America.* 9 vols. Boston, 1851–1884.
Ryerson, Stanley. *The Founding of Canada: Beginnings to 1815.* Toronto, 1960.
Trudel, Marcel. *The Beginnings of New France, 1525–1663.* Toronto, 1973.
——— *L'Esclavage au Canada français.* Quebec, 1960.
——— *Histoire de la Nouvelle-France.* 3 vols. Montreal, 1963–1978.

III. EARLY NORTHEASTERN ETHNOHISTORY

Much as the captivity narratives in this volume are best understood in the context of early New England and New France, so too are they enlightened by an understanding of northeastern Algonquian (and to some extent Iroquoian) culture. Relatively little is known about the Indians before contact with Europeans—only what archeological digs and the reports of the earliest explorers (inevitably distorted to some extent by the observers' ethnocentricity) reveal. There is, however, a substantial literature on native society in the seventeenth and eighteenth centuries and on the complex interaction of European and Indian cultures. Because it is all from the European side, it must be used cautiously.

The best guides to the ethnographic and ethnohistorical literature are George Peter Murdock and Timothy J. O'Leary, eds., *Ethnographic Bibliography of North America,* 5 vols. (4th ed., New Haven, 1975); Francis Paul Prucha, ed., *A Bibliographical Guide to the History of Indian-White Relations in the United States* (Chicago, 1977); Elizabeth Tooker, *The Indians of the Northeast: A Critical Bibliography* (Bloomington, Ind., 1978); and Dwight L. Smith, ed., *Indians of the United States and Canada* (Santa Barbara, Calif., 1975). An older but still useful guide to primary and secondary sources is William N. Fenton, Lyman H. Butterfield, and Wilcomb E. Washburn, *American Indian and White Relations to 1860: Needs and Opportunities for Study* (Chapel Hill, N.C., 1957). The most extensive and valuable reference work on the subject is *Handbook of North American Indians,* XV, *Northeast,* ed. Bruce G. Trigger (Washington, D.C., 1978) which largely supersedes the relevant sections of Frederick Webb Hodge, ed., *Handbook of Amer-*

BIBLIOGRAPHY

ican Indians North of Mexico, 2 vols. (Washington, D.C., 1907–1910). The latter
work remains useful, however, for topics not treated in Trigger's volume.

1. General Works on Indians and Early Intercultural Contact

Included below are works that treat early New England at least tangentially or
have important implications for its ethnohistory but are not primarily concerned
with that region. The list is necessarily highly selective. For other titles see the
bibliographies cited above, especially for works on the Iroquois, which this bibliography, with a few exceptions, does not include.

Ashburn, Percy M. *The Ranks of Death: A Medical History of the Conquest of
America.* New York, 1947.
Axtell, James. "The Ethnohistory of Early America: A Review Essay." *William
and Mary Quarterly,* 3rd ser., 35 (1978), 110–144.
———— "The European Failure to Convert the Indians: An Autopsy." In Wil-
liam Cowan, ed., *Papers of the Sixth Algonkian Conference, 1974.* Ottawa,
1975. Pp. 274–290.
———— *The Europeans and the Indians: Essays in the Ethnohistory of Colonial North
America.* New York, 1981.
———— "The Scholastic Philosophy of the Wilderness." *William and Mary
Quarterly,* 3rd ser., 29 (1972), 335–366. Reprinted with minor modifica-
tions in Axtell, *The School upon a Hill: Education and Society in Colonial New
England.* New Haven, 1974.
Axtell, James, and William C. Sturtevant, "The Unkindest Cut, or, Who In-
vented Scalping." *William and Mary Quarterly,* 3rd ser., 37 (1980),
451–472.
Berkhofer, Robert F., Jr. *The White Man's Indian: Images of the American Indian
from Columbus to the Present. New York,* 1978.
Bissell, Benjamin. *The American Indian in English Literature of the Eighteenth
Century.* New Haven, 1925.
Bond, Richmond P. *Queen Anne's American Kings.* Oxford, 1952.
Brasser, T. J. C. "The Coastal Algonkians: People of the First Frontier." In
Eleanor Burke Leacock and Nancy Oestreich Lurie, eds., *North American
Indians in Historical Perspective.* New York, 1971.
Ceci, Lynn. "Fish Fertilizer: A Native North American Practice?" *Science,* April
1975, 26–30; see also the "Letters" section of the succeeding volume.
Chiappelli, Fredi, ed. *First Images of America: The Impact of the New World on the
Old.* 2 vols. Berkeley, Calif., 1976.
Crosby, Alfred W., Jr. *The Columbian Exchange: Biological and Cultural Conse-
quences of 1492.* Westport, Conn., 1972.
———— "Virgin Soil Epidemics as a Factor in Aboriginal Depopulation in
America." *William and Mary Quarterly,* 3rd ser., 33 (1976), 289–299.
Day, Gordon, M. "The Indians as an Ecological Factor in the Northeastern For-
est." *Ecology,* 34 (1953), 329–345.

EARLY NORTHEASTERN ETHNOHISTORY

Driver, Harold E. *Indians of North America.* 2nd ed. Chicago, 1969.

Duffy, John. "Smallpox and the Indians in the American Colonies." *Bulletin of the History of Medicine,* 25 (1951), 324–341.

Flannery, Regina. *An Analysis of Coastal Algonquian Culture.* Washington, D.C., 1939.

Fussell, Edwin. *Frontier: American Literature and the American West.* Princeton, N.J., 1965.

Grumet, Robert Steven. "Sunksquaws, Shamans, and Tradeswomen: Middle Atlantic Coastal Algonkian Women During the 17th and 18th Centuries." In Mona Etienne and Eleanor Leacock, eds., *Women and Colonization: Anthropological Perspectives.* New York, 1980.

Hadlock, Wendell S. "War among the Northeastern Woodland Indians." *American Anthropologist,* n.s. 49 (1947), 204–221.

Hallowell, A. Irving. "The Backwash of the Frontier: The Impact of the Indian on American Culture." In Walker D. Wyman and Clifton B. Kroeber, eds., *The Frontier in Perspective.* Madison, Wis., 1957.

Hoover, Dwight W. *The Red and the Black.* Chicago, 1976.

Jacobs, Wilbur R. *Dispossessing the American Indian: Indians and Whites on the Colonial Frontier.* New York, 1972.

Jennings, Francis. *The Invasion of America: Indians, Colonialism and the Cant of Conquest.* Chapel Hill, N.C., 1975. Part I.

Josephy, Alvin M. *The Indian Heritage of America.* New York, 1968.

Knowles, Nathaniel. "The Torture of Captives by the Indians of Eastern North America." *American Philosophical Society Proceedings,* 82 (1940), 151–225.

Kupperman, Karen Ordhal. "English Perceptions of Treachery, 1583–1640: The Case of the American 'Savages'." *The Historical Journal,* 20 (1977), 263–287.

——— *Settling with the Indians: The Meeting of English and Indian Cultures in America, 1580–1640.* Totowa, N.J., 1980.

Lauber, Almon Wheeler. *Indian Slavery in Colonial Times within the Present Limits of the United States.* New York, 1913.

Leach, Douglas Edward. *The Northern Colonial Frontier, 1607–1763.* New York, 1966.

MacLeod, William C. *The American Indian Frontier.* New York, 1928.

Martin, Calvin. "Ethnohistory: A Better Way to Write Indian History." *The Western Historical Quarterly,* 9 (1978), 41–56.

Muldoon, James. "The Indian as Irishman." *Essex Institute Historical Collections,* 111 (1975), 267–289.

Nash, Gary B. "Notes on the History of Seventeenth-Century Missionization in Colonial America." *American Indian Culture and Research Journal,* 2, no. 2 (1978), 3–8.

——— *Red, White, and Black: The Peoples of Early America.* Englewood Cliffs, N.J., 1974.

BIBLIOGRAPHY

Pearce, Roy Harvey. *The Savages of America: A Study of the Indian and the Idea of Civilization.* Baltimore, 1953. Rev. ed. titled *Savagism and Civilization: A Study of the Indian and the American Mind.* Baltimore, 1965.

——— "The Metaphysics of Indian-Hating." *Ethnohistory,* 4 (1957), 27–40.

Pilling, James Constantine. *Bibliographies of the Languages of the North American Indians.* 3 vols., Washington, D.C., 1887–1894; repr. in 2 vols., New York, 1973.

Porter, H. C. *The Inconstant Savage: England and the North American Indian, 1500–1660.* London, 1979.

Ronda, James P. " 'We Are Well as We Are': The Indian Critique of Seventeenth-Century Christian Missions." *William and Mary Quarterly,* 3rd ser., 34 (1977), 66–82.

Sanders, Ronald. *Lost Tribes and Promised Lands: Origins of American Racism.* Boston, 1978.

Sheehan, Bernard W. "Indian-White Relations in Early America: A Review Essay." *William and Mary Quarterly,* 3rd ser., 26 (1969), 267–286.

——— *Savagism and Civility: Indians and Englishmen in Colonial Virginia.* Cambridge, Eng., 1980.

Slotkin, Richard. *Regeneration through Violence: The Mythology of the American Frontier, 1600–1860.* Middletown, Conn., 1973.

Smith, Marian W. "American Indian Warfare." *New York Academy of Science Transactions,* 2nd ser., 12 (1951), 348–365.

Snyderman, George S. "Behind the Tree of Peace: A Sociological Analysis of Iroquois Warfare." *Pennsylvania Archeologist,* 18, nos. 3–4 (fall 1948).

Swanton, John R. *The Indian Tribes of North America.* Washington, D.C., 1952.

Tebbel, John, and Keith Jennison. *The American Indian Wars.* New York, 1960.

Underhill, Ruth M. *Red Man's America: A History of Indians in the United States.* Rev. ed. Chicago, 1971.

Wallace, Anthony F. C. *The Death and Rebirth of the Seneca.* New York, 1969.

——— "Political Organization and Land Tenure Among the Northeastern Indians, 1600–1830." *Southwestern Journal of Anthropology,* 13 (1957), 301–321.

Washburn, Wilcomb E. *The Indian in America.* New York, 1975.

——— "The Moral and Legal Justification for Dispossessing the Indians." In James Morton Smith, ed., *Seventeenth-Century America: Essays in Colonial History.* Chapel Hill, N.C., 1959.

——— *Red Man's Land—White Man's Law: A Study of the Past and Present Status of the American Indian.* New York, 1971.

2. Early New England Ethnohistory

The most informative descriptions of Algonquian life in New England before it was undermined by English colonization are firsthand accounts by the rare colonists who set aside, to some extent at least, their cultural biases. Among the best are William Wood, *New England's Prospect* (London, 1634; modern ed. by Alden

T. Vaughan [Amherst, Mass., 1977]); Thomas Morton, *New English Canaan* (London, 1637; repr. New York, 1972); Roger Williams, *A Key into the Language of America* (London, 1643; modern ed. by John J. Teunissen and Evelyn J. Hinz [Detroit, 1973]); and Daniel Gookin, *Historical Collections of the Indians in New England* (Boston, 1792; repr. New York, 1972). Valuable too are the accounts of various settlers reprinted in Charles Lincoln, *Narratives of the Indian Wars* (cited above); Alexander Young, ed., *Chronicles of the Pilgrim Fathers of the Colony of Plymouth, 1602–1625* (Boston, 1841; repr. New York, 1971) and *Chronicles of the First Planters of the Colony of Massachusetts Bay, 1623–1636* (Boston, 1846; repr. New York, 1970); Charles Orr, ed., *History of the Pequot War* (Cleveland, 1897); and the Puritan missionary pamphlets, known collectively but not quite accurately as the "Eliot Indian Tracts," most of which are reprinted in *Massachusetts Historical Society Collections*, 3rd ser., 4 (1834). Also primarily concerned with missionary activities are Eliot's *Indian Dialogues* (Cambridge, Mass., 1671); and Daniel Gookin's *An Historical Account of the Doings and Sufferings of the Christian Indians in New England* (*Transactions and Collections of the American Antiquarian Society*, 2 [1836]). The writings of military and missionary leaders must, of course, be used with caution; the need to conquer or convert the Indians often distorted an author's perceptions. Additional sources on the Indians and on Indian-European contact are numerous but widely dispersed through colonial New England writings. A useful guide to early American sources is James Thomas Clancy, "Native American References: A Cross-Indexed Bibliography of Seventeenth-Century American Imprints Pertaining to American Indians," *American Antiquarian Society Proceedings*, 83 (1973), 287–341.

Listed below are modern studies, plus a few old but still valuable works, that analyze some aspect of New England's Indian culture or Anglo-Indian relations in the seventeenth and eighteenth centuries. As with other sections of this bibliography, the list is selective; for further titles see the bibliographic guides cited above.

Axtell, James. "The Vengeful Women of Marblehead: Robert Roules's Deposition of 1677." *William and Mary Quarterly*, 3rd ser., 31 (1974), 647–652.

Baxter, James Phinney. "The Abnakis and Their Ethnic Relations." *Massachusetts Historical Society Publications*, 58, 2nd ser., 3 (1892), 13–40.

Bennett, M. K. "The Food Economy of the New England Indians, 1605–75." *Journal of Political Economy*, 63 (1955), 369–397.

Burton, William, and Richard Lowenthal. "The First of the Mohegans," *American Ethnologist*, 1 (1974), 589–599.

Bushnell, David. "The Treatment of the Indians in Plymouth Colony." *New England Quarterly* 26 (1953), 193–218.

Campbell, Paul R. and Glenn W. LaFantasie. "Scattered to the Winds of Heaven—Narragansett Indians 1676–1880." *Rhode Island History*, 37, no. 3 (Aug. 1978), 67–83.

BIBLIOGRAPHY

Chase, Henry E. "Notes on the Wampanoag Indians." *Smithsonian Institution Annual Report.* Washington, D.C., 1883.

Cook, Sherburne F. *The Indian Population of New England in the Seventeenth Century.* Berkeley, Calif., 1976.

————— "Interracial Warfare and Population Decline Among the New England Indians." *Ethnohistory,* 20 (1973), 1–24.

————— "The Significance of Disease in the Extinction of the New England Indians." *Human Biology,* 45 (1973), 485–488.

Cooper, John M. "Is the Algonquian Family Hunting Ground System Pre-Columbian?" *American Anthropologist,* n.s., 41 (1939), 66–90.

Crosby, Alfred W., Jr. "God . . . Would Destroy Them, and Give Their Country to Another People." *American Heritage,* 29 (1978), 38–43.

Davis, Jack L. "Roger Williams among the Narragansett Indians." *New England Quarterly,* 43 (1970), 593–604.

DeForest, John W. *History of the Indians of Connecticut.* Hartford, 1851.

Gookin, Frederick William. *Daniel Gookin, 1612–1687.* Chicago, 1912.

Hare, Lloyd C. *Thomas Mayhew, Patriarch to the Indians, 1593–1682.* New York, 1932.

Jennings, Francis. "Goals and Functions of Puritan Missions to the Indians." *Ethnohistory,* 18 (1971), 197–212.

————— *The Invasion of America: Indians, Colonialism and the Cant of Conquest.* Chapel Hill, N.C., 1975. Part II.

————— "Virgin Land and Savage People." *American Quarterly,* 23 (1971), 519–541.

Johnson, Richard R. "The Search for a Usable Indian: An Aspect of the Defense of Colonial New England." *Journal of American History,* 64 (1977), 623–651.

Kawashima, Yasuhide. "Forced Conformity: Puritan Criminal Justice and Indians," *Kansas Law Review,* 25 (1977), 361–373.

————— "Jurisdiction of the Colonial Courts Over the Indians in Massachusetts, 1689–1763." *New England Quarterly,* 42 (1969), 532–550.

————— "Legal Origins of the Indian Reservation in Colonial Massachusetts." *American Journal of Legal History,* 13 (1969), 42–56.

Kellaway, William. *The New England Company, 1649–1776: Missionary Society to the American Indians.* New York, 1961.

LaFantasie, Glenn W. and Paul R. Campbell. "Covenants of Grace, Covenants of Wrath: Niantic-Puritan Relations in New England." *Rhode Island History,* 37, no. 1 (Feb. 1978), 15–23.

Leach, Douglas Edward. *Flintlock and Tomahawk: New England in King Philip's War.* New York, 1958.

Love, W. DeLoss. *Samson Occum and the Christian Indians of New England.* Boston, 1899.

Malone, Patrick M. "Changing Military Technology Among the Indians of

Southern New England, 1600–1677." *American Quarterly,* 25 (1973), 48–63.

Maloney, Francis X. *The Fur Trade In New England, 1620–1676.* Cambridge, Mass., 1931.

Pearce, Roy Harvey. "The 'Ruines of Mankind': The Indian and the Puritan Mind." *Journal of the History of Ideas,* 13 (1952), 200–217.

Roberts, William Iredell. "The Fur Trade of New England." Ph.D. dissertation, University of Pennsylvania, 1958.

Ronda, James P. "Red and White at the Bench: Indians and the Law in Plymouth Colony, 1620–1691." *Essex Institute Historical Collections,* 110 (1974), 200–215.

Ronda, James P., and Jeanne Ronda, "The Death of John Sassamon: An Exploration in Writing New England Indian History." *American Indian Quarterly,* 1 (1974), 91–102.

Russell, Howard S. *Indian New England before the Mayflower.* Hanover, N.H., 1980.

Sainsbury, John A. "Indian Labor in Early Rhode Island." *New England Quarterly,* 48 (1975), 378–393.

——— "Maintonomo's Death and New England Politics, 1630–1645." *Rhode Island History,* 30 (1971), 111–123.

Salisbury, Neal E. "Prospero in New England: The Puritan Missionary as Colonist." In William Cowan, ed., *Papers of the Sixth Algonquian Conference, 1974.* Ottawa, 1975. Pp. 253–273.

——— "Red Puritans: The Praying Indians of Massachusetts Bay and John Eliot." *William and Mary Quarterly,* 3rd ser., 31 (1974), 27–54.

Shuffelton, Frank. "Indian Devils and the Pilgrim Fathers: Squanto, Hobomok, and the English Conception of Indian Religion," *New England Quarterly,* 49 (1976), 108–116.

Simmons, William S. "Conversion from Indian to Puritan." *New England Quarterly,* 52 (1979), 197–218.

——— "Cultural Bias in New England Puritan Perceptions of Indians." *William and Mary Quarterly,* 3rd. ser., 38 (1981), 56–72.

——— "Southern New England Indian Shamanism: An Ethnographic Reconstruction." In William Cowan, ed., *Papers of the Seventh Algonquian Conference, 1975.* Ottawa, 1976. Pp. 217–256.

Slotkin, Richard, and James K. Folsom, eds. *So Dreadful a Judgment: Puritan Responses to King Philip's War, 1676–1677.* Middletown, Conn., 1979.

Speck, Frank G. *Penobscot Man: The Life of a Forest Tribe in Maine.* Philadelphia, 1940.

Stineback, David C. "The Status of Puritan-Indian Scholarship." *New England Quarterly,* 51 (1978), 80–90.

Stineback, David C., and Charles M. Segal. *Puritans, Indians, and Manifest Destiny.* New York, 1977.

263

BIBLIOGRAPHY

Tanis, Norman E. "Education in John Eliot's Indian Utopias, 1646–1675." *History of Education Quarterly,* 10 (1970), 308–323.

Vaughan, Alden T. *New England Frontier: Puritans and Indians, 1620–1675.* Boston, 1965; rev. ed., New York, 1979.

———— "Pequots and Puritans: The Causes of the War of 1637." *William and Mary Quarterly,* 3rd ser., 21 (1964), 256–269.

———— "A Test of Puritan Justice." *New England Quarterly,* 28 (1965), 331–339.

Vaughan, Alden T., and Daniel K. Richter. "Crossing the Cultural Divide: Indians and New Englanders, 1605–1763." *American Antiquarian Society Proceedings,* 90 (1980), 23–99.

Weis, Frederick L. "The New England Company of 1649 and Its Missionary Enterprises." *Colonial Society of Massachusetts Transactions,* 38 (1947–1951), 134–218.

Willoughby, Charles C. *Antiquities of the New England Indians.* Cambridge, Mass., 1935.

3. The Ethnohistory of French Canada

Indians in the areas of Canada bordering on New England are described in various early documents, including those cited above in part II. Other important sources are W. L. Grant, ed., *Voyages of Samuel de Champlain, 1604–1618* (New York, 1907); Chrestien Le Clerq, *New Relation of Gaspesia, with the Customs and Religion of the Gaspesian Indians,* trans. and ed. William F. Ganong (Toronto, 1910); J. F. Lafitau, *Customs of the American Indians Compared with the Customs of Primitive Times,* 2 vols. (Toronto, 1974–76); Nicholas Perrot, *Memories sure les moeurs, coustomes et religion des sauvages de L'Amerique septrionale* (Leipzig and Paris, 1864); Gabriel Sagard, *The Long Journey to the Country of the Hurons,* trans. and ed. George M. Wrong (Toronto, 1939); Nicholas Denys, *The Description and Natural History of the Coasts of North America,* trans. and ed. William F. Ganong (Toronto, 1908).

Listed below are modern studies of the Indians of eastern Canada south of Newfoundland (here defined as the Micmac, Maliseet, Passamaquoddy, and Abenaki, with their various subdivisions) plus the Huron. Although New England captives seldom came into direct contact with Huron tribesmen, their confederacy was a major force in eastern Canada during the sixteenth and early seventeenth centuries. Moreover, the Huron are probably the most thoroughly studied of all Canadian tribes; several recent investigations of Huron culture throw important, if indirect, light on the tribes most familiar to the New England captives.

Bailey, Alfred G. *The Conflict of European and Eastern Algonkian Cultures, 1504–1700: A Study in Canadian Civilization.* 2nd ed. Toronto, 1969.

Campeau, Lucien, ed. *La Première Mission d'Acadie (1602–1616).* Rome and Quebec, 1967.

Conkling, Robert. "Legitimacy and Conversion in Social Change: The Case of the French Missionaries and the Northeastern Algonkian." *Ethnohistory*, 21 (1974), 1–24.

Dickason, Olive P. "The Concept of *l'homme sauvage* and early French colonialism in the Americas." *Revue française d'histoire d'outre-mer*, 63 (1977), 5–32.

Gagnon, F. M. *La Conversion par l'Image*. Montreal, 1975.

Gonnard, René. *La Légende du Bon Sauvage*. Paris, 1964.

Hanzeli, Victor Egon. *Missionary Linguistics in New France*. The Hague, 1969.

Healy, George R. "The French Jesuits and the Idea of the Nobel Savage." *William and Mary Quarterly*, 3rd ser., 15 (1958), 153–167.

Heidenreich, Conrad. *Huronia: A History and Geography of the Huron Indians, 1600–1650*. Toronto, 1971.

Heidenreich, Conrad, and Arthur J. Ray. *The Early Fur Trades: A Study in Cultural Interaction*. Toronto, 1976.

Hurtubise, Pierre. "Le 'bon' et le 'mauvais' sauvage. Les *Relations* se contredisent-elles?" *Eglise et Théologie*, 10 (1979), 223–237.

Jaenen, Cornelius J. "Amerindian Views of French Culture in the Seventeenth Century." *Canadian Historical Review*, 55 (1974), 261–291.

———— "Conceptual Frameworks for French Views of America and Amerindians." *French Colonial Studies*, 2 (1978), 1–22.

———— "French Attitudes toward Native Society." In *Old Trails and New Directions: Papers of the Third North American Fur Trade Conference*, ed. Carol M. Judd and Arthur J. Ray. Toronto, 1979.

———— "The Frenchification and Evangelization of the Amerindians in the Seventeenth Century New France." *Canadian Catholic Historical Association, Study Sessions, 1968*, 35 (1969), 57–71.

———— *Friend and Foe: Aspects of French-Amerindian Cultural Contact in the Sixteenth and Seventeenth Centuries*. New York, 1976.

———— "The Meeting of the French and Amerindians in the Seventeenth Century." *Revue de l'Université d'Ottawa*, 43 (1973), 128–144.

———— "Missionary Approaches to Native Peoples." In D. A. Muise, ed., *Approaches to Native History in Canada*. Ottawa, 1977.

———— "Problems of Assimilation in New France, 1603–1645." *French Historical Studies*, 4 (1966), 265–289.

Johnson, Frederick. "Notes on Micmac Shamanism." *Primitive Man*, 16 (1943), 53–80.

Kennedy, J.H. *Jesuit and Savage in New France*. New Haven, Conn., 1938.

Leacock, Eleanor Burke. *The Montagnais "Hunting Territory" and the Fur Trade. American Anthropological Association, Memoirs*, 78. Menasha, Wis., 1954.

LeBlanc, Peter G. "Indian-Missionary Contact in Huronia, 1615–1649." *Ontario History*, 40 (1968), 133–146.

Martin, Calvin. "The European Impact on the Culture of a Northeastern Algonquian Tribe: An Ecological Interpretation." *William and Mary Quarterly*, 3rd ser., 31 (1974), 3–26.

———— "The Four Lives of a Micmac Copper Pot." *Ethnohistory*, 22 (1975), 111–133.

———— *Keepers of the Game: Indian-Animal Relationships and the Fur Trade.* Berkeley, 1978.

———— "Subartic Indians and Wildlife." In *Old Trails and New Directions: Papers of the Third North American Fur Trade Conference*, ed. Carol M. Judd and Arthur J. Ray. Toronto, 1980.

Martin J. Scott. *Isaac Jogues: Missioner and Martyr.* New York, 1927.

McGuire, Joseph D. "Ethnology in the Jesuit Relations." *American Athropologist*, 3 (1901), 257–269.

Mechling, William Hubbs. "The Malicite Indians, with Notes on the Micmacs." *Anthropologica*, 7 (1958), 1–160; 8 (1959), 161–274.

Parkman, Francis. *The Jesuits in North America.* Boston, 1867. See also Parkman's other volumes in his majesterial "France and England in North America," 9 vols., Boston, 1865–1892.

Patterson, E. P. *The Canadian Indian: A History Since 1500.* Don Mills, Canada, 1972.

Ray, Arthur J. *Indians in the Fur Trade.* Toronto, 1974.

Ronda, James P. "The European Indian: Jesuit Civilization Planning in New France." *Church History*, 41 (1972), 385–395.

Smith, Donald B. *Le Sauvage: The Native Peoples in Quebec Historical Writing in the Heroic Period, 1534–1663, of New France.* Ottawa, 1974.

Stanley, George F. G. "The First Indian Reserves in Canada," *Revue d'histoire de l'Amerique Française*, 4 (1950), 178–201.

———— "The Policy of 'Francisation' as Applied to the Indians during the Ancien Regime." *Revue d'histoire de l'Amerique Francais*, 3 (1949–1950), 333–348.

Surtees, Robert J. *The Original People.* Toronto, 1971.

Tooker, Elizabeth. *An Ethnography of the Huron Indians, 1615–1649.* Washington, D.C., 1964.

Trigger, Bruce G. "Champlain Judged by His Indian Policy: A Different View of Early Canadian History." *Anthropologica*, n.s., 13 (1971), 85–114.

———— *The Children of Aetaentsic: A History of the Huron People to 1660.* 2 vols. Montreal, 1976.

———— "The Destruction of Huronia: A Study in Economic and Cultural Change, 1609–1650," *Royal Canadian Institute Transactions*, 33 (1960), 14–45.

———— "The French Presence in Huronia: The Structure of Franco-Huron Relations in the First Half of the Seventeenth Century." *Canadian Historical Review*, 49 (1968), 107–141.

———— *The Huron: Farmers of the North.* New York, 1969.

———— "The Jesuits and the Fur Trade." *Ethnohistory*, 12 (1965), 30–53.

———— "Trade and Tribal Warfare on the St. Lawrence in the Sixteenth Century." *Ethnohistory*, 20 (1973).

Vachon, André. "L'eau de vie dans la société indienne." *Canadian Historical Association Report* (1960), 22–32.

Wade, Mason. "The French and the Indians." In Howard Peckham and Charles Gibson, eds., *Attitudes of Colonial Powers toward the American Indians*. Salt Lake City, 1969.

Wallis, Wilson D., and Ruth S. Wallis. *The Micmac Indians of Eastern Canada*. Minneapolis, 1955.

INDEX

269

INDEX

INDEX

Watertown, Mass., 38n
Week on the Concord and Merrimac Rivers, A, 28
Weems, James, 98
Weetamoo (Wettimore), 22–23, 43, 61
Wells, John, 199n, 221n
Wells, Me., 223
Wenimesset, *see* Menameset
Wept of Wish-Ton-Wish: A Tale, The, 27n
Wethersfield, Conn., 32, 185
Whitcomb, James, 74
White, Josiah, 71
White River Junction, Vt., 178n
Wigglesworth, Michael, 7, 8
Williams, Abigail Allen Bissell, 168
Williams, Eleazar, 175n, 196n, 213
Williams, Esther, 175n, 188n, 199n
Williams, Eunice (daughter), 175n, 188n, 209n
Williams, Eunice (mother), 16, 167, 175
Williams, John, 1, 6, 9, 10, 13, 15, 16, 19, 22, 23, 79, 167–226

Williams, Samuel, 175n, 180, 188n, 200n, 209, 210, 220, 224n
Williams, Stephen, 175n, 180, 188, 197, 199, 200
Williams, Warham, 175n, 188n, 209n, 210
Williams, Zebediah, 221, 222, 223
Williams River, 177n
Winthrop, Fitz-John, 199n
Winthrop, John, 4, 7
Wolverine, description of, 118
Women captives, literary perception of, 25
Wonderful Words of God, 8
Wooster River, 137n
Worcester, Mass., 163

Yamoyden, a Tale of the Wars of King Philip, 27
Yemasee, The, 27
York, John, 149–150